Marriage in James Hogg's Work

Scottish Cultural Review of Language and Literature

VOLUME 32

Marriage in James Hogg's Work

Plotting for Gender, Class, and Ethnic Equality

By

Barbara Leonardi

BRILL

LEIDEN | BOSTON

Cover illustration: Wedding dress, c. 1878–1879; Metropolitan Museum of Art (1979.339.2). Public domain.

Library of Congress Cataloging-in-Publication Data

Names: Leonardi, Barbara, author.
Title: Marriage in James Hogg's work : plotting for gender, class, and
  ethnic equality / by Barbara Leonardi.
Description: Leiden ; Boston : Brill, [2022] | Series: Scottish cultural
  review of language and literature, 1571-0734 ; vol 32 | Includes
  bibliographical references and index.
Identifiers: LCCN 2022020260 (print) | LCCN 2022020261 (ebook) | ISBN
  9789004519435 (hardback ; alk. paper) | ISBN 9789004519992 (ebook)
Subjects: LCSH: Hogg, James, 1770-1835–Criticism and interpretation. |
  Hogg, James, 1770-1835–Political and social views. | Marriage in
  literature. | Sex role in literature. | LCGFT: Literary criticism.
Classification: LCC PR4792 .L46 2022 (print) | LCC PR4792 (ebook) | DDC
  821/.7–dc23/eng/20220525
LC record available at https://lccn.loc.gov/2022020260
LC ebook record available at https://lccn.loc.gov/2022020261

Typeface for the Latin, Greek, and Cyrillic scripts: "Brill". See and download: brill.com/brill-typeface.

ISSN 1571-0734
ISBN 978-90-04-51943-5 (hardback)
ISBN 978-90-04-51999-2 (e-book)

Printed by Printforce, United Kingdom

To Tina and Gigi, my lovely mum and dad

∴

Contents

Acknowledgments

The present book is the result of a very long period of research, studies, and personal growth, during which time a few people have played a significant role. First of all, I thank Carla Sassi, my inestimable professional mentor throughout all these years, who transmitted me the love for Scottish literature, and encouraged me to pursue my dreams and to accept an Erasmus period of studies at Stirling University in Scotland, when I was a postgraduate student at the University of Verona. Giorgia Guerra was especially significant at this point, when suggesting I choose the spring term for my Erasmus period. The beauty of Stirling University's blossoming campus and the wild life on its loch at this time of the year inspired me to transition into a new stage of life. Stirling University's spring term also offered a course on Scottish literature thanks to which I discovered James Hogg and his energetic writings. The course was run by Suzanne Gilbert, an inspiring lecturer who became my extremely supportive and highly encouraging PhD supervisor: I will always be grateful for her kindness and professional advice at critical moments during my doctoral journey. It is also a pleasure to record my indebtedness to a number of scholars who have provided supportive feedback: Siobhan Chapman, Billy Clark, and Roger Sell for their guidance on the theoretical framework that I have used for this project; Ian Duncan, for his time and supportive feedback on various conference papers and writings that he kindly read; Adrian Hunter, for taking his time to read an early stage of the Introduction to this book. I feel especially grateful to Anders Pettersson for providing his fundamental advice on pragmatics linguistics applied to literature at a crucial moment of my research. I am also indebted to a number of friends and colleagues who proofread parts of this book to check my English: in particular, Matt Foley; Liz Speake; Carole Pitson; Heather Smith; and Angela Smith. I especially appreciate the kind, thorough, and extremely helpful feedback provided by Sarah Dunnigan in the very last stage of this book. I thank Stirling University for having formed me as a scholar through my doctoral and postdoctoral studies, and the Arts and Humanities Research Council for their generous funding of both. Above all, I thank Sheona Law who has been an outstandingly supportive friend during my Scottish life and whom I will always miss dearly. Last but not least, I thank my parents, Pierluigi Leonardi and Tina Loriga, for their unconditional love and for letting me pursue my dreams.

CHAPTER 1

Introduction: James Hogg, a Counter-culture Voice

Throughout his career, Scottish writer James Hogg (1770–1835) addressed gender issues in controversial ways, violating early nineteenth-century literary proprieties which discouraged the frank treatment of prostitution, infanticide, and the violence of war for imperial expansion which, by exploiting the myth of the indestructible and loyal Highlander, occasioned an outrageous waste of lives. Contemporary reviewers received Hogg's bluntness rather fiercely because, in so doing, he questioned the ideologies of chastity, marriage and military masculinities that informed emerging discourses of the British Empire. This book reveals the strategic use that Hogg made of early nineteenth-century gender stereotypes in their intersection with class and ethnicity in his texts, and Hogg's awareness of how contemporary writers exploited the same stereotypes to promote British ideology—the system of norms that Hogg questioned in his writing. The book then explores the significant reach of Hogg's works in North American magazines and newspapers during the first half of the nineteenth century.

The three major preoccupations of this book concern Hogg's challenges to, and constructions of, femininity and masculinity through the conventions of the marriage plot; Hogg's critique of Britain's imperial projects which were pursued at the expense of a marginalised population at home; and the reception of Hogg's works, which differed enormously depending on location. These concerns are interrelated, as contemporary gender stereotypes informed the political discourse of the imperial project. As explained in more detail later in this introduction, for example, the civilising ideal of the motherly heroine promoted British values of domesticity, while martial and sentimental masculinities supported the discourse of a strong but tamed national vigour.

The reception of Hogg's works was particularly influenced by Scottish reviewers who had their interests in promoting British ideals. In the early nineteenth century, Edinburgh was a centre of sophisticated culture, reflecting the legacy of the Scottish Enlightenment and the influence of eighteenth-century empiricists such as Francis Hutcheson, David Hume, and Adam Smith. These intellectuals had established 'absolute standards of taste' which mirrored 'elitist' attitudes towards autodidacts and, as Valentina Bold remarks, would greatly influence the subsequent early nineteenth-century Scottish *literati*'s opinion of Hogg who—being a 'peasant poet'—would

© KONINKLIJKE BRILL NV, LEIDEN, 2022 | DOI:10.1163/9789004519992_002

be regarded only 'on their own terms' (2007: 19). Hogg's writing was only accepted in the form of more rural genres, such as ballads and songs, as this was in line with the Romantic figures of the 'bard' and the 'rustic peasant-poet'. Hogg's image as the Ettrick Shepherd, however, would later become a problem for his literary career. Ian Duncan points out that it would struggle against 'a historiography which at once valorized the poet as voice of a primordial stage of society close to nature and depreciated him as an uncouth relic doomed to extinction by the logic of economic and cultural improvement' (2007b: 149). The same Edinburgh *literati* would have problems with Hogg's attempts at dealing with more urban and 'sophisticated' literary genres, such as the national tale, the historical novel, the drama, and the epic because Hogg's 'indelicacies' disturbed the British ideology which these works were meant to convey. Sense of propriety, norms of politeness and conformity to Englishness were subtly entangled with the tremendous financial power that the British empire offered to the Scottish ruling classes. For this reason, the next section briefly explains Scotland's economic transformation and involvement with the imperial project after the British Union, before returning to Hogg's themes and works.

As T. M. Devine explains, at the time of Hogg's writing, Scotland had gone through a prodigious 'economic transformation' due to 'a range of causes such as natural endowment, labour, enterprise, technology and others' (2004 [2003]: 326). In addition in 1815, after Waterloo and the end of the Napoleonic Wars, the British Empire was of colossal dimensions and it offered prodigious opportunities to Scotland. In 1707 the Glaswegian merchants involved in the tobacco trade had been reluctant to join the political union with England for fear of losing their commercial power in competition with the English traders. At the beginning of the nineteenth century, however, the economic advantages of the Union were unquestionable. The tobacco lords had direct access to the colonial trade and their ships 'were granted the protection of the Royal Navy' (Devine 2004 [2003]: 74). The capital gained through the tobacco trade in North America and sugar in the Caribbean was then invested in Scotland. T. M. Devine remarks that, although part of the merchants' fortune went into personal luxuries such as mansions, land, and precious furnishing, a great amount of capital was also invested in the manufacturing industry to supply the colonists with goods. The transatlantic market thus boosted the industrialisation of Glasgow and its hinterland (Ibid., pp. 330–31).

Moreover, as mentioned above, T. M. Devine explains that the rich merchants involved in the colonial trade invested their money in land around Glasgow:

Landownership not only provided social standing and the essential route to political prominence in the eighteenth century. It was also a secure asset, guaranteeing in most years a steady, passive and reliable income from rentals. This held a special allure for colonial merchants who were engaged in a very lucrative but also highly volatile business. Many had also come as younger sons from gentry families and aspired to the foundation of their own dynasties.

> 2004 [2003]: 332

However, as Mack points out, the money earned in the colonies supported an internal process of economic colonisation which affected rather seriously the peasantry and the labouring classes (2006: 58–62). In an essay published in Blackwood's *Quarterly Journal of Agriculture* (1831–32), Hogg exposes the loss of benevolence between master and servants among the peasantry, as the latter were not considered members of the family unit any longer. This is borne out by T. M. Devine's research, who explains that between 1760 and 1815, agricultural innovation had not benefited the labouring classes of Lowland Scotland, pointing out that

> on a number of estates a radical change in tenure was under way as proprietors converted more and more smaller holdings into larger individual tenancies, which meant that the capitalist farming class of the Agricultural Revolution of later years was already emerging in embryonic form. [...] The single farm under one master became the norm as holdings were united between 1760 and 1815. By 1830, most of those who toiled in Lowland agriculture were landless men and women servants. Their lives were often as much subject to the unrelenting pressures of labour discipline as those employed in the new industrial workshops and factories.
>
> 2004 [2003]: 320, 321, 326

It is important to highlight that the attenuation of feudalism—with the consequent decrease of masters' responsibility for their servants—was due to many causes, such as the rise of industrial capitalism, agricultural improvement, and the post-1745 legislation after the defeat of the Highland clans in the Battle of Culloden that undermined the authority of those 'masters'. Nonetheless, the traders who invested in multiple land properties would not have been interested in building the close, familial relationship between farmer and peasants that had characterised the past, as Hogg lamented (1985 [1831–1832]: 40–51).

As mentioned above, the colonial project also offered career opportunities to the younger sons of the laird class. There had been an increase in population during the eighteenth and early nineteenth centuries; this meant that the younger sons of the Scottish aristocracy had greater chances of survival than in the past. The system of primogeniture, however, did not allow them to inherit their father's land; yet, they still had to achieve 'gainful employment [...] which would not only provide income but an acceptably genteel position in society' (Devine 2004[2003]: 66). Robert Gordon of Cluny, one of these lairds, was particularly grateful for the chance that the imperial project bestowed on his younger son, as he 'had not estate whereby to make him a Scotch laird' (Landsman 1985: 87).

These aspirations developed an incredible system of Scottish patronage in the empire, which had its roots in the structure of the Scottish gentry. One of the most representative figures of imperial patronage during the eighteenth century was Henry Dundas. In his role, 'as sole Keeper of the Signet', taken up in 1779, Dundas had become 'the decisive influence over appointment to government posts in Scotland and systematically used his position to build up a complex network of clients, voters and local interests who depended on him for favours, places, promotions and pensions' (Devine 2004 [2003]: 249, 236). Such opportunism incited great antipathy in England where political caricatures gave birth to the image of the greedy Scot in the collective imagination (Mack 2006: 53). The British Union with England was thus pivotal to the modern development of Scotland, as 'virtually every other sphere of Scottish life, from economy to emigration, from rural transformation to political development, was fashioned in large part by engagement with empire' (Devine 2004 [2003]: 360).

As a self-educated shepherd, Hogg spoke from a position outside the dominant discourse. His 'outsiderness' allowed him to play with the culturally constructed categories of female delicacy and of Highland and sentimental masculinities that shaped the political discourse of the emerging British Empire. In so doing, Hogg was able to write more freely about prostitution, out-of-wedlock pregnancy, infanticide, and the violence of war by voicing people from the margins and revealing, in this way, gender politics and Britain's imperial aims. The ideal of the civilising, middle-class mother who taught and protected British moral values was an important discourse connected to imperial expansion, where Britain acted as a model of civilisation for the less supposedly civilised countries of the empire. Hogg's presentation of issues such as infanticide, countering the dominant role model of a protecting mother, therefore challenged the political role of Britain as mother country. Hogg's contemporary critics, and Scottish reviewers in particular as this introduction shows later, viewed the subjects he treated as violating the principles of literary politeness. Nevertheless, Hogg's obstinacy in addressing these issues throughout his career suggests that his aim went beyond challenging the expectations of decorum of his contemporary commentators. Hogg's poetry and prose questioned sexuality and gender as crucial categories of British national discourse. For example, Hogg's unorthodox depiction of female sexuality disturbed the ideology of the marriage plot, central to the narrative of the national tale and its promotion of a sound British Union founded on erotic and solid companionship as well as political bonds.

Hogg consistently adopted the marriage plot in his works and revisited this plot convention not only in the novel, but also in the short story, the narrative poem, the epic, and the drama, in order to interrogate the ideological assumptions on which the British Union based its political aims, as these were meant to advantage the top levels of society, while Hogg aimed to voice a more diverse social reality. As I have argued elsewhere (Leonardi 2018a: 1–3; Leonardi 2018b: 20–21), in his *Reflections on the Revolution in France*, Edmund Burke supported an English nationalism founded on the model of the white, heterosexual, bourgeois familial nucleus bound together by 'domestic ties' and 'family affections' (1982 [1790]: 120). In Burke's project, Deirdre Lynch explains, the 'lovely image' of the nurturing mother 'guarantees the nation's cohesion' (1996: 54), while Rajani Sudan points out that 'women's capacity to produce off-spring' is 'commodified to represent a morally healthy British nation and to regulate the feminine body' (1996: 77). This book sheds new light on Hogg's awareness of the social contradictions at the heart of Burke's family metaphor, pivotal in the national tale at the time of empire formation, where the political ties between Scotland and England were represented by the marriage plot that joined the two protagonists in a cross-national union. This study highlights Hogg's critical use of stereotypes of gender and language in relation to norms of class and ethnicity when deconstructing this plot convention.

With regard to the political union between England and Scotland, Douglas Mack has remarked that the Scottish ruling classes of the early nineteenth century had developed the notion of North Britain, 'a new name to match a new post-Union Scottish identity': lairds, aristocrats, lawyers, intellectuals, and politicians were willing to enjoy the fruits of the imperial economy; yet, in order to do so, they had to mould their 'cultural and linguistic norms' to those of 'polite England', as this cultural cleansing would smooth the path of their career in the colonial space (2006: 53). In her book *The Grammar of Empire*, Janet Sorensen clarifies that the middle classes' mastering of polite English was a way for marking their meritorious belonging to the higher levels of society, rather than acquiring such status through blood lineage. Polite English was an ideological formation that distinguished the ambitious members of the Lowland Scottish elite from both the 'uncouth' Highland warriors and the peasantry of the Scottish Lowlands, and made them feel at the same level of their English counterpart in the empowerment afforded by the British Empire (Sorensen 2000: 140–41, 151, 202). For this reason, Sharon Alker and Holly Faith Nelson conclude that those who did not conform, including 'working-class writers, particularly those who threatened to disturb moral and stylistic standards, were [...] carefully monitored by the literati' (2009: 9), as happened to Hogg.

Yet Sarah Mills indicates that both the production and the perception of politeness are a non-fixed continuum which changes according to the cultural and historical context, and which norms of class, gender, and ethnicity influence significantly (2003: 1). This linguistic phenomenon is borne out by how Hogg's works were received outside Scotland. For example, in North America Hogg's image of the Ettrick Shepherd was more in line with the rhetoric of the self-made man. This fact contributed to a more indulging acceptance of Hogg's supposed indelicacies, his works were successfully republished, and American periodicals reviewed them more positively. Using discursive (im)politeness theory (Christie 2000; Culpeper 1996; Mills 2009, 2011), this book reveals that Scottish, English, and North American reviewers received, interpreted, and evaluated Hogg's texts slightly differently. Although Hogg's social background influenced the patronising attitudes of all reviewers, those of Scottish reviewers were certainly the harshest (Leonardi 2019b). Hogg found himself censured by the literary elite for his persistent use of 'indelicate' topics and impolite language (i.e. Scots rather than English). This book argues that Hogg's recourse to these topics and languages was deliberate rather than inadvertent, and that his refusal to yield to contemporary notions of decorum expressed a concern with the causes of some contemporary social issues such as prostitution; the social stigma of out-of-wedlock pregnancy which could bring a woman to commit infanticide; as well as the violence of war in which many young soldiers lost their life in the name of British patriotism.

Sorensen explains that rules of decorum imply a certain degree of falsity, as 'polite conversation, far from being an open exchange of one's innermost sentiments, is more often a concealing of them' (Sorensen 2000: 214). Elsewhere I contend that in his first novel, *The Brownie of Bodsbeck* (1818), Hogg has Wat Laidlaw, a member of the peasantry, convey his ideals of honour in broad Scots. In my reading of the novel, Wat's Scottishness highlights his genuine nature, distinguishing him from the members of the Lowland ruling classes, whose use of proper English not only hid their Scottish identity but also masked their lucrative interests behind the British Union (Leonardi 2016a). This book traces both the advantages and disadvantages that the imperial project brought to Scotland, and how Hogg exposed them through a critical use of contemporary stereotypes of language and gender. It explores the tension between Hogg's individuality and the social forces that shaped the Lowland ruling classes—the middle class and the gentry formed by landowners both great and small—at the heart of the British Empire. Hogg's contemporary reviewers were rather surprised by Hogg's talent; nevertheless, they were also quick to dismiss his works by considering them as not relevant to their representation of the world. This book reveals *how* prejudiced those reviewers' reception of Hogg's works was and *why*, on the contrary, the same texts encountered a far more positive response in North America.

The chapters explore a wide range of texts and literary genres with which Hogg engaged: from well-known song lyrics and short stories, to longer narrative poems, as well as Hogg's major novels of the 1820s, including his most famous text, *The Private Memoirs and Confessions of a Justified Sinner*. The choice of texts spans from the early song 'Donald Macdonald', through the major works between 1815 and 1829, up to two original texts that Hogg wrote especially for the American periodical press in 1834: the ballad 'Bruce and the Spider' and the short story 'Tales of Fathers and Daughters'. Interestingly, though Hogg's later works show a retreat from his tendency to break the rules and an adjustment to moral conventions, the texts he wrote for the American press show more freedom in re-addressing his favourite themes, particularly his re-interpretation of the national tale where he debunks class barriers through the marriage plot. This project analyses Hogg's linguistic, stylistic and thematic choices in order to cast new light on the reasons for his obstinate violation of the literary proprieties of the period, thereby repositioning the significance of Hogg's oeuvre within the Romantic canon.

1   **Who Was James Hogg?**

James Hogg was a shepherd from Ettrick, in the Borders region of Scotland, who attended school for a very short period of time and who had to go to service at that age of seven as cow herder because his parents had lost their farm due to a decrease in the price of sheep and a few debtors' unpaid fees. At this time, Hogg experienced incredible hardships and suffered extreme hunger: 'From some of my masters I received very hard usage; in particular, while with one shepherd, I was often nearly exhausted with hunger and fatigue' (Hogg 2005 [1832]: 14). Gillian Hughes remarks that 'there is no doubt that' this experience 'conditioned his life-long identification with the dispossessed and the oppressed, and in various forms was transmuted into his subsequent writing' (2007: 9). Hunger, particularly for meat, is a recurrent motif in some of Hogg's works, where masters abuse their subalterns—see, for example, the embedded tale of 'Marion's Jock' in *The Three Perils of Man* (1822), later republished in *Altrive Tales* (1832), where the young protagonist kills a lamb after having been deprived of food for a very long period by his abusive master. The only master who treated Hogg with care was Mr Laidlaw of Black House, for whom Hogg worked for ten years since he was eighteen; he possessed a library of great value which Hogg perused with great passion, feeding his thirst for knowledge.

Hogg's first printed work was a pamphlet of poems that he published from memory in 1801 on a day he went to the Edinburgh market to sell some sheep. Yet the most significant encounter that eventually would transform his literary career was the one with Walter Scott, who went to Ettrick to collect some traditional ballads for his *Minstrelsy of the Scottish Borders* to meet Hogg and his mother, a holder of traditional lore who provided Scott with a few songs for his collection. Scott would subsequently inspire Hogg to publish his first book of poems and ballads, *The Mountain Bard*, in 1807.

A series of not very successful farming projects, as well as two daughters conceived out of wedlock, tarnished Hogg's reputation in Ettrick valley; so much so that in 1810, aged forty, he moved to Edinburgh to pursue his literary career. This is not to mean that Hogg was unwilling to take on his responsibility as a father but, rather, that he was 'dissatisfied with his profession as a shepherd and rather an unsettled sort of being' (Hughes 2007: 74). In fact, his Catherine 'married Hogg's much more stable cousin, David Laidlaw, in 1812' (Ibid., p. 74).

In Edinburgh, Hogg soon realised that no bookseller would be keen on employing a shepherd with no official education as a professional writer. For this reason, he decided to start his own weekly magazine, *The Spy*. At the time, the model for such publishing venue was the *Spectator* which demanded the observance of high levels of propriety. Hughes points out that the essay periodical was 'a form particularly associated with politeness, with manners and moral instruction, and readerly expectations were governed by the standard works of Joseph Adison (*The Spectator*), Samuel Johnson (*The Rambler*) and Henry Mackenzie (*The Mirror* and *The Lounger*)' (Hughes 2007: 90). After a few numbers, Hogg found himself in breach of such norms with the publication of a short tale, which he would later republish in the collection of *Winter Evening Tales* (1820) as 'The Renowned Adventures of Basil Lee'. This was a semi-autobiographical description of a not very successful farmer who impregnates one of his servant and flees to Canada to avoid the negative consequences of his actions. As a result, the literary audience of the time did not receive Hogg's story with pleasure and a high number of followers cancelled their subscriptions. Remarkably, in the metropolis Hogg survived thanks to his friend John Grieve, a hat maker with some literary interests, who took Hogg under his wing and house.

Notwithstanding his misfortunes, Hogg never renounced his writing ambitions and was always aware of his extraordinary talent; his good humour was never affected either. These are the years when he created some of his most ingenious works, such as the collection of poems *The Queen's Wake* (1813), *The Poetic Mirror* (1816)—a parody of the most renown authors of the period—, *The Brownie of Bodsbeck* (1818), Hogg's first novel, as well as numerous literary contributions to *Blackwood's Edinburgh Magazine*, a monthly periodical which Hogg helped to launch.

In 1815 the Duke of Buccleugh offered Hogg the lease of Altrive at a nominal rent for life, under the wish of his dearly departed wife who had always admired Hogg's literary talent, thereby fulfilling Hogg's wish to return to his beloved Ettrick and start farming again. Confident of his literary career as a source of extra income, Hogg took on a ten-year lease in Yarrow and married Margaret Phillips in 1820. This was a very happy marriage which gave birth to five children. In contrast, the farm of Yarrow proved to be a financial disaster, as Hogg was unable to stock it with enough animals. It was during this period that in order to pay off his accumulating debts, Hogg wrote prolifically, publishing some of his most genial works such as the romance *The Three Perils of Man* (1822), the two novels *The Three Perils of Woman* (1823) and *The Private Memoirs and Confessions of a Justified Sinner* (1824), the epic poem *Queen Hynde* (1824), as well as numerous contributions to *Blackwood's Edinburgh Magazine*, for which he received pecuniary compensation.

Towards the end of his life, Hogg grew disappointed with William Blackwood for various reasons: the dashed hopes of the publication of a collection of works added anger to Hogg's already disappointed mood caused by the incessant ridiculed figure of the Ettrick Shepherd, his literary persona, in the *Noctes Ambrosianae*. This was a fictional convivial debate about the literature of the period created by John Wilson and published periodically in *Blackwood's Edinburgh Magazine*, where Hogg was depicted as a coarse and rowdy shepherd. Gillian Hughes maintains that though the series was 'good publicity' for Hogg, 'it probably had a negative effect on the nature of his fame', so much so that when Hogg went to London in 1832, those used to his portrayal in the 'Noctes' 'were surprised to find him "so smooth, well-looking, and gentlemanly"' (Hughes 2007: 185–86, 249).

Hogg went to London to find a publisher for his collected works and here he started to collaborate with other London's periodicals such as *Fraser's Magazine*, *The Metropolitan*, and *The Royal Lady's Magazine*; the acrimonious relationship with Blackwood also led Hogg to try the American periodical market in 1834. Unfortunately, James Cochrane was able to publish only the first volume of Hogg's collected works, *Altrive Tales*, in 1832 as his publishing company went bankrupt. Hogg's dream was realised posthumously in 1837 by Blackwell & Son in Glasgow who published Hogg's *Tales and Sketches*, a bowdlerised and highly censored version of Hogg's works. This is how Hogg's writings came to be known to the Victorians and the future generations, a fact that has enormously contributed to belittling Hogg's literary talent and, most importantly, to hiding the fact that his works critiqued the inequality between the ruling classes and the margins of the period.

2   Exploding the Marriage Plot and the Family Metaphor for the Nation

In the early nineteenth century, the Scoto-British discourse was spread through the national tale and the historical novel, two novelistic genres which articulated the grand narrative of national progress endorsed by Adam Smith and other Scottish Enlightenment philosophers. Katie Trumpener maintains that the national tale originated in the Jacobin novel of the 1790s, later evolving into a new novelistic experiment undertaken by Irish writers Maria Edgeworth in *Ennui* (1809) and *The Absentee* (1812), as well as by Sydney Owenson (later Lady Morgan) in *The Wild Irish Girl* (1806) (1997: 124–32). According to Ina Ferris, the fortunate cross-national marriage between the main characters became an allegory of the political reconciliation between the British nations (2002: 48). It promoted, however, a distorted image of the British Union which, in line with Michel Foucault's notion of discourse, blocked and invalidated other knowledge (1990: 18) as, for example, the disadvantages that such political union had brought on the lower classes.

Ferris (2002) views the national tale as a narrative where Irish, mostly female, authors voiced early nineteenth-century national grievances for an English audience, hence mirroring the tension-rife contest generated by the creation of the United Kingdom. Trumpener, on the other hand, remarks that Walter Scott's historical novel 'repoliticized (and masculinized)' the national tale of his contemporary Irish female writers by shifting the emphasis from the characters' geographical movement across regions to their process of growth and loss through historical change (1997: 132). Maureen M. Martin and Kenneth McNeil contend that Walter Scott—a committed supporter of the union between Scotland and England—played an important role in developing the notion of romantic Highland Scotland. In his first novel *Waverley* (1814), he recreated the Jacobite rising of 1745 as a heroic romance in a mythical past, while glossing over the military attacks by the Highland clans, whose courage and unconditional loyalty to the chief he re-channelled into service to the British Union (Martin 2009: 20, 82; McNeil 2007: 21, 106). Scott's *Waverley* encompassed simultaneously the 1746 Jacobite defeat in the battle of Culloden and the assimilation of Scotland into an English-dominated Britain through the cross-national wedding of the two main characters.

Major criticism in the field, however, has noticed a change in Scott's representation of history after *Waverley*. Ferris, for example, points out that Scott's subsequent novels show 'ambivalence about the paradigm of progressive historical change standard in his day' (1991: 119), and that the remnant figure is a powerful container of energies of the past lingering in the present, thereby exposing the consequences of unresolved issues (Ferris 2009). Kenneth McNeil observes that in *Rob Roy* (1817), Scott re-articulates a more sophisticated representation of the Highlanders as less restricted and isolated by their land and cultural stereotypes, highlighting instead their 'participation in a globalising economy that necessitates a constant movement within and across regional boundaries', thus representing the relation between Highlanders and Lowlanders in more fluid terms (2007: 53). Ian Duncan remarks that in *Rob Roy*, Scott distances himself from previous teleological representations of history, where the Highland myth is relegated to the past, depicting 'the historical simultaneity of different worlds [...in which] savagery and commerce sustain rather than cancel one another, constituting the uncertain, cryptic field of the present' (2007: 110). It must be argued, however, that although Scott in his later novels undoubtedly re-articulated a more fluid relation between Highlanders and Lowlanders as Scots who, by sharing a less threatening Highland imagery for the union, kept a distinctive national identity from the English with whom they now were equal partners in the British imperial project, yet Scott's rethinking of this relationship was rather classist, as he tended to downplay the negative effects of the union on the margins of both Scottish regions.

In view of what Scott was promoting in the Waverley novels, Hogg's rewriting of the national tale in his first novel *The Brownie of Bodsbeck* was radical and extreme, as here he does not provide a marital resolution to Scotland's social inequalities, highlighting instead the failure of Burke's familial trope in the construction of a British nation that does not account for its ethnic, gender, and class diversity. However, Hogg's shift from the family metaphor to a single woman as a new political symbol of Scotland threatened the continuation of the nation: Katharine's lack of progeny implicates a resistance to progress because, as Cynthia Enloe remarks, 'no nation can survive unless its culture is transmitted and its children are born and nurtured' (2014: 119). As a consequence, Hogg's *Brownie* deconstructs the British discourse of mother country, depicting the disintegration of Katharine's family of origin and hence countering the national tale's ideology of erotic desire. Hogg's novel, on the contrary, supports the male coalition between Katharine's Lowland father and a Highland soldier, thereby questioning the ideology of the marriage plot (Leonardi 2016a).

The national tale as practised by Sydney Owenson and Charles Maturin was also subversive of middle-class conventionality. Heather Braun notes that in *The Wild Irish Girl*, Owenson 'recast[s] Ireland as a place where desire is fulfilled, an image that disturbs imperialist portrayals of Ireland as disagreeable and woefully dependent on Britain for its survival' (2005: 35); while Esther Wohlgemut claims that 'the cosmopolitan heroines of Germaine de Staël and Charles Maturin [in *Corinne, or Italy* (1807) and *The Milesian Chief* (1812) respectively ...] challenge romantic fantasies of national union, marking the point at which [...] the social mechanism "creaks,"' thereby questioning the political correlation between domestic femininity and national stability by the interplay between national and cosmopolitan heroine (2002: 192). Hogg was thus not alone in subverting the ideology of romantic love in the political union endorsed by the national tale; nonetheless, he was challenging those 'romantic fantasies of national union' by proposing a more inclusive social milieu in his texts and by encompassing the margins usually silenced or kept in the background among contemporary authors.

Anne McClintock observes that the traditional figure of the family was fundamental to the construction of British national identity. The subordination of wife to husband and of children to adults provided a language to articulate British relations between the margins and the centre in familial terms, so that the infantilisation of colonials, women, and members of the lower classes resulted in the perception of differences in class, gender, and ethnicity as natural and legitimate (McClintock 1995: 43–45). In line with this discourse, Edgeworth felt compelled to remove the inter-racial marriage between the secondary characters Lucy (an English farm-girl) and Juba (a black servant) in the 1810 edition of *Belinda* (1801). Moreover, though Thomas Tracy points out that in *The Wild Irish Girl* Sydney Owenson 'argues for increased equality both between Britain and Ireland and between women and men' (2004: 91), it must be argued that such gender equality was still contemplated within an aristocratic and upper- and middle class social milieu.

In some ways, the efficacy of the national tale was already collapsing by the time Hogg was writing. Juliet Shields remarks that 'Scottish national tales sought to enable, through sensibility, the integration of a racially and culturally homogeneous and distinct Highland people into a heterogeneous British nation and empire'. In *Clan-Albin* (1815), Shields explains, Christian Isobel Johnstone represents 'Highlanders as paragons of domesticity and familial affections' rather than as 'uncouth savages governed by blind allegiance to a lawless chieftain', thus integrating them in the present through 'the social virtues most cherished by civilized southern Britons'; while in *Marriage* (1818), Susan Ferrier 'envisions a hybrid Anglo-Celtic Britishness formed [...] through an open-minded and observant toleration of cultural difference', where only a marriage 'founded in rational affection will produce lasting harmony' (Shields 2010: 112, 114, 129–30). Shields's account of these novels suggests a renewal of the national tale's formula by admitting the Highlanders and emphasising companionate marriage. Hogg's particular intervention was thus occurring at a time when the ideology of the national tale was been reshaped to encompass the new demands of the British political project.

The courtship plot had had a long history before its allegorical re-appropriation by the national tale. Patrick Parrinder explains how it had mediated class difference in the consolidation of English national identity since Samuel Richardson's *Pamela* (1740), which he considers a 'female variant' of the *Bildungsroman*, where 'the maidservant marries her former mistress's son' (2006: 30). Parrinder remarks that 'the story of courtship portraying a young girl's awakening has remained the typically English form of the novel, since it is sharply opposed to the dangerously adulterous liaisons of classic European fiction' (Ibid., pp. 30–31). Hogg's treatment of the marriage plot hence derives from a long literary tradition of 'English domestic novels' that endorsed 'family values', and 'offered both instruction in the social proprieties and the indulgence of (licit or illicit) desire' (Ibid., p. 31) with the aim to educate the young middle-class readers. 'Sexual desire in English fiction is famously muted', Parrinder explains, as the 'novel's great task was to make its middle-class heroes and heroines visible by representing them as newcomers eligible for admission into the charmed spectacle of upper-class society' (Ibid.). Arguably, Hogg's rewriting of the courtship plot and his portrayal of wayward female characters share more in common with Daniel Defoe's *Molls Flanders* (1722) and *Roxana* (1724) than with Walter Scott's Rose and Flora in *Waverley* (1814) or Sydney Owenson's Glorvina in *The Wild Irish Girl*, even though Hogg's fallen female characters are morally more sound than Moll Flanders and Roxana. In the works where Hogg uses the marriage plot as national allegory, the supposedly 'impure' woman, the fallen daughter that a father eventually redeems, poses as a more historically realistic, ethnically diverse and socially inclusive figure for the nation than the morally pure, middle-class, motherly heroine who has never been exposed to the social reality suffered by women on the other side of the social spectrum.

This is born out by two further social concerns that Hogg portrays in some of his works and which debunk the ideology of progress inherent in the family metaphor: illegitimate pregnancy and infanticide. In the early nineteenth century, this reality clashed with the Enlightenment idea that society's treatment of children is one of the signs of Western civilisation. In his *Theory of Moral Sentiments*, Adam Smith claims, 'Can there be greater barbarity [...] than to hurt an infant? [...Yet] we find at this day that this practice prevails among all savage nations' (1976 [1759]: 209–10). At the time of Hogg's writing, Smith's notion was exploited to support the imperial economic expansion under the cover of civil improvement. Josephine McDonagh observes that '[t]he historical memory borne by the figure of child murder [...] complicates the conventional teleology of historical narrative, and opens the possibility of counter-histories that question the authority of conventional, progressive accounts' (2003: 12). It must be noticed, however, that Hogg was not alone in dealing with this issue, as both Walter Scott in *The Heart of Midlothian* (1818) and, subsequently, George Eliot in *Adam Bede* (1859) address infanticide. However, Scott and Eliot place their plots in the past, while Scott's novel blames a vagabond, not the mother, for the child's death. Chapter 4 shows that infanticide was a reality still extant in Scotland, not just 'among all savage nations', as Smith argued (1976 [1759]: 201), and that illegitimate motherhood affected the lives of a number of women, sometimes not only among the lower classes.

3   Hogg, Literary Dialogism, and Early Nineteenth-Century Politeness

With reference to other contemporary writers, Massimiliano Morini maintains that Jane Austen avoided any kind of confrontation with the ideology of her time by appearing to simultaneously endorse and critique the *status quo*. In Austen's novels, Morini explains, '[t]he narrator's position in his/her ideological and linguistic world is at one and the same time acquiescent and subversive, parasitic and critical' (2009: 76)—a fact which certainly contributed to the positive reception of Austen by contemporary critics.[1] On the other hand, other critics argue that Austen's works *are* critically engaged with their social conditions. For example, Sheryl Craig observes that each of Austen's novels refers to the financial situation of England at the time when it was composed. Craig maintains that considering Austen's work as a mere form of love story escapism means missing 'the political message that would have been obvious to Austen's original readers' (2015: 18). Similarly, Rachel M. Brownstein observes that in *Sense and Sensibility* (1811), Austen's 'satire on selfishness and greed' is meant to expose the 'social structure and institutions that shape, alter,

---

1   The 1815 review of Austen's *Emma* in the *Quarterly Review* by Walter Scott (*QR*, 14, 1815: 188–201), though dated October 1815, did not appear until March 1816.

and inflect human nature—marriage and the family, primogeniture, assumptions about gender and rank' (2015: 98). Stephanie M. Eddleman observes that Austen's culture 'privileges youth and beauty, especially for females, and her novels reflect this influence', though she also shows 'awareness of and resistance to this regrettable reality', as in the portrayal of Anne Elliot in *Persuasion* (1817), through which Austen critiques society's restrictions 'of the joys of life only to the very young' (2015: 131, 132, 134). Likewise, David Sigler observes that Austen's novels comment 'on sexual difference and its discursive, cultural, and economic implications, even as it trains readers to accept the inevitability and desirability of marriage' (2015: 58). Finally, Lauren Miskin points out that in *Northanger Abbey* (1818), Henry Tilney's 'fashionable taste' for Indian muslin shows a new masculine identity based on the consumption of the products derived from the expansion of the British Empire, while 'his interest in "true Indian muslin" indicates [...] his political allegiance to larger structures of imperial and patriarchal oppression' (2015: 6). Nevertheless, Austen's criticism of her society was never direct and her elusive technique in exposing social issues represents the exact contrary of the narrative strategies that Hogg employed in his works, where such negotiation is completely and purposefully disregarded.

Austen was highly skilled at mastering what LuMing Robert Mao views as the 'two competing forces shap[ing] our interactional behaviour: the ideal social identity and the ideal social autonomy' (1994: 451). Mao holds that the perception of keeping or losing face and the norms of polite behaviour are shaped by a tension between a centripetal force towards adherence to social norms and a centrifugal force towards individual freedom (1994: 472). In the same line, in some of his works Hogg exhibits a strong wish to express his own personal criticism against the false assumptions behind literary norms of propriety, as well as a desire to be accepted by the Edinburgh literary elite; it is thus no wonder that when reviewing *Winter Evening Tales*, *Blackwood's Edinburgh Magazine* accused Hogg of being 'too fond of calling some things by their plain names, which would be better expressed by circumlocution' (vol. 7, 1820: 154).

In considering the publishing conventions of early nineteenth-century Edinburgh, Alker and Nelson observe that 'Hogg's *ability* to conform to the genteel expectations of the marketplace was not in question. It is his *desire* to do so that is at issue' (2009: 10, emphases original). Roger Sell assumes that nineteenth-century fiction largely mirrors the 'interweaving of politeness with class and power' (2015 [1991]: 210). Hogg's writing that violate nineteenth-century principles of literary decorum show this dynamic at work well. Yet a self-educated shepherd who refused to conform could not be considered a serious writer, and Hogg's boldness was thus condemned as being inappropriate for middle-class female readers. As I have argued elsewhere, in the short story 'Basil Lee' (1820), for example, Hogg challenges the dichotomy between conventional heroine and fallen woman by presenting Clifford, a prostitute, endowed with higher moral values than the supposedly Highland hero who deserts the imperial war in Quebec (Leonardi 2012a). Ian Duncan has noticed that though Hogg removed Clifford's considerations about the British army in the 1821 edition of *Winter Evening Tales*, he kept 'the Clifford Mackay plot', even though it had provoked a negative response from contemporary critics (2004: 533). While Hogg's collection in 1820 had been received very enthusiastically, the *Monthly Review* had judged 'Basil Lee' the worst story because its grappling with prostitution and illegitimate pregnancy offended 'the best regulated modesty' (n.s., 93, Nov. 1820: 264); whereas *Blackwood's Edinburgh Magazine* had argued that 'not a few passages [...] would require an intrepid person to read aloud to boys and virgins' (vol. 7, 1820: 154). Duncan observes that 'it seems that Hogg took care to present the story as a challenge to middle-class morality, not a lapse from it; and to the very end he refused to alter it' (Duncan 2004: 534). Yet, as Duncan points out, Edinburgh was not ready.

Only in *Queen Hynde* Hogg 'seems' to have achieved a balance between his ideal of self-expression and his adaptation to conventional values, thanks to the ironic tone with which he addresses the young Edinburgh ladies, the implied readers of this poem. Here Hogg exploits what Jonathan Culpeper defines as 'mock impoliteness', that is, 'impoliteness that remains in the surface, since it is understood that it is not intended to cause offence' (1996: 352). Thanks to such negotiation Hogg was thus able to claim his intellectual freedom and to earn positive criticism on this point, even though *Queen Hynde* was not a literary success and other critics dismissed it. Yet Suzanne Gilbert and Douglas S. Mack have noted that Hogg's work was censored in press (1998: 224). As a result, the excisions must have contributed to an apparently achieved balance between his own desire to depict women without any hypocritical constraints of false delicacy and his own wish to be accepted and acknowledged as a valuable author in his own right. Gilbert and Mack point out that a comparison between Hogg's own manuscript and the first edition of *Queen Hynde* shows that many passages where the wayward Wene, Queen Hynde's maid of honour, plays her mocking tricks were deleted by the alert activity of Ballantyne's copy-editors, who removed what they considered indelicate (Gilbert and Mack 1998: 224). As a consequence, the deletions in the first edition decrease enormously the impact of Wene's symbolism of freedom, hence blurring Hogg's implicit critique of nationhood based on the gender discourse of women's sense of propriety (see Chapter 5).

This book suggests that assumptions about politeness also illustrate Mikhail Bakhtin's understanding of literary dialogism. Politeness theory assumes that participants observe power and social hierarchies by respecting (or threatening) their interlocutor's face. Likewise Bakhtin's dialogism assumes that the varieties of language an author confers on the characters of a text expose a social dimension which may be placed at various points of either closeness to or distance from what is ideologically regarded as the standard language in the world outwith the text at the time of the author's writing. For Bakhtin—and similarly to what Mao discusses about the tension between individual freedom and the desire to be socially accepted—the use of various languages in the novel mirrors the social tension between a unifying force towards a standard language that represents the main discourse and a decentralising tendency towards other language varieties which Bakhtin calls *heteroglossia* (1981: 67). Each character in the novel represents a social dimension, for their speech is always ideologically marked (Bakhtin 1981: 334); this is why Hogg's contemporary Scottish reviewers were rather critical of Hogg's extensive use of broad Scots in place of polite English, as this did not align with the politics of Englishness they had been promoting since the political union in 1707. For example, Scottish reviewers demystified Hogg's use of Scots by representing Hogg's supposedly uncouth behaviour through his literary persona, the Ettrick Shepherd of the 'Noctes Ambrosianae' published in *Blackwood's Edinburgh Magazine*. This was an ideologically devised image influenced by stereotypes of class: by placing the Ettrick Shepherd as the 'other', Scottish reviewers helped construct the identity of the Scottish ruling classes as more genteel and in line with the norms of politeness of the English, with whom they were competing for the conquest of the British Empire (see Leonardi 2019b). This book reveals that the potentials of politeness phenomena are enormous for investigating the adherence to and the challenge of the *status quo* in those literatures whose goal is to voice realities other than the socially accepted ones, as in Hogg's case.

Yet Hogg was not alone in using vernacular styles in his works. Murray Pittock observes that Robert Burns's different variants of Scots provide 'alternate readings of the same poem', Walter Scott's vernacular 'takes place within a closure of Unionist conformity', while Hogg's tension between forms of dialects and proper English challenges 'that very closure' (2011: 4). Sorensen remarks that 'the naming of a particular usage as "dialect" or nonstandard' indicates a social struggle (2000: 67), thus revealing that acceptable language represents only one side of the social scale. In Scotland's case, 'the polite language of the Lowland elite signalled their society's advanced status in a four-stage chronology of human societal development [... and i]t is likely on these terms that Scottish "improvers" could comfortably celebrate Burns' (Sorensen 2000: 153, 155). On the other hand, contemporary Scottish reviewers felt threatened by Hogg's use of broad Scots, failing to admit his sophisticated use of languages. For example, in *The Brownie of Bodsbeck* Hogg's fluid alternation between English and Scots in the same social scale counters the rhetoric of inclusion/exclusion implicit in the dialectic between Standard English and vernaculars, so fundamental to the discourse of Englishness of the British Empire. The dissonance between Katharine's Englishness and her father's Scottishness exposes the performative nature of British national identity through language, destabilising the ideology of Standard English and, thus, disintegrating class distinctions (Leonardi 2016a: 64–65). This book shows that Hogg's sophisticated use of language and gender questions the ideology of Englishness, Scottishness and Britishness that shaped the ruling classes of early nineteenth-century Britain. Hogg's diverse and flexible use of languages destabilises the hierarchy between Standard English and regional Scots at a time when the use of dialect was not only associated with the province and the peasantry but also with a primitive past, an earlier historical stage seemingly superseded by urban standards of progress. On the other hand, Hogg's particular use of Englishness and Scottishness challenges contemporary constructions of British progress, showing how such supposedly modern developments had profoundly affected the life of the inhabitants of the Scottish margins.

It must be noted that though early nineteenth-century Scottish reviewers were not captivated by Hogg's outrageous depiction of female sexuality, his use of broad Scots, and the violence of war, outside Edinburgh Hogg's reputation seems to have been less affected by his audacity (Leonardi 2019b). London reviewers, for example, were far more lenient with Hogg's work. *The Eclectic Review* published a very positive assessment of Hogg's long poem *The Pilgrims of the Sun*, where Hogg is quite critical of the devastation of war, contending that

> It is no easy task for a young man, without either title or name that may ensure attention, to force his way through the hosts of versifiers that crowd the levee of Fame with their obstreperous claims; and in spite of fashion, prejudice, or envy, to stand forward as the rival or compeer of Southey and Wordsworth, of Byron and Campbell, of Montgomery and of Scott.
>
> n.s., vol. 3, March 1815: 280

Indeed, *Blackwood's Edinburgh Magazine* would have never compared Hogg to such high-profile names.

Suzanne Gilbert points out that in early nineteenth-century North America, 'Hogg was popular [...] because his personal narrative appealed to Enlightenment ideals of "improvement" and self-help, and because the democratic and humanitarian impulses of his work paralleled those current in American political discourse' (2012: 44). American reviewers writing for abolitionist periodicals were inclined to highlight Hogg's literary achievement from obscurity, and to set his self-education as an example of democracy to ex Afro-American slaves, for whom education would have made a difference in finding a path in their newly emancipated condition. Hogg's reception in America is the topic of Chapter 6, which shows how the different socio-historical reality of North America contributed to a less offensive and problematic perception of his works. Here Hogg's texts were received more favourably because their democratic values aligned with contemporary American anti-slavery campaigns; American democratic politics; and with cultural commitment to demotic and popular styles.

4   Hogg's Intersectional Dialogue with Stereotypes of Gender, Class, and Ethnicity

In recent years, James Hogg has been the subject of various books on British and Scottish Romanticism. In *Scott's Shadow: The Novel in Romantic Edinburgh* (2007), Ian Duncan explores Walter Scott's novelistic genre to capture the history of the Scottish nation, developing a comparative analysis with James Hogg's and John Galt's historical representations of regional, national, and imperial accounts. Penny Fielding's *Writing and Orality: Nationality, Culture, and Nineteenth-Century Scottish Fiction* (1996) investigates Scottish national identity and culture in the nineteenth-century fiction of Walter Scott, James Hogg, R. L. Stevenson, and Margaret Oliphant, focusing on the link between speech writing and orality. In *Scotland and the Fictions of Geography: North Britain 1760–1830* (2011), Fielding explores Scottish Romantic literature to expose the roles of England and Scotland in the shaping of the British nation. Her analysis of Burns, Hogg, antiquarian and travel writing sheds new light on the relationship between Scottish history, literature and geography. Douglas S. Mack's *Scottish Fiction and the British Empire* (2006) explores how Hogg questioned the imperial ideology of his time from a class perspective. The present book is indebted to Mack's portrayal of Hogg's voicing of the margins; however, it departs from Mack by shedding new light on Hogg's strategic use of nineteenth-century stereotypes of language and gender in intersection with class and ethnicity to voice those margins.

Hogg has also being the subject of two essay collections. *James Hogg and the Literary Marketplace: Scottish Romanticism and the Working-Class Author* (2009), edited by Sharon Alker and Holly Faith Nelson, explores Hogg from a labouring class lens, highlighting how he questioned the aesthetic conventions embraced by his contemporaries writers. The essays contribute to acknowledging how ideas about oral culture, nationalism, trans-nationalism, intertextuality, class, colonialism, empire, psychology, and aesthetics illuminate Hogg's originality as a working-class author in Scottish Romanticism.

The Edinburgh Companion to James Hogg (2012), edited by Ian Duncan and Douglas S. Mack, gathers the research of sixteen international experts on Hogg, shedding new light on the contexts and debates that shaped his texts. The essays discuss Hogg's personal life and experience, how Hogg dealt with the publishers of his time, how his texts were received, Hogg's position with ideas about politics, religion, nationality, class, sexuality and gender, and his fascinating engagement with a large array of literary genres: from the ballads, to popular songs, poems, the theatre, short stories, novels, and the writing which he published in the periodicals press.

Recently, Meiko O'Halloran's *James Hogg and British Romanticism* (2016) argues for 'Hogg's centrality to British Romanticism through his radical experiments with literary form and his creative reconfiguration and parodic interrogation of the values of the early nineteenth-century literary marketplace' (pp. 1–2), focusing on Hogg's reinvention of particular literary genres and on his effort to 'prompt readers to exercise their own critical reflexes' (p. 2). Finally, Karl Miller's *Electric Shepherd* (2003) is a biographical reflection on Hogg's eclectic personality and remarkable resilience which enabled him to raise among the most prolific literary figures in the Romantic period.

My book differs from all of these discussions by focusing on Hogg's unorthodox treatment of the marriage plot and on representations of masculine as well as feminine gender types in their intersection with class and ethnicity. It also provides an overview of Hogg's reception in North America, where the works of the Ettrick Shepherd were received more positively. These key topics are peripheral to the above discussions, with the exception of Silvia Mergenthal's essay entitled 'Hogg, Gender, and Sexuality', published in *The Edinburgh Companion to James Hogg* (2012). Mergenthal touches briefly on questions of Highland and Lowland ethnicities with regard to military masculinities when discussing Hogg's novella 'Basil Lee'. My book adds to Mergenthal's analysis by highlighting the astute use that Hogg made of such gender and ethnic constructions during the expansion of the British Empire to expose the negative effects of such discourses on the Scottish margins. Hogg engaged pro-actively with nineteenth-century concepts of class, gender, and ethnicity thus exposing the important role that such assumptions played in shaping the discourse promoted through the marriage plot and in construction of English, Scottish and British identities for the ruling classes at the expense of the Scottish margins.

Surprisingly, despite Hogg's engagement with these aspects in his works, and with the exception of Alker and Nelson's collection of essays (2009) and other articles (2006: 69–70; 2001) exploring Hogg as labouring author, and Douglas Mack's study of Hogg's voicing of the margins (2006), there has been no substantial study of the overlapping of class, gender, and ethnicity in Hogg's works, nor of Hogg's more positive reception in North America in the nineteenth century. This book hence contributes to revealing Hogg's sophisticated engagement with such variables in relation to early nineteenth-century constructions of Scotland, the British nation and empire, as well Hogg's outstanding international literary outreach during the same period.

5   Summary of the Chapters

Chapter 2 explores how Hogg re-articulates his own version of the national tale in the two novels *The Three Perils of Man* (1822) and *The Three Perils of Woman* (1823). Though apparently conforming to this novelistic genre through the prosperous unions of the protagonists, Hogg questions the ideology behind the marriage plot through the secondary characters in the subplots of both novels. In Peril First of *Perils of Woman*, the female protagonist Gatty is temporarily reduced to a body incapable of articulating the costs of her marriage to the hero, namely the death of her less socially privileged cousin Cherry, the secondary heroine. Antony Hasler observes that Gatty's 'marriage to a Highland gentleman finally seals the heroine's moral progress in an allegory of national renewal' (2002: xvii). Chapter 2 reveals that by portraying the transformation of Gatty's body into an automaton, Hogg counters the progressive assumptions of that promising end.

Ian Duncan (1994) maintains that in *Perils of Woman*, Hogg's management of contemporary literary conventions is so subtle that it requires great effort on the part of a modern reader to grasp its satirical aspects, as Hogg's novel encourages a critical distance from the dominant literary conventions of his time, even though inhabiting those very narrative modes. Katherine Inglis views the maternal bodies in Hogg's novel, Gatty's in 'Peril First' and Sally's in 'Peril Third', as 'an uncanny form', arguing that 'that which in the ideology of the national tale or the historical novel is the repository of national meaning, agency and continuity, becomes instead an emblem and agent of the disruption of history' (2011: 62). Drawing on Bakhtin's notion of novelistic dialogism and on recent developments in the pragmatics of literary communication, Chapter 2 suggests that the temporary paralysis of Gatty's body conveys

Hogg's sharp criticism of the primary heroine as symbol of national progress in both the national tale and the historical novel.

To this end, I draw on Suzanne Rosenthal Shumway's Bakhtinian reading of Sandra Gilbert and Suzanne Gubar's *The Madwoman in the Attic* (1979) (Shumway 1994). In their reading of Charlotte Brontë's *Jane Eyre* (1847), Gilbert and Gubar view Bertha Rochester's madness, and her consequent reclusion, as subverting the moral assumptions of the primary narrative by 'function[ing] as [an] asocial surrogate for [a] docile sel[f]' (2000 [1979]: xi). Similarly to Shumway's re-visitation of this imagery of female enclosure and insanity, I view the lunatic asylum where Gatty's family hides her from social gaze as a Bakhtinian chronotope: Gatty's spatial confinement and her three-year physical transformation are in intrinsic relation to each other as they symbolise the costs of Gatty's marriage to the hero and her punishment for Cherry's death, hence questioning the ideology of the marriage plot in the national tale.

In the same book, the wedding between Rickleton, a Northumbrian landowner, and a Scottish Lowland prostitute in the secondary plot further complicates the idealised marriage of the main plot between Gatty and M'Ion. This male character is discussed in more details in Chapter 3 because its transformation into a tamed type of masculinity is a topic in line with what is discussed in that chapter. Rickleton's recognition of his wife's son from a previous lover shows a real 'man of feeling', who accepts the consequences of the system of primogeniture that such an acceptance implies for the inheritance of his land (see Leonardi 2012b: 33). Rickleton is an honest model of sentimental masculinity, evolving from an untamed to a sensible man who truly sympathises with his wife, thereby performing the anti-hypocrisy that was needed to correct the middle-class conventionality of the national tale, its 'anti-mimetic model', as Ina Ferris would call it (2002: 47).

In Peril Third of the same novel, Hogg moves back in time to the Culloden massacre of the Highland clans in order to destabilise the romanticised union between Gatty and M'Ion of Perils First through the physical consequences of the violence of that war on the bodies of Sally Niven and her child. The class-crossing marriage of convenience between this Lowland servant and a Highland gentleman does not protect the former from death. Hogg here exposes the catastrophic effects of a war violating a maternal body, thereby leaving, once again, a symbol for the Scottish nation without progeny for the future.

In *Perils of Man*, Hogg hints briefly at the celebration of the royal wedding between Princess Margaret and Lord Douglas, while conferring a longer narrative space to the comical performances of the friar's mule infuriated at the vain behaviour of one of the knights, and transgressing class boundaries through

the union between the English Lady Jane Howard and the poor, but honest, Scottish warrior Charlie. Hogg then counteracts the majesty of the royal
wedding with the fantastic marriages between the witches and the devil. The
hyperbolic caricature of the old wives' terrifying deaths thwarts the auspicious
unions of the royal couple. In *Perils of Man*, the grotesque destruction of the
witches' bodies suggests their union to the devil to be an 'emblem of all worldly
grandeur' which, eventually, turns out to be 'unreal and unsubstantial' (Hogg
1996 [1822]: 525).

Chapter 3 addresses the various types of masculinities that, in the early
nineteenth century, informed the construction of Scottish, English, and British identities. Hogg was concerned with the waste of human lives provoked by
nearly two decades of war with France for imperial expansion. T. M. Devine
maintains that 'empire and militarism were linked together like Siamese twins',
as the colonial dominion 'had to be achieved on many battlefields across the
world and by the unrelenting application of massive naval force on the high
seas' (2004 [2003]: 291). The myth of the indestructible and loyal Highlander
served a double purpose, as it shaped the militaristic power of the British
Empire as well as the identity of the Scottish nation. Maureen Martin reveals
that although in the eighteenth century the Scottish Enlightenment had played
an important role in the cultural achievements of the sophisticated Lowlands,
by the nineteenth century Scotland as a whole came to be identified with a
wild hyper-masculinity located in the Highlands. The prowess of the enduring
Highlanders threatened the masculinity of the Scottish Lowlanders who thus
suffered a double invasion: the economic and political control on the part of
England on the one hand, and the cultural supremacy of Highlandism on the
other, all aspects that affected the construction of a stable Scottish national
identity (Martin 2009: 2, 13).

During the visit of King George IV to Edinburgh in August 1822, Walter Scott
promoted the '"Celtification" of Scotland' through a 'gaudy overuse of "tar-
tanry"' (McNeil 2007: 52). In Scott's royal spectacle, the Highland militaristic
discourse positioned Scotland as an indispensable partner for the virilisation
of the more feminised commercial England, the centre of the British Empire,
and more interested in trade-related affairs than in male, honour-based questions of national identity. Juliet Shields contends that the charisma of the
Highlander did not affect English manliness, as the latter was founded on
contemporary discourses of sympathy and sensibility which shaped a more
sophisticated sense of masculine vigour, tamed by self-control. Once considered an exclusively 'feminine virtue' that distinguished middle-class women
and made them suitable mothers and wives, besides 'justifying' their 'confinement to the safety of the domestic sphere', sensibility came to be assimilated

into an idealised 'benevolent patriarchy', supposedly exercised by men of the middle and upper classes (Shields 2010: 9).

The Lowland Scots endured a further cultural stigmatisation which the English exploited in order to contain the economic power of Scotland in the imperial conquest: the stereotype of the rapacious Lowlander, based on the assumption that Lowland Scots had bribed the parliament to influence the approval of the 1707 Union with England, in order to take advantage of the economic potential offered by the exploitation of the colonies (Martin 2009: 112). The English felt threatened by the Scots' economic potential in the British Empire, and the 'penny-pincher' caricature, 'popular in English newspapers [...] deflate[d] both the intimidating masculinity of the untamed [Highland] Scottish warrior figure and the commercial success of the ambitious [Lowland] Scottish entrepreneur with whom Englishmen had found themselves in competition since the Union' (Martin 2009: 110). Chapter 3 exposes that this cultural stereotype, however, mirrored only part of the Scottish social spectrum, namely what Douglas Mack has defined as the 'avaricious nature of the Glasgow of the Imperial "sugar and tobacco-trade"' (2006: 155), and what Martin describes as 'the lucrative renting of Highland estates throughout the century, first to sheep farmers and then to English sportsmen' (Martin 2009: 110) by Highland landlords. Hogg believed that this cultural assumption was rather unfair to the lower classes of Scotland, as they did not prosper in the political union with England, nor did they enjoy the financial gains from the empire but, rather, had either to emigrate to Canada and North America or to enrol in the army for the Napoleonic Wars in order to survive.

Chapter 3 maintains that the social status of Hogg's characters is a pivotal element in Hogg's engagement with Highland, Lowland, and sentimental masculinities. For example, the popular song 'Donald Macdonald' (first published c. 1803) parodies the mystique of the Highlander by displaying an unquestionably loyal soldier who would offer his soul to the devil to fight for King George in the Napoleonic Wars. The long poem 'Wat o' the Cleuch', included in Hogg's collection *The Poetic Mirror* (1816), revises the stereotype of the avaricious Lowlander by exposing the reality of a Lowland Scots from the margins, whose robberies and craving for meat—a symbol of wealth and prosperity—hint at the exploitation of the peasantry by the Lowland gentry, the ones really prospering in the British Union. Finally, the ideological assumptions inherent in early nineteenth-century constructions of sentimental and Highland masculinities are explored, once again, through the character of Rickleton in *Perils of Woman*.

Chapter 4 opens with an historical overview of the Scottish Kirk, prostitution, illegitimate pregnancy, and the issue of infanticide in late eighteenth- and early nineteenth-century Scotland, in order to prepare the ground for the analysis of Hogg's following works and characters: the long narrative poem *Mador of the Moor* (1816), the short story 'Maria's Tale' (1820), and the figure of the prostitute Bell Calvert in *The Private Memoirs and Confessions of a Justified Sinner* (1824). In *Mador*, Hogg focuses on Ila Moore, a forsaken young woman from the 'woodland', who is seduced, abandoned and made pregnant by the King of Scotland in disguise, and who has to endure the social stigmatisation of her condition—contrary to the 'counter-history' of the Palmer's upper-class lover who, in the same poem, kills her baby to avoid public shame. For this reason, Ila deserves to become a queen and she eventually marries the King of Scotland. On the other hand, in 'Maria's Tale' Hogg reveals what happens when a young female servant hides her out-of-wedlock pregnancy and a child birth goes wrong: a reality well represented in the Scottish ballad tradition but which did not accord with the ideology of the motherly heroine in the national tale. The chapter concludes by exploring Hogg's outspoken treatment of prostitution in *The Private Memoirs and Confessions of a Justified Sinner* through the figure of Bell Calvert, a fallen lady of the upper class who has to resort to this means of survival to keep both herself and her child born out of wedlock. Chapter 4 assumes that by being so explicit about these matters, Hogg challenged the progressive assumptions of British civilisation inherent in the ideology of motherhood and mother country.

Chapter 5 shows that in the short story 'Tibby Hyslop's Dream' (1829 [1827]), Hogg fuses the primary and the secondary heroine in a unique character who does not engage in any courtship with the hero. Jennifer Camden maintains that in the marriage plot, the hero's repressed attraction towards a more rebellious secondary heroine poses a threat to the nation's stability, as his real feelings return like the Freudian 'uncanny' to 'destabilize' and 'complicate' the 'national ideals' embodied by the primary heroine (2010: 2). According to Camden, the hero's hidden feelings for the secondary female character expose 'national anxieties', thus 'pointing to the instability of national identity' (2010: 6). Camden draws on the models of nationhood devised by Benedict Anderson (2006 [1983]) and Katie Trumpener (1997) to shape a paradigm for the tension between the primary and the secondary heroine (Camden 2010: 3). Anderson's view of 'nationhood as an imperial construct' where 'the nation is defined by the majority' as an 'imagined community' which 'excludes the "other" in the interests of group cohesion' supplies Camden with a theory for conceptualising the role of the primary heroine, whose marriage to the hero represents 'the basic unit on which the larger nation is constructed'; Katie Trumpener's idea of nationalism as located on the border provides instead a model for the 'rebel, outcast, or merely forgotten' secondary heroine who 'pulls readers' attention to the margins' (Camden 2010: 3). The unmarried condition of Hogg's heroine in 'Tibby Hyslop's Dream', however, leaves Scotland without an offspring for the future to 'ensure the continuation of the nation': a trait that Jennifer Camden associates with the secondary heroine (2010: 4), but which Hogg incorporates in this female protagonist. Abusing Tibby's body is the only interest of the two male characters. Tibby thus performs a cultural role within Hogg's tale, setting spinsterhood as a dignified solution when there are no heroes, and revealing the harsh reality of female servants in the early nineteenth-century Scottish Borders. Sadly, women had to defend their chastity to keep their reputation, though they could also lose their position if they did not yield to the amorous requests of their masters.

Chapter 5 concludes with the analysis of *Queen Hynde*, in which Hogg portrays the marriage plot between the two Celtic peripheries of the British Isles: Ireland and Scotland. Ian Duncan notes that Maria Edgeworth's *Ennui* (1809), rather than engaging in the typical national tale's plot of 'Anglo-British Union [...] casts Scotland as Ireland's future. A Scottish Enlightenment ethos of scientific improvement and professional discipline provides the model for Irish accession to modernity within the British state' (2007: 258). In *Queen Hynde*, Hogg exhibits a reversal of Edgeworth's agenda since, rather than supporting the Scottish grand narrative of historical improvement, he poses M,Houston—King Eiden of Ireland disguised as a Scottish peasant—as an ethical model to the Scottish aristocrats of Queen Hynde's entourage. M,Houston fights bravely against the Norse King Eric, the invader of Scotland, while the Scottish aristocrats lack the courage to defend their queen. M,Houston's honourable behaviour thus leads Queen Hynde to choose him as her royal husband.

In the subplot of this epic poem, Hogg then portrays a proactive secondary heroine, the charming and rebellious Wene, one of the ladies of Queen Hynde's train who, by playing the game of love with Prince Haco, advances her position in the social scale to the rank of queen of Scandinavia. Wene's progression symbolises Hogg's independence from literary conventions of propriety and his aspiration to establish himself at the top of the list of Romantic poets as the 'king o' the mountain and fairy school' (Hogg 2004 [1834]: 9).

Finally, Chapter 6 is devoted to the reception of Hogg in North America. It returns to politeness theory in exploring Hogg's reception in the US, where he was praised as a self-made man. In North America, Hogg's works were received very positively for the high sense of democratic values that they conveyed at a time when some North American periodicals and newspapers were promoting not only abolitionism, emancipation and anti-slavery campaigns, but also the discourse of the American dream through the ideal of the self-made man. Chapter 6 discusses Hogg's presence in the American periodical press of a wide political spectrum: from journals that openly promoted and supported slavery, to those who supported a more gradual emancipation, up to the most fervent abolitionist ones. Towards the end of his literary career, Hogg wrote a few works especially for the American press, such as the ballad 'Bruce and the Spider' and 'Tales of Fathers and Daughters'. The latter engages with the themes of gender, ethnicity and inter-class marriage, thereby providing a transatlantic coda to the marriage plot discussed in the previous chapters.

Chapter 6 also discusses the incredible reach of Hogg's texts in North America thanks to newspapers' habit of clipping essays, poems and stories from the most prestigious literary reviews of Boston, New York and Philadelphia. For example, 'Epitome of War' from the essay 'Soldier' in *Lay Sermons* (1834) was a particularly popular one, similarly to 'A Scotchman's Advice to his Daughter' from *Perils of Woman*, where Daniel Bell warns her daughter Gatty on how to behave in the 'sin' city of Edinburgh. The chapter develops a comparative analysis between British and American reviews of Hogg's works, exploring differences and similarities through a class lens. The scope is to illustrate how the emerging United States of America re-appropriated and re-adapted British stereotypes in an attempt to distinguish themselves from their mother country and to lay the foundations of their newly born nation.

Thanks to the Stirling / South Carolina Research Edition of the Collected Works of James Hogg, published by Edinburgh University Press (which is reaching its end with nearly forty volumes published), today Hogg's works have reached an audience beyond Scottish Studies. The aim of this book is to highlight the stature of this Scottish author who deserves to be included in the conversation with other canonical Romantic writers. Hogg's legacy is evident in the interest that his works have raised among postmodern and postcolonial scholars who have responded favourably to Hogg's particular use of the Scots language, as this shows that in the nineteenth, as well as in the twentieth and twenty-first centuries, Englishness is still a national ideology strictly entangled with structures of power and wealth.

CHAPTER 2

Exploding the Marriage Plot

1   The Three Perils Novels and the Ideology of the Marriage Plot

This chapter shows how in the two novels *The Three Perils of Man* (1822) and *The Three Perils of Woman* (1823), Hogg questions the ideology of the marriage plot as developed in the two grand narratives of the national tale and the historical novel where the cross-national wedding of the two protagonists supported an unquestioned stability of the British Union. By showing the effects of a marriage of convenience on the bodies of both the primary heroines and some secondary female characters, Hogg counters the progressive assumptions of the marriage plot in both narratives, thereby exposing the ideology behind this plot convention and the contradictions at the heart of empire formation.

In the first book of *Perils of Woman*, Hogg interrogates the supposedly blissful union between Gatty and M'Ion in the central plot through the boisterous figure of a secondary character, Richard Rickleton, a Northumbrian laird who marries a Scottish prostitute (see Chapter 3). In the same novel, Hogg also sets the wayward, but honest, cousin Cherry in intra-textual relation with the self-restrained Gatty. In so doing, Hogg defies the expectations of middle- and upper-class women in contemporary conduct books, which promoted the ideal of the delicate lady as carrier of British moral values. Hogg articulates his critique through Gatty's grotesque body: the carnivalesque transformation of this female character, who falls into an apparent state of coma for three years, is the consequence of a malady the cause of which Hogg never clarifies and which has stimulated a fierce debate among twentieth-century critics, as this chapter later explains. No scholar, however, seems to have explored the significance of Gatty's physical change, hence missing Hogg's pointed critique of the ideology of the marriage plot, where the female protagonist is meant to act as a repository of British moral values.

Twentieth-century critics of *Perils of Woman* have mostly focused on the negative reception of Hogg's novel both at its time of first publication in 1823 and among modern scholars who, until recently, have regarded this novel as one of Hogg's minor works, a poor imitation of conventional fiction for women, thus failing to grasp its sophisticated satirical aspects. Antony Hasler contends that in 1823 the novel received the most negative reception of Hogg's entire literary production (2002: xiv), a fact which has influenced its negative reputation until recently. David Groves maintains that the readers of Hogg's time

© KONINKLIJKE BRILL NV, LEIDEN, 2022 | DOI:10.1163/9789004519992_003

regarded *Perils of Woman* as a terrible failure for its blasphemous language, its lustful heroines, and its lack of respect for polite social mores (1986: 192). Emma Letley (1990) observes that the disturbing prayers of Gatty's father, Daniel Bell, in his native tongue during his daughter's illness caused accusations of blasphemy at the time of the novel's first publication. When compared with other nineteenth-century authors, Letley contends that Hogg used the Scots language in a distinctive way; surprisingly for his time, he brought it into the courtroom and the church—two important centres of authority from which it had been banned. Hogg's placement of Scottishness in these two institutionalised spaces defied the rhetoric of early nineteenth-century Englishness which Hogg's contemporary Scottish reviews actively promoted.

Groves argues that a real appreciation of Hogg's novel only began in the 1980s, when scholars such as Nelson C. Smith and Douglas S. Mack started to perceive the satirical tone behind its seeming imitation of conventional fiction for women (1992: 80). Ian Duncan (1994) holds that Hogg's management of contemporary literary conventions is so subtle that it requires great effort on the part of a modern reader to grasp its satirical undertones, as Hogg's novel encourages a critical distance from those conventions, even though engaging in those very narrative modes. Katherine Inglis views the two pregnant bodies of Gatty's in 'Peril First' and Sally's in 'Peril Third' as 'uncanny form[s]', arguing that in Hogg's novel 'that which in the ideology of the national tale or the historical novel is the repository of national meaning, agency and continuity, becomes instead an emblem and agent of the disruption of history' (2011: 62). Drawing on Bakhtin's notion of novelistic dialogism and on recent developments in pragmatics linguistics for literary communication, this chapter views the temporary paralysis of Gatty's body as Hogg's critique of the primary heroine as symbol of national progress; while in the third book of the same novel, the deaths of Sally Niven and her daughter dash any hope for the future of the Scottish nation.

Seemingly in line with the narrative requirements of both the national tale and the historical novel, *The Three Perils of Man* ends with a series of marriages. Hogg sets this long narrative in the Scottish Borders at the time of Robert II and its beginning has a chivalric tone. It starts with the English Lady Jane Howard demanding Sir Philip Musgrave conquer the castle of Roxburgh as a test of his love. The Scottish Princess Margaret Stuart requests the same task of her suitors, adding a further demonstration of love: the winner of Roxburgh will have her in marriage but, should he lose, he will also lose all his possessions. The only suitor who accepts these conditions is Lord Douglas. The early chapters of the novel relate the first attempts of the Scots guided by Lord Douglas to dislodge Sir Philip Musgrave and his English garrison from the castle of Roxburgh. Princess Margaret Stuart (who, disguised as a valet in the early part of the novel, is thought to have died in the siege) turns out to be still alive and marries Lord Douglas; while Lady Jane Howard is given in a national class-crossing marriage to Charlie Scott in reward for his loyalty to Sir Ringan and Lord Douglas.

Princess Margaret's sense of restlessness, however, calls into question her marriage with Lord Douglas. Margaret is a highly proactive female character when compared to other heroines of contemporary fiction, one who, as Graham Tulloch explains, is able 'to turn [her] position of vulnerability into a position of strength by forcing men to play the chivalric game on [her] behalf' (2004: 41), and by demanding men 'risk their life under the pretence of honour', as Jason Mark Harris points out (2003: 52). Margaret also utilises various male disguises in order to cross the border between domestic and public sphere, and to control the events of the dispute between the English and the Scots in the conquest of the castle of Roxburgh. At the end of the novel, however, Tulloch remarks that the marriage that Margaret so hoped and fought for 'controls and contains her' (2004: 41), as she is no longer able either to play the chivalric game nor to engage in her carnivalesque masquerades.

Hogg parodies the series of royal marriages at the end of *Perils of Man* through the hyperbolic caricature of the witches' own weddings to the devil in disguise, through which he exposes the dramatic consequences of the marriage plot on the female body. Hogg then presents his own version of this plot convention, transgressing class boundaries in the union between the English Lady Jane Howard and the poor but honest Scottish warrior Charlie Scott, a character who contrasts the selfishness of Lord Douglas. The latter mirrors the opportunism of the Scottish ruling classes of Hogg's time who, thanks to the 1707 political union with England, had derived a great deal of wealth from the exploitation of the British empire at the expense of the Scottish margins. Likewise, Lord Douglas is so absorbed by his own economic interests in the conquest of the castle of Roxburgh that he does not recognise Princess Margaret in male disguise, thereby putting both her life and honour at risk, in addition to sacrificing the lives of many of his subordinates in the vain conquest of the Castle of Roxburgh.

As mentioned above, the reception of both novels was rather negative at the time of their first publication. The thirteen anonymous reviewers of *Perils of Woman* did not appreciate Hogg's use of the Scots language nor his 'indelicacies'. The *Literary Gazette* summarises the general opinion, acknowledging that Hogg was 'a man of a strong but undisciplined imagination', accusing his text of blasphemy, 'coarseness and gross vulgarity', as well as of being characterised by 'a dialect of unintelligible gibberish'; also 'the frequent allusions to women of ill-fame, and especially Gatty's letter about them, [which] are in the worst possible taste', were criticised (no. 345, 1823: 546, 547). Concerning *Perils of Man*, the twelve anonymous reviewers were against Hogg's use of the supernatural, his parody of the language of the Scriptures in the voice of the Gospel Friar, and the use of Hogg's 'unintelligible' Scots language.[1] In *Perils of Woman*, Hogg interrogates the notion of the 'pure' lady as a national signifier and he deconstructs the ideology of the marriage plot that he had started in *Perils of Man* in 1822 with the carnivalesque portrayal of the witches' marriage. Hogg's subtle questioning of what had become conventions of the two novelistic genres, however, contributed to the negative reception of both novels.

2   The Witches' Marriage to the Devil: A 'True Emblem of All Worldly Grandeur'

In *Perils of Man*, the character of Princess Margaret has to be read within a nineteenth-century context, where the ruling classes would abuse their subalterns: though a medieval romance, this long narrative clearly exposes itself to questions about Hogg's contemporary monarchical and arbitrary power. This is hinted at when Princess Margaret, with the promise of some social advancement, has a young valet die in her place, in order to cover her masquerades.

The the royal marriage between Princess Margaret and Lord Douglas has also cost the unnecessary death of many young subordinates in the skirmishes between English and Scots, the violent depiction of which mirrors the waste of human lives incurred by British soldiers in the imperial expansion during the Napoleonic Wars. Significantly, the anonymous reviewer of the *Monthly Censor* did not appreciate Hogg's violent depiction of the battles, claiming that 'Mr. Hogg [...] ought to blush for having painted the race from whom his countrymen are sprung, in such black, and hideous colours' (vol. 1, 1822: 468). Evidently, the supporters of the British Union were not ready to admit the casualties that Hogg so graphically portrayed and that echoed the devastation of a war that had ended only seven years before the publication of *Perils of Man* with the battle of Waterloo in 1815.

Tellingly, the narrator decides to cut the description of the royal weddings, only remarking that '[t]he streets of the city, and the square of the fortress, that had so lately been dyed with blood, now "ran red with Rhenish wine"' (Hogg

---

1   Both lists of journals can be retrieved from *Literary Reviews in British Periodicals 1821–1826*, compiled by William S. Ward (New York: Garland, 1977), p. 116.

1996 [1822]: 491).² Instead, he dedicates a far longer narrative space to the comic adventures of the friar's mule, 'Goliah of Gath', during the royal games, through which Hogg exposes class-related pride:³

> It chanced one day that the knight of Kraeland entered the list alone. [...] He was a goodly youth, but uplifted above the earth with vanity, and of his vapouring and airs there were no end. [...] The lookers on were all beginning to get sick of him, and to view his vaporous manoeuvres with disdain, but amongst them all there was none so much moved to spleen as Goliah of Gath. From the first moment that the knight entered the list that uncircumcised Philistine began to manifest a mortal dislike towards him: the more so it was believed that he was mounted on a milk white steed, a colour peculiarly disagreeable to the mule's optics. [...] the malevolent eye of Goliah [...] became moved with so much indignation that he would no longer be restrained, either by bit or spur, soothing or threatening [...] fixing his long teeth in the horse's shoulder, till [...] the white steed was overturned.
>
> HOGG 1996 [1822]: 492–93

As I have remarked elsewhere (Leonardi 2012b), in the final part of *Perils of Man*, Hogg chooses to portray the more unconventional marital unions between the witches and the devil. Silvia Mergenthal contends that these marriages 'are, respectively, an uncanny foreshadowing of, and an unkind commentary on, the disillusionment experienced by the knights and the ladies in their marriages' (2012: 85). Yet the witches' carnivalesque unions to the devil also question the ideology of the marriage plot as represented by the royal weddings. Considering that the witches are poor women who have accepted to work for the wizard Michael Scott under the promise of a marriage of convenience, their grotesque death mirrors the exploitation of the lower classes in Scotland as a consequence of the empowerment that the ruling classes had acquired through the union with England.

---

2 Hogg also exploits the same motif of the streets dyed with blood which later 'ran red with Rhenish wine' in a previous ballad, 'Thirlestane', contained in the collection *The Mountain Bard*; for further details see *The Mountain Bard*, ed. by Suzanne Gilbert (Edinburgh: Edinburgh University Press, 2007), first published in 1807 (pp. 79, 81).

3 In a letter to William Stewart Rose (18 March 1823), to whom he dedicated *The Three Perils of Man*, Hogg states that John Gibson Lockhart considered the friar's mule 'the hero of the romance', *The Collected Letters of James Hogg*, ed. by Gillian Hughes, associate editors Douglas S. Mack, Robin MacLachlan and Elaine Petrie, 3 vols (Edinburgh: Edinburgh University Press, 2004–08), vol. 2, pp. 183–85.

Gibbie Jordan, who in Hogg's novel is a bearer of old tradition, provides an account to the Queen of Scots and her attendants who find him during a visit to Aikwood castle. In regards to the witches' wedding to the devil, Gibbie reports that

> The marriage ceremony itself, always performed by a demon in the habit of a friar, was a piece of the most horrid blasphemy ever conceived; and every night one of the witches was married to the devil in disguise. Sometimes the bridegroom made his appearance as a gay cavalier, sometimes as a country squire, a foreign merchant, a minstrel, and a moss-trooper [...] and though she seemed always aware of the deceit in a certain degree, from former experiences, yet it was wonderful with what avidity each of the old creatures clung to her enamoured and goodly husband!
>
> HOGG 1996 [1822]: 523

Here Hogg shows his negative commentary on contemporary progressive assumptions inherent in the marriage narrative. Though set in the fourteenth century, the witches' violent death mirrors the costs of the British Union on the margins during Hogg's life. Time and again, the witches marry the devil in a magnificent celebration, only to die a terrible death soon after. Hogg portrays the horrible consequences of these marriages of convenience by depicting the murder of one of the witches, 'writhing to death in the arms of a huge and terrible monster, that squeezed her in its embraces, and hugged her, and caressed her till the spark of wretched life was wholly extinguished' (Hogg 1996 [1822]: 524). Hogg then focuses on the witch's disintegrated body, 'squeezed almost to a jelly, and every bone broken as if it had been smashed on an anvil', 'literally dashed in pieces' (Ibid., pp. 525, 527). Through Gibbie's voice, Hogg describes the witches' marriages as 'true emblem[s] of all worldly grandeur' which eventually turn out to be 'all equally unreal and unsubstantial' (Ibid., p. 525).

3   The Chronotope of the Asylum: A Subversive Literary Space

Drawing on Bakhtin's notion of carnival as the momentary disruption of social norms, Clair Wills reads both nineteenth-century hysteria and medieval witches as women's rebellion against patriarchal repression at different historical moments. However, while medieval carnival reversed rules in the public sphere and witches were punished before an audience, the hysteric was contained within the private space (2001: 88–90). Similarly, while in *Perils of Man* Hogg articulates his critique of the marriage plot through the hyperbolic portrayal of the witches' sensational punishment for pursuing 'worldly grandeur', in *Perils of Woman* he questions the ideological assumptions of this plot convention through Gatty's psychological derangement which her family contains within the private space of the asylum.

'Peril First' of *Perils of Woman* narrates the love-triangle between Gatty Bell (the daughter of a rich farmer in the Borders), her cousin Cherry Elliot, and M'Ion of Boroland, a Highland student of medicine in Edinburgh. Though in love with M'Ion, Gatty does not reveal her feelings to him because her nurse has warned her against the rashness of youthful love. Meanwhile Gatty, her brother Joseph, and Cherry move from the Scottish Borders to Edinburgh accompanied by their nurse in order to improve their education. Gatty's father rents the first flat he comes across, failing to notice that it is located in the very red-light district of Edinburgh. Strange as it may sound, M'Ion lives in the same building. When Gatty notices the anomalous inhabitants of the lodging, she writes a letter to her father, asking him to bring her back home, while cousin Cherry remains in Edinburgh. Feeling rejected by Gatty, M'Ion turns his attentions to her cousin and they become engaged, but when Cherry discovers that M'Ion still loves Gatty, she releases him from his promise. Eventually, M'Ion and Gatty celebrate their wedding and the three go to live in the farm of Gatty's father. Broken-hearted, Cherry becomes mysteriously ill and dies. Feeling guilty for her cousin's death, Gatty falls into a state of coma for three years, meanwhile giving birth to a son. Recovered from her illness, Gatty moves to the Highlands with her husband who inherits an estate, and they live happily thereafter.

Hogg's twentieth-century critics have never agreed on whether Gatty's illness is due to venereal or psychological causes. David Groves (1987) contends that the illness has to be read as venereal; Barbara Bloedé (1992) and Valentina Bold (1992) support a psychological origin in hysteria; while Douglas S. Mack (1990) believes in a moral and religious cause, viewing Gatty as a sacrificial victim due to her family's involvement in Cherry's death. Mack concludes that in order to grasp the complexity of Hogg's novel, a reader should allow the possibility of multiple interpretations for the origin of Gatty's illness. Along the same lines, Richard D. Jackson suggests that it is more likely that Hogg was 'temperamentally inclined' to leave Gatty's illness 'the subject of wonder' (2003: 6).

In *Three Perils of Woman*, the third-person narrator never clarifies the origins of Gatty's disease:

M'Ion still took it for the nervous shiver of a disturbed sleeper, and maintained his point that she [Gatty] was not dead, but fallen into a deep sleep,
or rather a trance. In what state she then was, it will never be in the power
of man to decide. The issue turned out so terrible, that the whole matter
has always appeared to me [the narrator] as much above human agency
as human capacity; if any [among the readers] can comprehend it from a
plain narration of the incidents as they succeeded one another, the definition shall be put in their power; but further I take not on me to decide.

HOGG 2002 [1823]: 196–97

Hogg leaves areas of ambiguity, exploiting what recent studies in pragmatics
linguistics define as the cooperative principle of communication. Research in
conversational strategies (Grice 1989: 22–40), which have also been applied to
the dynamics of literary communication (Sell 2000: 51–59, 221–22; Mey 2001:
68–78), contends that a speaker may purposefully decide to be uncooperative
with a hearer in order to communicate an indirect message. The speaker's uncooperative behaviour alerts the hearer, who starts to wonder why the speaker
did so, looking for an 'implicature', namely a hidden meaning behind it. Flout-
ing what Grice defines as one of the sub-maxims of manner—avoid ambiguity
(1989: 27)—Hogg indirectly hinted at the raise in the number of prostitutes
and venereal diseases in early nineteenth-century Edinburgh. Yet raising attention to this problem in an open and unashamed manner could have defied the
principles of politeness of early nineteenth-century Englishness that the big
reviews alertedly policed. Three years earlier, though Hogg's collection *Winter
Evening Tales* (1820) had been generally well received, *The Monthly Review* had
judged 'Basil Lee' a troublesome story because its not-so-hidden portrayal of
prostitution offended 'the best regulated modesty' (n.s., vol. 93, Nov. 1820: 264);
while *The Scotsman* had argued that Hogg should have tried to read his tales to
his then newly married wife and 'strike out every paragraph which, either as to
thought or expression, offend[ed] her delicacy' (29 April 1820: 143). This may
explain why in *Perils of Woman*, Hogg decided to leave the causes of the illness
that affects the love triangle unexplained.

In order to avoid defying what Roger D. Sell terms as 'selectional politeness' in literary texts, namely the author's choice of topics which may offend
a particular readership (2000: 221–26), in *Perils of Woman* Hogg chose to be
ambiguous about the consequences of prostitution. However, though he may
have exploited a certain ambiguity at the level of 'what is said' about Gatty's
illness, at the level of 'what is implicated' Hogg suggested a series of disturbing
circumstances, which were actually inferred by his contemporary reviewers

who rebuked Hogg's choices. The *Literary Chronicle* felt threatened by Hogg's indirect hints since he judged *Perils of Woman* a novel 'for our own right understanding and gratification, and not for that of our family, to whom, we soon found, we must make it a sealed book' (vol. 228, 27 Sept 1823: 615). That is to say, this reviewer thought that Hogg should have left bourgeois women—the symbolic signifiers of the British nation—unaware of the disturbing reality of prostitution in their position at the other end of the social spectrum.

Gatty's monstrous physical transformation into an 'animated corpse' (Hogg 2002 [1823]: 200) symbolises Hogg's resistance to middle-class assumptions of proper feminine behaviour:

> The body sprung up with a power resembling that produced by electricity. It did not rise up like one wakening out of a sleep, but with a jerk so violent that it struck the old man [Gatty's father] on the cheek, almost stupefying him; and there sat the corpse, dressed as it was in dead-clothes, a most appalling sight as man ever beheld. *The whole frame appeared to be convulsed, and as it were struggling to get free of its bandages.* It continued, moreover, a sort of hobbling motion, as if it moved on springs [...] It was now like the dead countenance of an idiot,—the eyes were large and rolled in their sockets, but it was apparent that they saw nothing, nor threw any reflection inward on an existing mind. *There was also a voice, and a tongue, but between them they uttered no intelligible word, only a few indistinct sounds like the babble of a running brook.* No human heart could stand this; for though the body seemed to have life, it was altogether an unnatural life; or rather, the frame seemed as if agitated by some demon that knew not how to exercise or act upon any one of the human powers or faculties [...] there the creature sat struggling and writhing, using contortions both in body and feature that were truly terrific. No one knew what to do or say; but as they were all together in the same room, so they clung together, and neither sent for divine nor physician, *unwilling that the deplorable condition of the family, and the nakedness of their resources, should be exposed to the blare of the public voice.*
>
> HOGG 2002 [1823]: 200–201, emphases mine

Drawing upon a contemporary vogue for the studies led by Luigi Galvani on the ability of electricity to re-animate corpses,[4] Hogg portrays the symptoms of

---

4 Ian Duncan discusses both the influence of galvanism on Hogg's fictional construction of Gatty's body and the latter transformation into a 'maternal body' through the deliverance of a child during her three-year comatose state in the asylum (2007: 207–12).

Gatty's illness as a 'staging' of Bakhtin's carnival. He depicts her body as a symbol of resistance to the 'civilising' discourse endorsed by Gatty's mother who, in *Perils of Woman*, is the guardian of early nineteenth-century Englishness, shown by her continuous rebuking of her husband's use of the Scots language.[5] As I have argued elsewhere, early nineteenth-century Englishness was a set of values that not only regulated the Scottish ruling classes' use of Standard English but also how they dressed and behaved (Leonardi 2019b). Mrs Bell displays an excessive preoccupation with appearance and she polices the conduct of her daughter. However, Gatty's 'whole frame appeared to be convulsed, and as it were struggling to get free of its bandages' (Hogg 2002 [1823]: 200), namely the dead-clothes that Mrs Bell has put on her seemingly dead body—a metaphorical representation of the 'civilising' values that she is attempting to instil in her daughter.

The critical value of the Bakhtinian grotesque body lies in its openness to public gaze, so as to articulate its commentary on social issues but, as Wills explains (1989: 88), in the case of nineteenth-century discourse on hysteria, the disruptive potential of mentally deranged women had to be contained within the private sphere. The identity of the middle classes that Hogg portrays in *Perils of Woman* relies on differentiation from Gatty's monstrous body, a symbol of disgust which must be hidden from public gaze. The members of Gatty's family are 'unwilling that the[ir] deplorable condition [...], and the nakedness of their resources, should be exposed to the blare of the public voice' (Hogg 2002 [1823]: 201). This is why 'it was judged proper [...] that she [Gatty] should be conveyed to a private asylum [...] so that the country might never know the real circumstances of the case' (Ibid., p. 203).

Bakhtin defines the chronotope as the intersection of the novel's spatial and temporal coordinates which, in addition to providing a setting, also shape the plot (1981: 84–85). For example, Suzanne Rosenthal Shumway explains that in *Jane Eyre* the attic where Rochester hides his mad wife is an important chronotope with the function of 'subverting and distorting the primary narrative' (1994: 157). According to Shumway,

> Within the chronotope of the asylum centrifugal language gains the upper hand over centripetal language. *Laughs, screams, even silence are valorised in this narrative space, rather than utterances.* In short, in the chronotope of the asylum lies the key to an intense linguistic freedom

that exists just beyond sanity [...] The chronotope of the asylum [...] thus
becomes an arena in which subversion—and in particular a feminine
form of subversion—can be articulated.

SHUMWAY 1994: 157, emphasis mine

Likewise in Hogg's *Perils of Woman*, the chronotope of the asylum becomes the
only space where Gatty can articulate the uneasiness derived from her following the appropriate code of conduct for ladies of her social status. Though in
the asylum Gatty is only able to utter 'a few indistinct sounds like the babble of
a running brook' (Hogg 2002 [1823]: 200), her incomprehensible words stage
Hogg's subversion of the ideology behind the marital narrative of the national
tale which, in the novel, has caused Cherry's death.

Gatty's cultural repression opens the pages of *Perils of Woman*, where she
addresses herself before a mirror, in so doing performing an example of what
Bakhtin refers to as 'super-addressee', the judging self which restrains her
behaviour in a similar fashion to a Freudian super-ego. Bakhtin remarks that
the super-addressee is a third authoritative voice against which an author
shapes the language of the text (Bakhtin 2004 [1986]: 126), while Jacob L. Mey
argues that this hidden third party mirrors a text's 'power and dominance'
(2000: 283). Its presence, however, becomes apparent only when characters
talk to themselves using the 'you' voice while evaluating the social consequences of personal choices by imitating the voice of an institutional authority
that the super-addressee represents. In Hogg's *Perils of Woman*, Gatty's double-
voiced monologue reflects the policing of her behaviour by the Scottish Kirk,
the rules of Englishness, and her nurse that have been restraining her natural
attraction towards M'Ion:

What is the matter with you, naughty Agatha, that you cannot pray to
your Maker this morning, as you have long been wont to do and that with
so much delight?

Because I am ashamed of the thoughts and feelings of my heart this
morning, and I never was before.

And because you are ashamed of your thoughts, do you therefore
propose to set up a state of independence of your Creator, and to ask no
more guidance or counsel of Him? If you think it sinful and shameful to
be in love, cannot you pray that you may never be so?

No.—Oh dear me! I cannot pray for that neither.

Then cannot you pray that you may love with all your heart, and be
beloved again?

Oh! No, no, no, no! I would not pray that for the whole world; it is so home a thrust, and comes so near one's heart, it must be very bad. My dear parents and my pastor have always taught me the leading duty of self-denial; to pray for such things as these would be anything but self-denial. To love with all my heart, and be beloved again! Oh! Goodness, no. I cannot, cannot ask such a thing as that! I am sure, at least fear, it is wrong, very wrong, but—I would not care to try.

HOGG 2002 [1823]: 2

The mirror is a window into Gatty's internal fight between culture and nature. This is why she never dares to look at herself into it until she has exercised some form of self-control by reciting 'a short prayer', wearing 'her clothes', and 'put[ting] her exuberant locks'—a symbol of her femininity—'under some restraint for the day' (Hogg 2002 [1823]: 1). John Berger maintains that a woman's identity contains a double perspective: the perspective of the male surveyor and the one of the surveyed female who inspects 'everything she is and everything she does', since the way a woman appears determines how society will treat her (1972: 46). In *Perils of Woman*, the mirror dismantles such double policing, putting Gatty before her real feelings for M'Ion. A dream triggers Gatty's self-awareness who, careless of any sense of decorum, looks at her real self, acknowledging her desires. Gatty's freedom is short-lived, though, as the super-addressee in the 'you' voice, referring to her 'dear parents' and 'pastor', as well as addressing her with the more official proper noun 'Agatha', regains control over Gatty. Nonetheless, the tension between culture and nature turns again towards freedom as, in the last sentence of the above passage, Gatty admits that even though her feelings are 'very wrong', she 'would not care to try' (Hogg 2002 [1823]: 2). Here, though Hogg seems to be embracing the saccharine features of the sentimental novel, he actually portrays a more authentic representation of Gatty's female desires than what twentieth-century critics believed.

Similarly to Susan Ferrier's *Marriage* (1818), which Hogg particularly loved, *Perils of Woman* describes a cycle of ignorance which middl-class women kept alive through their daughters.[6] Rather than opposing two twin sisters, Hogg compares two cousins, Gatty and Cherry, showing how Gatty's mother has

---

6   In a letter to William Blackwood of 28 June 1824, Hogg writes that 'never was there such a painter as she is [...] if the author of MARRIAGE and THE INHERITANCE be a woman I am in love with her and I authorise you to tell her so'; see *Collected Letters*, ed. by Hughes and others, vol. 2, p. 202.

passed her own Englishness on to her daughter, while Cherry, being orphaned and hence less culturally conditioned, is able to give full vent to her nature. Cherry and Gatty speculate over whether showing one's amorous feelings towards M'Ion, whom they both love, is appropriate for a lady. Cherry opens up the dialogue:

> I love him so dearly, that I feel just as I could take him all to my heart!
>
> Bless me, child, you must not speak out your foolish thoughts in that ridiculous manner. I hope you would not repeat such a sentiment to anybody else. If ever such a shameful thought cross your inexperienced mind again, for Heaven's sake suppress it, and say the very reverse of what you feel!
>
> Would I, indeed? Catch me there! A fine lesson, truly! You would first persuade me that I am a child, and then teach that child to be a systematic liar. *No, no, cousin, I will always think as I feel, and express what I think, for I shall never take up a trade that I think shame of*; and if I should love Mr M'Ion ever so well, and die for him too, what has anybody to say? So I will do both if I think proper.
>
> [...]
>
> Well, I protest, child, that *no young lady of this country ever expressed herself in such a style*. I am utterly ashamed to hear you.
>
> And yet you have had the same feeling a hundred times [...] So you are changing colour, are you?—*Who is the child now?*—*She that professes one thing, and feels quite the reverse, say I.* Good bye cousin.
>
> HOGG 2002 [1823]: 28–29, emphases mine

Hogg opposes Gatty—the young lady, carrier of British moral values—to Cherry—a symbol of honesty; even though, eventually, Cherry's genuine nature is punished with death. This female pair represents Hogg's own 'co-adaptation' between his appreciation of young women's spontaneity and what the norm of contemporary Englishness demanded of them, in line with what Mao (1994) argues with regard to how individuals negotiate their own desires with what is demanded of them by society when negotiating the social rules of face and politeness, as well as with what Roger Sell views as the 'empathetic movement' between a writer and the cultural values of their time.[7]

---

7   An anonymous reviewer, probably John Wilson, received Cherry as a 'warm-hearted creature towards M'Ion' and 'very innocent and piquante', even though viewing 'her prattle' too 'tedious'; see *Blackwood's Edinburgh Magazine* (vol. 14, 1823: 434).

In an essay to 'Young Women' published in 1834, Hogg claims that

> [t]here is an ingenious frankness which I am far from condemning, which consists simply in shewing the mind as it is. It is the purity which has nothing to conceal, *nothing to be ashamed of*, nothing to counterfeit, and nothing to affect [...] Nothing great is expected from her [a young lady], which makes her little sallies the more pleasant; and such a picture of happy cheerfulness cannot fail to be reflected even from the breast of a cynic. It is like music at a feast [...] a sweet fragrance on a passing breeze–a savour for delight, which cheers and amends that heart.
>
> 1997 [1834]: 18–19, emphasis mine

When considered in intertextual relationship with *Perils of Woman*, these words seem to portray the character of Cherry herself: similar to a Bakhtinian polyphonic orchestration, Hogg hides behind the voice of this secondary heroine, thus questioning the ideology inherent in the primary heroine as carrier of British moral values.

4   Violating a Maternal Body

According to Ian Duncan, in *Perils of Woman* Hogg depicts the development of the Scottish novel from 'domestic national tale' to Walter Scott's historical novel, with the aim of questioning those very narrative conventions 'from which he felt more and more alienated' (1994: 155). The aim of the following discussion is to show *how* Hogg interrogates the historical novel in 'Peril Third'. To this end, this section provides an analysis of the narrative techniques, literary tropes, and human feelings that Hogg exploits to articulate his own version of the marriage plot.

No critic seems to have engaged with Hogg's use of the feeling of jealousy in 'Peril Third' as an organising trope for the narrative structure. By signposting a chain of events through this basest of emotions, and by adding touches of humour and suspense when tracing a number of its causes and consequences, Hogg seduces the reader in order to achieve a more important goal. Hogg exposes the negative consequences of war on Sally Niven and his daughter, whose tragic death renders the end of 'Peril First'—in which the union of Gatty and M'Ion reconciles the Highlands and the Lowlands—rather utopian, a reality that Hasler defines as 'far distant from the vision of history as meaningless violence' (1990: 43). In 'Peril First' of *Perils of Woman*, Hogg hints at the exploitation of the Highlands by Lowland investors through Daniel Bell, who talks about the possibility of breeding sheep in M'Ion estate once he marries his daughter Gatty, all in all thinking the match with the Highland heir better than the one with Rickleton:

> And our daughter is likely to be a great Highland lady too; [...] and I think it will be a better speculation, after a', than Mrs Rickleton of Burlhope; for ye see, by way o' tocher [a bride's dowry] good, I shall double M'Ion's yearly income to him.
>
> HOGG 2002 [1823]: 127

At the time when Hogg wrote the novel, the Highland Clearances caused the eviction of tenants to make room for sheep breeding, which had started soon after the Culloden massacre in 1746, the time when 'Peril Third' is set.[8]

Significantly, Hogg reverses Walter Scott's progressive movement of the historical novel by starting with a tale set at his time of writing in the 1820s and then going backwards in 'circles'—rather than in linear chapters—to 1746, the year of the battle of Culloden—which Scott sidesteps in *Waverley*—in order to expose its resulting devastation of the Highland clans through Sally Niven's eyes. Antony Hasler remarks that Hogg views history as inexorable and inscrutable, as it tends to reiterate some of its negative patterns rather than to progress towards civilisation (2002: xxv-xxxi). This is why Hogg divides *Perils of Woman* in 'circles' rather than chapters, thereby suggesting that in human history wars are motivated by the same basic drives for violence, greed, and power on the part of those 'princes and great men [... who] generally live in luxury in their palaces, far from the battle's alarm, and are but little sensible of the miseries that accompany the wars that they themselves have raised', as Hogg argues in his essay 'Soldiers', when reflecting upon the Napoleonic Wars (1997 [1834]: 40).

Transgressing class boundaries, in *Perils of Woman* Hogg continues the critique of the marriage plot started in *Perils of Man*, where the union between the English Lady Jane Howard and the poor, but honest, Scottish warrior Charlie Scott contrasts the opportunism of Lord Douglas and, by extension, of Hogg's contemporary Scottish ruling classes, the ones who profited from the British union with England. In 'Peril First' of *Perils of Woman*, Hogg portrays the wedding between a Scottish prostitute and an English squire in the subplot as more honourable than the union between the protagonists of the main plot (see Chapter 3). In 'Perils Second' and 'Third', Hogg then depicts Sally Niven, a

---

8   See editorial note 127 (d) in Hogg's *Perils of Woman*, p. 445.

Lowland servant, unwittingly climbing the social scale: for her help in the Stuart cause, she is offered a Highland gentleman in marriage as a reward—even though this rise in social status, with relative adjustment to domesticity and renunciation of her sexual freedom, eventually causes her death.

Likewise, Peter Gow (Sally's previous lover) climbs the social ladder by marrying a lady of the upper class as a reward for having behaved 'heroically'. He, in fact, defeats 'the Earl of Loudon's grand expedition to catch Prince Charles' (Hogg 2002 [1823]: 333) at the castle of Balmillo by a trick, with the only help of eleven old men who 'placed themselves […] behind bushes on each side of the road […] and then […] running fire at considerable intervals' (Ibid., p. 323), they pretended to be two Highland clans surrounding the advancing troops of the Earl of Loudon.

The narrator points out that Lady Ogilvie (one of the Highland ladies supportive of the Stuart cause), upon knowing Sally's and Peter's heroism, remarked that

> [i]t would be the highest imprudence of these two to be united; for that they were both well entitled to change their places in society, from the lowest to the highest. If they were married, they were in a manner compelled to remain in the same humble sphere which they at present occupied.
>
> HOGG 2002 [1823]: 356

'Peril Third' then shows the tragic consequences of Peter's and Sally's abandonment of their 'humble sphere' thanks to their 'highly ranked' unions.

Hogg catalyses the plot of the second story around four fits of jealousy. At the end of 'Peril Second', Sally's 'leasing' (her 'flirtatious lying') provokes the jealousy of Peter and the minister of Balmillo who, for this reason, abandon Sally to her destiny, leading her to accepting a marriage of convenience to a Highland gentleman, Alexander Mackenzie. The second fit of jealousy is Sally's who, on seeing her husband with a supposed lover, flees away, setting in motion a chain of misunderstandings that lead to the final catastrophe of the tale: 'What toil, what sorrow, what misery one single word at that decisive moment would have prevented! But JEALOUSY, that fiend of internal descent, […] prevented her from […] inquiring […] into the connexion between her husband and supposed rival' (Hogg 2002 [1823]: 380), who turns out to be Alexander's half-sister. Sally's escape contributes to a third fit of jealousy: this time, her husband Alexander's, with the result that he and Peter wound each other. The fourth outburst of this feeling is that of Peter's wife who, in retaliation for her husband supposedly abandoning her for Sally, 'haunted as she was by the tormenting fiend of jealousy' (Ibid., p. 401), reveals Peter's location to the Duke of Cumberland's soldiers, who find and kill Peter and Alexander. In line with one of Hogg's aesthetic principles according to which, what appears to be true is not necessarily so, no cause of such outbursts of jealousy proves to be real; yet once ignited by such a potent feeling, the plot momentum cannot be arrested and Hogg arranges his critique of the marriage plot around these four cardinal fits.[9]

Sally's Highland husband, soon after their marriage, is involved in the battle of Culloden. Not knowing what has become of him, Sally experiences a strong feeling of abandonment, which is further exacerbated by the members of her husband's family who, notwithstanding her heroism in the Stuart cause, have never accepted her low origins. Cross-dressed as a man, Sally trespasses the borders of her safe domestic sphere and starts her adventure in the public space, in search of her spouse.

Appealing to a contemporary vogue for touring, Hogg portrays the journey of his cross-dressed heroine through the Highlands, juxtaposing picturesque sceneries with the atrocious effects of Culloden upon women and children, which he shows through Sally's eyes. Using noun phrases and adjectives that emphasise femininity, such as 'beautiful Lowland boy' (Hogg 2002 [1823]: 372) or 'fine Lowland stripling' (Ibid., p. 373), Hogg suggests how Sally's improbable Highland garb highlights her continuous risk of having her real gender revealed. This poses a great threat to Sally, because the English and the Highland soldiers might rape her; after Culloden, 'all the posts [were] occupied by a licentious military' (Ibid., p. 361). In such a state of uncertainty, Sally meets Davie Duff, the bizarre sexton of Balmillo, a Bakhtinian fool whom Hogg endows with the important literary function of exposing the human suffering derived from the battle of Culloden in 1746.

---

9   In his Preface to *The Hunting of Badlewe*, Hogg discusses the dynamics of his creative process in the organisation of dramatic action. The same principles seem to motivate the plot construction of 'Peril Third' around the feeling of jealousy. In that preface Hogg claims that

a chain of interesting events connected with and arising out of one another, affords infinitely more scope and chance of success to the poet,—more opportunities to the actor, of displaying his powers in the representation of nature, and more interest and delight, whether to spectators or readers, than can possibly be produced, if the rules are adhered to which criticism and custom have established.

See James Hogg [J.H. Craig of Douglas], 'Preface', in *The Hunting of Badlewe: A Dramatic Tale*, written by James Hogg (London: Colburn, 1814), pp. v–viii (p. vii). Meiko O'Halloran (2012) also discusses the great influence of the theatre on Hogg's successive fiction, where he adopts 'several provocative storytelling techniques' that he had experimented with in *The Hunting of Badlewe* ('Hogg and the Theatre', in *The Edinburgh Companion to James Hogg*, ed. by Duncan and Mack, pp. 105–12 (p. 110)).

The narrative voice hints at the dehumanising effects of this war by providing a melancholic description of the aftermath of Culloden, where the grotesque sexton appears:

> All was ruin and desolation. Hamlet, castle, and villa, had shared the same fate; *all were lying in heaps of ashes*, and not a soul to be seen save a few military, and stragglers of the lowest of adverse clans scraping up the poor wrecks of the spoil of an extirpated people. Among others, whom should they overtake but daft Davie Duff, *walking merrily along*, with a spade over his shoulder.
>
> HOGG 2002 [1823]: 362, emphases mine

Davie is a ludicrous figure, totally alien to the real world, as the juxtaposition of the verbal phrase, 'walking merrily along', with a semantic field of words describing human suffering suggests. The imagery of Davie compulsively burying corpse after corpse, which he finds 'lhying tier above tier, and rhank pehind rhank' (Ibid., p. 363),[10] reveals a universe indifferent to the atrocities committed in the Culloden battle, where death has erased all social hierarchies.

Hogg shows the horrendous effects of the battle on the 'half roasted' bodies of women and children (Hogg 2002 [1823]: 365), while later conveying his criticism through Davie's *heteroglot* Gaelic voice:

> His Mhachesty te Tuke of Chumperlhand pe a fery cood shentleman, but, Cot tamn! he should nhot have persecuted te poor prhetty mhaiteans, and wifes, and lhittle pabies to teath. Fat (what) ill could they doo to himsel or his mhaister? And ten te plack crow, and all te vhile creedy bhaist, would fall on te lhittle dhear innocent crheatures, and would tak out teir eyes, and te tongues out of teir mhouths. And ten tey would pe dhigging into teir hearts, and thaking out all teir bowels; and, O Lort, would pe mhaking a vhery pad chob of it.
>
> Ibid., p. 394

The genuine comments of this 'fool' figure, however, offended the anonymous reviewer of the *British Magazine* who, feeling that Hogg had gone too far in his

---

10 In presenting the Highland-English of native Gaelic speakers, Hogg follows a well-established literary convention: the de-voicing of the voiced consonant [b] to [p] (as in *peing* for *being* and *pe* for *be*); *ta* for *the*; *she* for *I*, and sometimes also for *you, he, it*. Other features include the substitution of *c* for *g*, and *t* for *d*, so that *God* becomes *Cod*. From Note 62(d) on p. 443 of *Perils of Woman*, ed. by Hasler and Mack.

graphic descriptions, accused him of being a violent Jacobite and of spreading 'absurd false hoods about the sanguinary cruelty of English soldiers, whom Mr. Hogg pretends to have butchered women and children for sport' (vol. 1, 1823: 374). The *British Critic*, though acknowledging Hogg's talent, judged the tales of 'Leasing' and 'Jealousy' as 'clumsy attempts to interweave a tissue of imaginary adventures on an historical groundwork [...] with little regard to manners, language, facts or character' (n.s., vol. 20, 1823: 361). The reviewer of *Blackwood's Edinburgh Magazine*, supposedly John Wilson, regarded Hogg to be skilled at writing ballads, but found him ridiculous when attempting more prestigious genres, as 'in one page, we listen to the song of the nightingale, and in another, to the grunt of the boar' (vol. 14, 1823: 427). These reviewers appear to have perceived Hogg as a threat to the rules of Englishness and politeness which the major reviews of the time controlled and promoted. The portrayal of the results of such extreme violence was not in line with what these reviewers would allow to publish, preferring to view Hogg's truthful descriptions as the result of his low social background and 'poor' education. Indeed, Wilson would have never described Hogg's language as 'the grunt of the boar' had Hogg belonged to his social milieu.

As I have argued elsewhere (Leonardi 2019b: 203–204), (im)politeness theory helps clarify the dynamics between social status and the occurrence of prejudices based on class stereotypes. Wilson's harsh review is an example of what Juhani Rudanko has defined as 'aggravated impoliteness' (2006). Jonathan Culpeper, D. Bousfield and A. Wichman explain impoliteness as 'communicative strategies designed to attack face, and thereby cause social conflict and disharmony' (2003: 1546). To this definition of impoliteness, Rudanko adds the notion of 'aggravated impoliteness', arguing that '[t]he difference between the two is not one of kind, but one of degree' (2006: 838; see also Rudanko 2017: 4, 14). Arguably, Wilson intentionally designed to chastise Hogg's literary figure, with no consideration for his public face as a writer. Sachiko Ide (1989) discusses the important role that politeness plays in revealing the status that an individual holds on the social scale (qtd in Mills 2011: 24). John Wilson's comments arguably attacked Hogg for not keeping his 'proper' place.

The second catalyst in Hogg's plot, Sally's jealousy at the sight of her husband and his supposed lover, leads our cross-dressed heroine to experience what David Groves describes as 'a descent into a world of confusion which engulfs physical, spiritual, and psychological aspects of human life' (1988: 19). Hogg exploits this motif, appealing to his contemporary readers' taste with a scene that is 'a mixture of the serene, the beautiful, the sublime, and the tremendous, as the wilds of Caledonia cannot equal' (Hogg 2002 [1823]: 370). The narrator portrays Sally descending

> into the bottom of the ravine, on a path made by the feet of the goat and the wild-deer; it was a gully, fifty fathom deep; all the rocks on both sides were stripped with marble, and the silver current was pouring alongst its solid bed, which for all the world, had the appearance of the hide of the zebra.
>
> Ibid., p. 371

Surrounded by this scene, Sally lives her psychological torment at its extreme; but after having gone through 'exhilarating emotions' (Ibid., p. 370), she ascends stronger than ever. Sally then 'strip[s] off her hose and brogs' (Ibid., p. 372), symbols of Highland masculinity, abandons her old greedy and self-interested Highland guide, and changes the direction of her journey towards her Southern home, still cross-dressed though now as a 'beautiful Lowland boy' and 'little caring about the consequences' (Ibid.).

Sally's improbable cross-dressing is not a new motif in Hogg's writing. In *Perils of Man*, without informing the reader of their real gender, the narrator describes Princess Margaret's and Lady Jane's masquerades in a similarly unconvincing way. Silvia Mergenthal observes *how* in Hogg's romance none of the cross-dressers can really pass as men because they consistently show signs of femininity (2012: 88). But *why* does Hogg engage in such a failed gender performance? In *Perils of Man*, the narrator depicts Lady Jane with 'a sweet, delicate voice' (Hogg 1996 [1822]: 27), 'blushing deeper than it behoved a knight to do' (Ibid., p. 32), and Princess Margaret with 'dark raven hair that parted on a brow of snow, a black liquid eye, and round lips, purer than the cherry about to fall from the tree with ripeness' (Ibid., p. 31). Hogg insists on a dense use of lexical items and metaphors related to feminine stereotypes typical of the sentimental novel, thereby leaving little doubt as to the real gender of both characters, so much so that Lord Douglas's failure to recognise Princess Margaret in disguise strikes the reader as a significant implicature, suggestive of his self-centredness and neglect of Princess Margaret.

Similarly, in *Perils of Woman* the narrator describes Sally as a 'fine Lowland stripling' (Hogg 2002 [1823]: 373), whose 'loud and piercing shriek' (Ibid., p. 374) points to her real gender. Once again, Peter Gow, her former lover, fails to recognise Sally, as 'he took a light, examined the features, recognized an acquaintance with the face, but could give no account when or where he had seen it' (Ibid.). In this case, Peter himself voices the implicature of Hogg's failed gender performance. When Sally asks him the whereabouts of his wife, he replies that

> she is well enough, and safe enough, for anything that I know; but Culloden men have had so much ado to escape from the cruelty of our beastly and insatiate foes, that really *we have been compelled to let the wives shift for themselves.*
>
> Ibid., p. 375, emphasis mine

When Peter asks Sally the whereabouts of her husband, she replies by ironically echoing his previous words, claiming that she feels as 'an outcast creature, abandoned to the world and to my fate. You warriors have enough to do in taking care of yourselves; *you are obliged to leave your wives to shift for themselves, you know*' (Ibid., emphasis mine). In this way, Hogg conveys his implicit criticism of the war of Culloden, whose soldiers—absorbed as they are by the rhetoric of war—have become oblivious to their wives' fate at home. Earlier in the narrative, Hogg anticipates the effects that such neglect will have upon his heroine through a prophetic dream, where a soldier runs his sword through Sally's body in the presence of an irate but impotent Peter.

Sally's husband, Alexander Mackenzie, is the victim of the third outburst of jealousy, when a series of misleading clues lead him to believe that Sally and Peter are still lovers. Alexander attacks Peter but the latter reacts, with the consequence that both men seriously injure each other and have to remain in a remote hut of the Highlands until their wounds have healed. This is the site where Hogg shows how war deforms human nature thanks to two secondary characters: Dr Frazer and, once again, David Duff, who respectively play the Bakhtinian roles of rogue and fool (see Bakhtin 1981: 158–67). Dr Frazer, the rogue, still maintains a contact with the real world, while David Duff, the fool, is totally alien to it and blind to the wicked intentions of other characters.

The remote hut in the Highlands is the site where both Dr Frazer and David Duff take care of the two wounded men and Sally—the latter showing the first signs of a deranged mind. The narrative voice introduces Dr Frazer as 'a country surgeon [...] who accounted the life of a man of no more value than the life of a salmon' (Hogg 2002 [1823]: 390) and who, in the particular context of the Culloden aftermath, has grown

> accustomed to so many scenes of misery, despair, and extermination, that his better feelings were all withered, and a certain distortion had taken place in the bias of his mind. He perceived Davie to be a rude copy

of something within himself, and he hankered after him as one deformed object lingers round another, either from sensation or disgust, or a diabolical pleasure in seeing some creatures more loathsome than itself. There the two strayed together, the one relating what deaths, pinings, and ravings, he had seen during the summer; and the other, what miserable corpses he had found and interred in the wastes.

> Ibid., p. 393

Lost in their own personal distorted world, both characters highlight each other's idiosyncrasies, thus exposing the horrifying effects of the war of Culloden on their desensitised behaviour. Yet neither of them has completely gone astray, as later both show a few signs of humanity.

David has been able to survive thanks to his ability to bury corpses, for which the Duke of Cumberland rewards him. From some previous episodes in the novel, the reader understands that Davie has a penchant for accumulating money, probably a fixation that derives from what, in modern terms, could be termed as a mental condition in the autistic spectrum. Culloden has exacerbated David's autism: not only has 'burying [...] grown into a passion with Davie' (Hogg 2002 [1823]: 391), but he has acquired the gruesome habit of cutting the ears from the corpses as evidence for the Duke of their burial. Nonetheless, though on the surface David's macabre fondness seems to be driven by a financial gain, his primary reason for burying the corpses of women and children is the disgust he feels when the crows dig into their hearts, 'mhaking a vhery pad chob of it' (Ibid., p. 394).

When Dr Frazer cuts off David's earlobes as a punishment for how he earns his living, the doctor's callous act highlights his shallow reason, as he has violated the ears of a living man, not those of a corpse. After such a tremendous injury,

> Davie went away cursing, to the burn in the corrie, where he washed his mutilated ears and bound them up; and taking the severed parts, he rolled them carefully up with the rest, deeming the trick played to him, upon the whole, not a very bad speculation.
>
> HOGG 2002 [1823]: 395

Such a naive reaction makes the reader sympathise with Davie. Dr Frazer, however, is not that heartless either, as he later shows the signs of a man of feeling notwithstanding his apparent cruel disregard for Davie. When Sally shows her feelings of loneliness and abandonment: 'Where can I go? [...] I have neither home nor friend to which I can go—nothing beyond the walls of this hut', the narrative voice remarks that 'Dr Frazer cursed her for a whining jade, but, at the same time, *the tears were running over his sallow cheeks*' (Ibid., p. 397, emphasis mine). The doctor is then overwhelmed by 'a cloud of the deepest melancholy' when he sees that Sally, Peter, and Alexander have recovered from their respective psychological and physical wounds, as he still suspects that a worse injury is hanging over them, namely treachery by Peter's wife's 'fiend of jealousy'. When Dr Frazer takes leave of them, the narrator admits that 'though cursing them for fools and idiots, *the words growled through showers of tears*' (Ibid., p. 400, emphasis mine). Hogg transforms a Bakhtinian rogue into his complete opposite, a Mackenzian man of feeling, thus highlighting that Dr Frazer's previous villainy was a mask meant to cover the negative effects of the battle of Culloden on his emotions.

The fourth and final, plot-shaping fit of jealousy—through which Hogg deconstructs the marriage plot—is on the part of Peter's wife. This lady 'of some rank', believing that her husband has eloped with his former lover Sally, starts to be 'haunted [...] by the tormenting fiend of jealousy' (Hogg 2002 [1823]: 401), thereby revealing the location of her husband to the soldiers of the Duke of Cumberland. At this turn of events, Hogg depicts the horrendous effects of the rhetoric of war on the men involved in the battle of Culloden, subjugated as they are by violence and revenge.

The narrator depicts the English soldiers as having grown 'accustomed for three months bygone to regard the lives of Highlanders merely as those of noxious animals' (Hogg 2002 [1823]: 402), with no respect for military law and killing their prisoners 'with the most perfect *sang froid*' (Ibid.) on any small occasion. Hogg's narrator then describes, in great detail, the trivial reason for which they murder Peter and Alexander. One of the subordinate soldiers opposes the English sergeant's cruel proposal to kill both men. Perceiving such resistance as an outrage to his rank, the sergeant kills Peter Gow to reaffirm his authority. Here, Hogg's criticism in his essay 'Soldiers' comes to mind. There he compares the beginning of wars to an argument he witnessed between two boys, who 'eyed each other with rather *jealous* and indignant looks, and with defiance on each brow' (Hogg 1997 [1834]: 42, emphasis mine), thus fighting with all their might in a quarrel without knowing 'the why or wherefore' (Ibid., p. 41) everything had begun. Hogg points out that the anecdote of the two boys mirrors the dynamics of history: 'the rulers of kingdoms have often kindled up the flames of war, they scarcely knew why or wherefore; so that upon a retrospective view, historians and politicians have been quite at a loss how to account for it' (Ibid.). The feeling of jealousy, 'that fiend evil' which propels the narrative plot of the last 'Peril', is an extended metaphor mirroring the same driving force of the sergeant who kills Peter Gow as a result of what has become of him after the battle of Culloden which, like any war, 'originate[s] in the evil and malevolent passions of our nature, which seem to form a primitive part of our constitution, and which neither the reasonings of the philosopher, nor the injunctions of religion have been able to eradicate' (Ibid., p. 44).

Though the anonymous reviewer of the *British Magazine* criticised Hogg for describing the English soldiers as butchers who kill 'women and children for sport' (1823: 374), it must be argued that in *Perils of Woman*, Hogg describes the same 'evil' behaviour on the part of the Highland soldiers. When Dr Frazer and the M'Phersons return to the hut to move Sally, Alexander and Peter to a safer place, they discover that the two men have been murdered. They hence leave in search for the killers and, after having vindicated their deaths, significantly forget to return to the hut to bury the two corpses and to recover Sally, who is still alive.

Only Davie, the grotesque sexton, comes to the hut 'carrying his spade over his shoulder, and bringing also some cordials and refreshment for his old friends'; though '[h]e had been inured to scenes of carnage; and, indeed, they were become so familiar to him, that he delighted in them', the narrator suggests that 'natural affection, though blunted in him, was not obliterated' (Hogg 2002 [1823]: 405). Though a ludicrous scene ensues where Davie, assuming Sally to be dead, starts searching for some hidden money in her bosom before burying her, his logic is not as horrible as the tremendous effects of the battle of Culloden, which Hogg soon after describes.

In the previous passages of this tale, the narrator alludes to Sally's pregnancy and portrays her delirious despair for having been forsaken. She talks 'about an ideal orphan babe, the total destitution of which seemed to haunt her wandering imagination' (Hogg 2002 [1823]: 398), while later she starts 'speaking to a cropt flower, as if it were a deserted babe' (Ibid., p. 401). Once again, Hogg shows the negative impact of a tragic historical event on the female body. Though Davie saves and brings Sally to the hut of an elderly lady, after a while she flees away. Subsequently, one of the M'Pherson brothers (the ones who had not come back to the hut where they had abandoned Sally, Peter and Alexander) finds Sally accidentally. The boy sees her 'rocking and singing over the body of a dead female infant', but when he comes back with his brothers, both mother and child lie 'stretched together in the arms of death, pale as the snow that surrounded them, and rigid as the grave-turf on which they had made their dying bed' (Ibid., p. 407). Here Hogg ends his tale, having depicted the catastrophic effects of a marriage of convenience, of a war violating a maternal body, and of a cyclically inexorable history that keeps repeating itself, both at Culloden and in the more recent Napoleonic Wars.

In both *Perils* novels, Hogg presents his heroines as national symbols that do not resolve Scotland's grievances in the marriage plot. Hogg shows them in a circling trajectory that begins in *Perils of Man* with Princess Margaret's marital discomfort mirrored in the witches' carnivalesque caricature; continues in *Perils of Woman* with its depiction of Gatty's grotesque body—a symbol of paralysis rather than civilised progress; and then concludes the tragic deaths of Sally and her daughter, and no procreative future for Scotland. Apparently, a political marriage of convenience with England was not the solution for healing Scotland's collective grievances, and all social spheres, from royalty to peasantry, were destined to perish if the imperial enterprise only favoured the interests of the ruling classes.

CHAPTER 3

Scottish Masculinities and the British Empire

1 More Than Just Highlanders

In the discourse of imperial expansion, the mystique of the Highland soldiers played the role of invigorating Britain through their archaic code of honour and manly courage. Yet Highland vigour did not affect English masculinity because, Martin explains (2009: 84), England was a solid economic and political force and, Shields remarks (2010: 9), at the beginning of the nineteenth century English manliness began to be characterised by the discourse of sensibility,[1] which shaped a more tamed and less violent sense of manhood than the one symbolised by the 'rugged' Highlander.

The notions of sympathy and sensibility were informed by the philosophers of eighteenth-century Scottish Enlightenment such as David Hume who, in his *Treatise on Human Nature*, argues for a sympathy determined by closeness and similarity that enables the exchange of emotions among human beings. Hume contends that

> [n]o quality of human nature is more remarkable, both in itself and in its consequences, than the propensity we have to sympathize with others, and to receive by communication their inclinations and sentiments, however different from, or even contrary to our own. This is not only conspicuous in children, who implicitly embrace every opinion propos'd to them; but also in men of the greatest judgement and understanding, who

---

1 Mike Goode observes that

historical epistemology underwent a shift over the course of the long nineteenth century from being a *feeling* of history to being an *idea* of history and that [...] this epistemological shift was enacted [...] through a complex political and philosophical struggle over the nature and social importance of feeling, especially over the relation of feeling and manliness.

See Mike Goode, *Sentimental Masculinity and the Rise of History, 1790–1890* (Cambridge: Cambridge University Press, 2009), p. 3. Glenn Hendler explores the logic of sympathy in the nineteenth-century American novel, arguing that authors like Mark Twain and Henry James show that this feeling was not strictly private and individual, but rather a public one that shaped contemporary social institutions and political movements; see Glenn Hendler, *Public Sentiments: Structures of Feeling in Nineteenth-Century American Literature* (Chapel Hill: The University of North Carolina Press, 2001).

find it very difficult to follow their own reason or inclination, in opposi-
tion to that of their friends and daily companions.

1965 [1739]: 316

However, Shields points out that Hume's notion of sympathy as a trait developed by 'like-minded individuals raises the question of whether sympathy
that transcends cultural, political, or national boundaries is possible' (2010:
10). Adam Smith, in his *Theory of Moral Sentiments* (1759), answers this point
by arguing instead for a learnt sympathy which 'requires both the self-control
necessary to regulate or moderate emotion and the sensibility necessary to
imaginatively change places with others' (Shields 2010: 11).

Smith claims that sensibility and self-control work together in the formation of manhood, as sensibility restrains the roughness of martial features,
while self-control deters the emotional overindulgence that would 'destroy
the masculine firmness of character': self-control hence converts sensibility
into a less passive quality 'founded on humanity' (Smith 1976 [1759]: 204).
Shields contends that the idea of a sensibility tamed by self-control served the
purpose of representing the British nation as a community bound by learnt,
shared sympathies rather than economic and political interests at a time when
the late nineteenth- and twentieth-century 'paradigm of nation-state' was still
distant (2010: 9).

Hogg engaged with these different stereotypes of masculinity in some of his
works, challenging their cultural assumptions. For example, the Highland regiments employed for imperial expansion during the Napoleonic Wars, which
Scott supported, were constituted largely by young soldiers whose lives were
wasted as a consequence of the arbitrary power to which they were subjected.
As I have argued elsewhere (Leonardi 2019c), Hogg explicitly highlights this
aspect in *The Pilgrims of the Sun* (1815) and in 'The Field of Waterloo' (1822), a
long and a short poem which, though published at different times, were composed in the same year of Napoleon's defeat in Waterloo. In these texts, Hogg
reflects on the negative consequences of the Napoleonic Wars upon human
lives. He then conveys the critique of these wars more implicitly some years
later in *The Three Perils of Man* (1822), where the hunger for meat—along
with the carnivalesque transformation of Sir Ringan's warriors into bulls to
'feed' the enemy—is an extended metaphor meant to expose the destructive-
ness of tyrannical power (Leonardi 2019c: 139–60).

This chapter explores Hogg's questioning of sentimental masculinity
through the character of Rickleton in *Perils of Woman*; Hogg's deconstruction of the myth of the Highland soldier in the song 'Donald Macdonald';

and Hogg's parody of Walter Scott's poetic style through the stereotype of the avaricious Lowland Scots in 'Wat o' the Cleuch', through which Hogg exposes the reality of the margins in the Scottish Lowlands at the time of imperial expansion.

The long relationship between Hogg and Scott is complex and pivotal to Hogg both as a person and as a writer, and an exhaustive review of it is beyond the scope of this chapter. Ian Duncan, however, provides a perceptive description of this thirty-year long friendship, arguing that

> [s]cholars[hip] engaged in the modern revaluation of Hogg [...] mystifies Scott's influence by reading it in sheerly negative terms. Zealous to reclaim Hogg as original genius, it takes too little account of the social and dialogical construction of such genius, Scott's as well as Hogg's; it yields instead the Romantic myth of Hogg as victim of a literary system that remained external to him, and overlooks Hogg's vigorous agency in entering that system, taking part in it, and using its terms. Literary influence, rather, is the social and psychological medium in which Hogg wrote himself into being. Enthralled as he remained by Scott's seemingly irresistible example and authority, Hogg worked out his literary identity (a literary identity that was never solely his) in a complex, strenuous dialectic of emulation and resistance, in which—in the last analysis—the act of resistance cannot be separated from the act of emulation.
>
> 2007: 153

The following section provides a review of how both authors engaged with contemporary stereotypes of masculinity in the early nineteenth century, before proceeding to an analysis of these specific texts by Hogg.

As Murray G. H. Pittock explains, although Scott exploits the Highland myth and the romance of Scottish Jacobitism's resistance to the union, he also presents them as 'a lost cause [...] based on emotion not fact'. Certainly, Pittock remarks, 'Scott's Jacobite lords [...] are potent [...] figures', but their violence is 'childish' and has 'no place in the peaceable interchange of civilized society' offered by the British Union. To this 'childish' Scottish patriotism, Scott instead opposes a more 'adult' British patriotism, represented by the main character's achievement of common sense (Pittock 1991: 84–85). Yet McNeil contends that, in so doing, Scott also 'emptied Jacobite ideology of its political force' (2007: 7). This is the politically threatening content that, conversely, Hogg kept in his *Jacobite Relics of Scotland*, a collection of songs that the Highland society of London[2] commissioned him in order to celebrate 'Scottish heroism in the context of the Napoleonic Wars', and which appeared in two series between 1819 and 1821 (Pittock 2002: xiii). Pittock points out that, particularly in the *Second Series*, Hogg failed to observe the contemporary post-Ossianic taste for 'heroism and sensibility', which de-historicised the radicalism of Jacobite songs, therefore mirroring a too heavy 'Scottish politics of resistance from the eighteenth century' (2002: xviii, xiii). Indeed, Pittock explains, Hogg appears to have produced 'spurious' versions of 'songs dealing with the melancholy aftermath of Culloden', probably to allude implicitly to the contemporary Highland Clearances, but also failing in this way to produce the 'sanitized' 'image of Scotland' demanded of him by the Highland society of London (2003a: xiii, xvii).

Sadly, Hogg was never paid by the Highland Society of London for his *Jacobite Relics*, though he had been promised a contribution of £50 by Colonel Stewart of Garth (1772–1829) via George Thomson. Pittock points out that Stewart, trying 'to cover his own faults', sent a letter to Hogg attacking him 'in terms which would hardly have been used to a man closer to his social status', and in which he claimed that Hogg had failed to show 'Scottish songs as "equal to if not superior to any other country"' (Pittock 2003a: xvii).[3] The way in which Stewart addressed Hogg reflects the dynamics between politeness and class prejudice discussed in Chapter 2 with regard to Wilson's review of Hogg's *Perils of Woman* in *Blackwood's Edinburgh Magazine*. Similarly, what Stewart judged here is not the literary value of Hogg's *Jacobite Relics*; rather, Stewart dismissed the potential threat that Hogg's work represented to the ideology of Englishness playing with stereotypes based on class prejudices, as (im)politeness theory bears out. Douglas S. Mack maintains that in a letter to

---

2 Kenneth McNeil (2007) writes that

"[i]n May 1778, a group of twenty-five expatriate Scots met at the Spring-Garden Coffee-House where they agreed to form the Highland Society of London. Their principal aims were the restoration of the Highland dress [which had been banned after the second Jacobite uprising in 1746]; the preservation and cultivation of Highland music, literature, and language; the establishment of institutions devoted to aid Highlanders such as Gaelic schools, churches, and asylums for Highland children orphaned upon the death of their soldier fathers; honoring the achievements of Highland regiments; and, lastly, the promotion of agricultural improvement in the Highlands. [...] The Highland Society was a key force in disseminating, institutionalizing, and popularizing ideas about the Highlands in the Romantic era." (pp. 1–2)

In the same book, McNeil adds that in subsequent years, the Highland society of London also welcomed members from foreign countries, a fact that highlighted not so much a corruption as an evolution of the society's 'original criteria [...] given [...its] awareness of the difficulties in delimiting the "Highlands"' (p. 19).

3 See also Hogg's letters to Thomson of 14 December 1821 and 14 February 1822, *Collected Letters*, ed. by Hughes and others, vol. 2, pp. 133, 142.

William Blackwood of 7 October 1820, Hogg laments the negative reception of his *Jacobite Relics* by the *Edinburgh Review*, in which 'Lesley's March to Long-maston Moor' was condemned as coarse (vol. 34, Aug. 1820: 155).[4] Hogg writes that '[t]he principle is absurd for a collector of relics must take them as they are and one would have left out Lesly's [*sic*] March ought to have been damned the taste is not mine but the taste of the age' (*Collected Letters*, vol. 2, p. 47).

McNeil (2007) remarks that during King George IV's visit to Edinburgh in August 1822, Scott exploited the Highland myth promoting the '"Celtifica-tion" of Scotland' through an ostentatious display of Scottish imagery (McNeil 2007: 52). For Mack, the King's visit represents a significant moment in the history of Scotland, a return of the King to his ancient origins, as George IV descended from 'a daughter of James VI, one of the Stuart Kings of Scots' (2008: xxx, xxxiii). Exploiting the cultural trope of 'kinship ties' in 'Highland social identity' (McNeil 2007: 71), and having the Hanoverian king wear the Stuarts' tartan, Scott presented George IV as a modern, updated version of the absolute monarchy of the past and as 'the legitimate heir of the Stuarts and of Scotland's hero-king, Robert I (the Bruce)', whose memory was still alive among the Scots for having 'secured the country's pre-Union independence' in the 1314 battle of Bannockburn (Mack 2008: xxxiv–xxxv). In this way, Scott re-established Scotland's position within the British Union not just as an equal partner with England but as a fundamental one, from which the King was descended. Mack argues that by asserting people's loyalty to the Hanoverian king, Scott also reaf-firmed the status quo, kept at bay any revolutionary threat from France, and 'weaken[ed] support for radical political change [...] establish[ing], instead, an understanding of Scottish identity based on loyalty to George IV as King of Scots, and as a monarch of the united kingdom of Britain' (Mack 2008: xxxiv).

McNeil contends that Walter Scott's tartan pageantry was also influenced by Adam Ferguson's notion of 'soldiering as the instrument to rebind society' and to 'masculinize' 'the relative effeminacy' 'of the modern commercial state' (2007: 71–72). Likewise, when discussing the dynamics between manhood and commerce, J. G. A. Pocock (1985: 114) observes that the efficient, money-making man was perceived as 'feminized, even an effeminate being' in the eighteenth century, but as a 'masculine conquering hero' in the nineteenth (qtd. by Martin 2009: 6). Yet, Martin contends that

> modern masculinity could not be created out of whole cloth; to feel authentic, it had to incorporate older measures of masculinity too. Few

---

4   'Song III. Lesley's March to Scotland', in *The Jacobite Relics of Scotland* (*First Series*), ed. by Pittock, pp. 5–7, see editorial note on Hogg's *Collected Letters*, vol. 2, p. 48.

men living in commercial Britain had direct access to warrior skills or experience, yet the traditional martial values of hardihood, fearlessness, and fighting ardour lingered and demanded integration into the new manhood. [...] The construction of Scotland as a source of rugged primal masculinity helped respond to this demand [...] to an English civilization that sometimes seemed too civilized, the desire to internalize Scottish wildness was an attempt to ensure that, beneath the manly self-control, that crucial volcanic core of masculinity still burned.

2009: 6

Hence Walter Scott's tartan spectacle presented Scotland as a key partner for the virilisation of England.

Nevertheless, some critics have argued that Scott's pageantry did not represent the entire spectrum of the Highlands' reality, obscuring instead a fundamental historical issue: the Highland Clearances, at which Hogg had hinted in his *Jacobite Relics* and which, during the King's visit, were at one of their highest peaks. Juliet Shields observes that Highland landlords, who once had been chieftains of their own clans, now favoured 'economic interest over affective bonds' and 'export[ed], like so many surplus goods, Highlanders and their virtues', to repopulate their estates with sheep (Shields 2010: 123). McNeil argues that the 'continuous emigration and clearances throughout the era of "external colonialism" points to the simultaneous process of empire at work both inside and outside the nation' (2007: 12). Duncan indicates that Christian Isobel Johnstone's *Clan-Albin* (1815), a novel published soon after Scott's *Waverley* (1814), depicts self-interested landlords 'clearing their estate for sheep' and 'forc[ing] their tenants to choose between Canadian emigration and service in the French wars' (2007: 99). Hogg, too, in some of his works hints at the paradoxical synchronicity between the myth of the Highlander and the Clearances after Culloden, the negative effects of which he depicts in 'Peril Third' of *Perils of Woman* (see Chapter 2).

Yet Hogg grew aware of the effects of Culloden rather late in his life. In his early thirties, by undertaking a series of journeys to the Highlands, he acquainted himself with 'the economic problems facing Highland landlords'; nevertheless, as H. B. de Groot observes, 'at this stage in his life' Hogg still 'idealised the Highland chiefs' (2010: xxxiii). Hogg had in mind to start his own farm in Harris (Currie 2010: 231–42), and 'was committed to a major expansion of sheep-farming in the Highlands, while at the same time advocating the granting of secure tenancies to those already on the land' (de Groot 2010: xxxiv). In 'An Essay on Sheep-Farming and Population', Hogg writes that sheep are the most eligible stock for the greatest part of the Highlands; for the proprietor and farmer, they certainly are so. In a political point of view, however, the scheme must certainly be prosecuted with leisure, caution, and tenderness; nor must we drive the people from their poor, but native huts and glens, until some other source of industry is opened to them, which, by persevering in, they may become more useful members of the commonwealth.

HOGG 2010: 215

However, as de Groot points out, '[t]he two [views] were simply not compatible' (2010: xxxiv). Later in his life, Hogg realised this incongruity and voiced his criticism of the Highland Clearances in *Perils of Woman*, *The Forest Minstrel* (1810), the two series of *Jacobite Relics*, and the *Songs by the Ettrick Shepherd* (1831). de Groot writes that by this time, Hogg had begun 'to see the essential connections between the terrorising of the Highlanders from 1746 on, the growth of sheep-farming and the Clearances, and the development of tourism' (2010: lv). Even earlier, Hogg had already shown some internal contradictions, as in his *Highland Journeys* he writes that while he was

traversing the scenes, where the patient sufferings of the one party, and the cruelties of the other were so affectingly displayed, I could not help being a bit of a Jacobite in my heart, and blessing myself that in those days I did not exist, or I had certainly been hanged.

2010: 81

The King's visit to Edinburgh in 1822 offered Hogg the occasion to pronounce his own view on the Scottish Clearances, while Scott saw the same event as 'an opportunity to heal the old wounds of the Jacobite/Hanoverian conflict by presenting George IV as the legitimate heir of the Stuarts [...and] ignoring some important and painful realities' (Mack 2008: xl), particularly the Clearances. In his own contribution to the king's visit, *The Royal Jubilee* (1822), Hogg did not ignore these social issues. Although playing with the same cultural tropes that Scott was exploiting in his pageantry, probably hoping to earn a royal pension to alleviate his financial straits, Hogg concludes his masque in a rather unconventional way. Mack points out that he replaces the 'authoritative figure' which, at the end, should 'restore harmony and order' with a conclusion where '*all the spirits*' '[*e*]*xeunt, in different directions*', thereby suggesting that the return of the king was not a 'sufficient' action to restore 'harmony' in Scotland (Mack 2008: xliii). Scott exploited the tartan pageantry to convey a martial and masculine essence of Scottish national identity, so as to pose Scotland as a vital associate with England in the British partnership; this ideological construct, however, obscured the tragic reality of the Highland Clearances.

McNeil provides a perceptive analysis of the dynamics at work in the cultural construction of Highlandism at the time of Hogg's writing, which he views as 'a set of anthropological assumptions', whereby the isolated and harsh nature of the land itself

> produces a "natural warrior" who from childhood develops a propensity for warfare [...a] geographical determinism [...] which reinforces an imperialist epistemology that assumes the universal condition of other "primitive" mountain people and spaces set apart from normative, civil "lowland" peoples and space. [...] Highlandism is crucial to the rise in popularity of the figure of the Highland soldier-hero in the late eighteenth and early nineteenth centuries. Without Highlandism, it is safe to say, there would have been no Highland soldier-hero and, quite possibly, no regiments in the British army uniquely designed as "Highland." [...M]ost crucial to Scott's attraction to highlandism, is the powerful code of absolute loyalty, which is fomented by the difficult conditions of mountain life and the patriarchal ties that bind family to family and isolate the clans within their narrow glens. [...] For Scott, it is this code of loyalty [...] that separates the Highland fighting man from his English counterpart, making him an ideal "natural soldier." [...T]he Scottish Highlander soldier-hero, as it moves to a colonial setting, is transformed [...] as an essentialized category of race that works to affirm the innate superior qualities of British colonizers [...] a powerful spectacle of British prowess in action, while simultaneously registering as exotic.
>
> 2007: 86, 92–93, 120–21

McNeil concludes his discussion by stating that Highlandism's essentialism— the soldier-hero's martial qualities that are linked to his land of origin— represents the limit of such cultural construction since, as a result, the Highlander cannot be upheld as a model to be imitated nor is he suitable for anything else. The Highland regiments, however, were not always populated exclusively by soldiers from the Scottish Highlands, though this was the general impression. This is an aspect that Hogg highlights in 'Basil Lee', the eponymous protagonist of which is a good-for-nothing Lowlander employed in the Scottish regiments (Leonardi 2012a).

The incorporation of Highland masculinity into the construction of British national discourse had a double ideological purpose: besides uniting Scotland and England in the imperial enterprise, Highlandism answered a Scottish national need to keep a distinctive character without compromising the union with England. As argued by T. M. Devine (2006a [1999]: 233–36, 244) and Peter Womack (1989: 145), when Lowland Scotland became economically similar to England, it turned to the Highlands to mark its difference. Walter Scott's 1822 pageantry showed that the myth of the Highland warrior enhanced the masculinity of England because, as Martin explains, 'a heart of Highland masculinity animate[d] Scotland's [...] history and culture [...] an undying heart that, because Scotland [wa]s part of Britain, c[ould] beat for Britain as a whole' (2009: 38). During the Napoleonic Wars—the period when the Hogg texts that are discussed in this chapter were mostly written or published—the reputation of the kilted Highland regiments, depicted as the direct descendants of the clans, conferred great prestige on the British army.

By exploiting the cultural stereotypes of class, gender and ethnicity of his time, Hogg parodied both notions of Highland and Lowland Scottish masculinities, demystifying the heroism of the Highland soldier in his famous song 'Donald Macdonald', and questioning the stereotype of the greedy Lowland Scots in 'Wat o' the Cleuch'. Hogg instead exposed a different reality, revealing that the peasantry of the Scottish Lowlands not only did not benefit from any material advantage from the colonial enterprise, but that they also suffered the negative consequences of a deteriorated relationship between master and servant. In the *Quarterly Journal of Agriculture* (1831–32), Hogg claims that

> ever since the ruinous prices made every farmer for the time a fine gentleman, how the relative situations of master and servant are changed! Before that time every farmer was first up in the morning, conversed with all his servants familiarly, and consulted what was best to be done for the day. Now, the foreman, or chief shepherd, waits on his master, and, receiving his instructions, goes forth and gives the orders as his own, generally in a peremptory and offensive manner. The menial of course feels that he is no more a member of a community, but a slave; a servant of servants, a mere tool of labour in the hand of a man whom he knows or deems inferior to himself, and the joy of his spirit is mildewed. He is a moping, sullen, melancholy man, flitting from one master to another in hopes to find heart's ease and contentment,—but he finds it not; and now all the best and most independent of that valuable class of our community are leaving the country.
>
> 1985 [1831–1832]: 44–45

Here Hogg provides a very different image from the stereotype of the avid Scot as represented in the English collective imagination. Though from one perspective Hogg seems to be arguing for a benevolent feudalism and hence may be criticised as backward-looking, he maintains that the new imperial economy had enriched the Scottish landlords, who were now 'expect[ing] feudal obedience without assuming feudal responsibility', as Katie Trumpener (1993: 694) observes in her analysis of the Irish condition in Maria Edgeworth's *Ormond* (1818). David Groves holds that

> [p]olitically the Shepherd was a moderate and traditionalist, equally opposed to radical innovation, on one side, and to the new '*aristocracy of farming*' on the other. Both the Whig and Tory policies of the day, he maintained, were destroying community spirit by making 'the distance between master and servant wider and wider'.
>
> 1988: 140, emphasis original

For this reason, a section of this chapter is devoted to the carnivalesque figure of 'Wat o' the Cleuch' in *The Poetic Mirror* (1816), the Borderer moss-trooper that Hogg depicts in his parody of Scott's poetry, and whose voracious hunger for meat represents the peasantry's harsh conditions in the Scottish Lowlands at the time of imperial expansion.

2   British Masculinities

Ian Duncan observes that in *The Private Memoirs and Confessions of a Justified Sinner* (1824), Hogg parodies Adam Smith's notion of sympathy, conflating it with Enlightenment notions of physiognomy—the search for a correspondence between 'facial forms' and 'immortal soul'—through the chameleon nature of Gil-Martin, the protagonist's *alter-ego* who can change his features by entering into someone else's feelings (2007: 267). I contend that Hogg deconstructs the conflation of the Enlightenment vogue for physiognomy and Adam Smith's conceptualisation of sympathy through the unruly figure of Rickleton in *Perils of Woman* since this character, despite being 'a real clod-pole—a moss-jumper—a man of bones, thews, and sinews' (Hogg 2002 [1823]: 56), turns out to be one of the most humane types among the characters that Hogg ever conceived. Hogg poses the relation between the emphasised physicality and the psychological evolution of this disruptive character, whose wedding with a prostitute exposes the ideological assumptions of the marriage plot in the national tale, as a double critique of both sentimental and Highland masculinities.

Viewing the processes of writing and reading as ruled by communicative strategies influenced by contemporary cultural assumptions, this section explores how in *Perils of Woman* Hogg demystifies the masculinity of the Highland soldier-hero through the carnivalesque duel between Rickleton and 'captain' M'Turk. It then shows how Hogg's treatment of Rickleton interrogates the supposed 'honesty' of contemporary British conventions of sentimental masculinity, as this character evolves from an extremely stubborn, hyper-masculine type to a more balanced man, capable of genuinely sympathising and 'feeling *with*' his wife. Significantly, Rickleton accepts to be the father of the son that his wife conceived with another man and, in so doing, he gains the respect of Simey Dodd of Ramshope, his worst enemy, on whom Rickleton founds his manly value.

David Groves views Rickleton's subplot in *Perils of Woman* as involving a descent into chaos and confusion since, after the discovery that his wife's pregnancy is due to a former lover, Richard endures 'the amorphous uncertainty at the centre of human relationships', a cathartic cleansing which allows his subsequent forgiveness and acceptance of the child as his own, and the abandonment of male revenge, thereby gaining 'social happiness' (1982: 206). No twentieth-century critic, however, appears to have explored the dialectics between this quarrelsome character and the cultural assumptions of both sentimental and Highland masculinities at the time of Hogg's writing.

Rickleton, introduced by the third-person narrator, enters the scene as follows:

> That very evening, who should arrive with the Pringleton coach, but our good friend Daniel Bell [Gatty's father], and with him his nephew-in-law, that is, his wife's brother's son, Richard Rickleton, Esq. of Burl-hope, and farmer of seventeen thousand acres of land, on two sides of the Border. He was a real clod-pole—a moss-jumper—a man of bones, thews, and sinews, with no more mind or ingenuity than an owl; men nicknamed him *the heather-blooter*, from his odd way of laughing, for that laugh could have been heard for five miles around, on a calm evening, by the Border fells,—and, for brevity's sake, it was often contracted into *the blooter*. But, with all these oddities, Richard Rickleton was as rich as Croesus; at least he was richer, by his own account, than Simon Dodd of Ramshope, and that seemed to be the ultimatum of his ambition.
>
> HOGG 2002 [1823]: 56, emphases original

In this passage, the narrator first introduces Rickleton through his social status, 'Esquire' and 'farmer' of an extended land. He then describes him through a series of noun phrases that highlight his physical strength, as Rickleton is depicted as 'a real clod-pole', 'a moss-jumper', and 'a man of bones, thews, and sinews' (Ibid.); while, soon after, the narrator contrasts Rickleton's physicality to his little common sense, describing him 'with no more mind or ingenuity than an owl' (Ibid.).[5] The narrator then alludes to Rickleton's personality running to extremes by referring to him with his nickname *'the heather-blooter'* (Ibid.), 'a common snipe' with 'a low, rasping call' which epitomises Rickleton's extravagant way of laughing.[6] Finally, Simon Dodd of Ramshope appears on the scene—Rickleton's competitor in physical strength and material possessions and, apparently, the most potent signifier of his masculine identity. In a single paragraph, Hogg manages a masterly introduction of a secondary character who defies the ideological assumptions of the marriage plot embodied by the two primary characters, Gatty and M'Ion, and who interrogates contemporary stereotypes of Highland and sentimental masculinities.

Rickleton's figure encompasses a farcical, parodic depiction of manly traits that highlight his subsequent evolution into a more sensible gentleman in whom '[s]ensibility and self-control work dialectically', and where '[s]ensibility moderates the potentially offensive harshness of martial virtues', as Shields observes concerning eighteenth-century constructions of British manhood (2010: 30). Through Rickleton, Hogg presents a more honest model of sentimental masculinity than the one encouraged by contemporary assumptions of sympathy informing the relation between Scotland and England—a hypocritical mask that hid the more materialistic political rationale of the British Union.

Invoking the epistolary novel, Hogg shows Rickleton's emotional evolution into 'a man of feeling' through a series of letters to his cousin Joseph Bell, a student of law. Bell is dealing with the divorce between this Northumbrian Esquire and his wife because, according to the patriarchal system of primogeniture, all of Rickleton's possessions should go to Katie's son, conceived with a previous lover, an aspect that the former is not yet able to accept.

The epistolary mode also serves Hogg's the purpose of showing the tension between Rickleton's *heteroglot* voice and Standard English. Though in contemporary or late eighteenth-century fiction vernacular languages were usually exploited for comical reasons (see, for example, Tobias Smollet's *Hamphry Clinker*), Hogg bestows Rickleton's hilarious speech an important message. Though Rickleton's idiolect is 'translated' in his letters for an English

---

5   Though conventionally an owl is an animal thought to be wise, the Oxford English Dictionary reports an example by M. E. Braddon of this bird as being stupid: 'I must go and get my siesta, or I shall be as stupid as an owl all the evening' (*Mt. Royal* 1882, I. viii., p. 243), <WWW.OED. com> [accessed 27 April 2013].

6   See *Perils of Woman*, ed. by Hasler and Mack, editorial endnote, p. 442.

audience because, as he states, '[i]f I had not the master of the academy to write for me, and put my feelings on paper, I never could' (Hogg 2002 [1823]: 233), Rickleton does not appear to be satisfied with such translations. When dictating the conversation he had with his wife in the letter to his cousin, Rickleton critiques his speech 'adaptations' and exclaims, 'I shall give you our conversation in our own words; [...] spelling and all. [...W]rite it and spell it as that one delivers it to you', yells Rickleton at the master, 'and be cworsed to thee for a dwomonie, although thou calls thyself measter of the academy!' (Ibid. p. 228). Rickleton's Northumbrian speech, interspersed with a few Scots terms, represents a fluid linguistic dimension at the borders between Scottishness and Englishness. Being a character not yet fixed in the sentimental category of 'man of feeling', Rickleton is thus able to evolve into an honest, real sentimental man.

The *heteroglot* passages of his direct speeches signal the crucial moments of this evolution. On meeting his wife with her new-born in her arms, Rickleton— in a voice translated by the master's pen—writes,

> *How fain would I have clasped them both to my bosom and wept too!—But honour,—stern and magnificent honour interposed, and I was obliged, against my inclination, to assume a deportment of proud offence.* 'How's this, my dear?' says I. 'It's to be hoped that same baby is not yours?'
>
> She kept rocking the child as formerly, and weeping over it still more bitterly; but she neither lifted her eyes nor moved her tongue in answer to my question. *My heart was like to melt; so I saw there was a necessity for rousing myself into a rage in order to preserve any little scrap of honour and dignity that remained to me.* Accordingly, I turned to the doctor; and, *tramping my foot violently on the floor*, I said, 'There's for it now, sir! There's for it! That comes all of your d—d prescriptions!'
>
> HOGG 2002 [1823]: 233–34, emphases mine

The prescriptions Rickleton refers to are the nutritional 'regimen' his wife had hinted at in a previous letter, as prescribed by the doctor for her supposed 'illness' (namely her pregnancy), which Rickleton had mistaken for a 'regiment' of soldiers. This humorous misunderstanding, though apparently playing with Rickleton's poor education, hints at more serious social issues, specifically prostitution and its abuse by the supposedly 'honourable' Highland soldier-heroes, as I discuss later in regard with Hogg's deconstruction of Highland masculinity through Rickleton's voice. In the extract above, Rickleton's internal struggle shows a tension between his wish to re-establish the law of the father by 'rousing' himself 'into a rage'—so as to preserve his culturally-acquired notion of patriarchal 'honour and dignity'—and his capacity to feel sympathy with a 'heart [that] was like to melt'. Through Rickleton's hilarious behaviour, Hogg reveals that gender-, class-, and ethnic-conditioned assumptions of masculinity are a burden both for women's and men's personal and social happiness.

The tragic situation of Rickleton's wife also mirrors Hogg's critique of the Scottish Kirk, whose system of patriarchal values would not allow christening a child born out of wedlock (see Chapter 4). On Rickleton asking his wife to renounce her son and to come back to him, she replies,

> Poor little innocent! He is an outcast, both of God and man; for, owing to his father's circumstances, as a married man, I cannot get him introduced into Christian church. No reverend divine will, out of pity or commiseration, pronounce a blessing on his unhallowed head, bestowing on him the holy ordinance of baptism.
>
> HOGG 2002 [1823]: 253

Rickleton's subsequent sincere act of forgiveness towards his wife and the acceptance of her child as his own represent the honourable manly values which Hogg advocates in *Perils of Woman*. Rickleton's actions eventually gain him the admiration and respect of Simon Dodd of Ramshope, his fierce enemy and male signifier who admits, 'You have done a deed of generosity, of which I was incapable, and which proves you, with all your obstreperous oddities, to be possessed of a more gentle, forgiving, and benevolent heart, than almost any other of your sex' (Ibid., p. 257). Simey Dodd will offer himself as the guarantor of Rickleton's honour by supporting the child's baptism—one of the most important religious celebrations for the Scottish Kirk and utmost symbol of social respectability.

Through Rickleton, Hogg also reveals the anthropological assumptions that shaped the essentialist paradigm of Highlandism, according to which the Scottish Highlands produced natural warriors whose loyalty to their clan chief was later transferred to the British king. This ideology, however, did not always correspond to reality, and though among the clans of previous times there must certainly have been honourable Highlanders who would have given their life for their chief (as Walter Scott depicts in *Waverley*, when Evan Dhu undergoes a trial and the death penalty for his chieftain Fergus Mac-Ivor), the reality of the Highland regiments during the imperial wars was rather different. In the above-mentioned anecdote of the 'regiments', Rickleton claims that the Highland soldiers were mostly 'a horde of rude, vulgar, and beastly dogs' (Ibid., p. 231)—the same 'dogs of havoc and war' which Hogg, however, some years later in his essay 'Soldiers' would view as the poor victims of arbitrary power (Hogg 1997 [1834]: 40–47).

Rickleton fights with M'Ion, M'Turk, and Callum Gun in a series of carnivalesque duels because they have derided his two nick names: 'heather-blooter', which refers to his boisterous way of laughing; and 'wolf-dog', an epithet originating from an unfortunate past liaison that Rickleton had with a married lady. Despite their hilarity, such contests are not mere moments of comic relief. They occupy different lengths of discourse time, that is text, with a major narrative space of seven pages dedicated to the comical preparations for the fight between Rickleton and M'Turk, including the narrator's and a few characters' comments on questions related to the valour of the Highland hero, the difference between Lowland manliness based on individuality and Highland sense of collectiveness, considerations about human fear, and a seemingly re-appropriation of the real value of Highland masculinity as represented by Callum Gun. Yet the duel between the latter and Rickleton occupies only a short paragraph, ending with both men wounded and with an equal achievement of honour on the part of both competitors. Hogg appears to interrogate the ideological assumptions of Highlandism in the duel to which he dedicates the longest narrative space—the one between Rickleton and M'Turk—through which he conveys this critique to the readers of his time.

Hogg interrogates the ideology of the Highland warrior through M'Turk's not-so-honourable behaviour, as the latter tries to envisage a stratagem to avoid the duel with Rickleton, to the point of omitting to bring him the sword, in addition to his own, as had been previously arranged. What follows is the core of the duel between the two. M'Turk opens up the dialogue in his *heteroglot* Highland speech:

"Dhear, sir, te mhatter is peyond te law, and peyond all shenteel pehaviours," said the Ensign, bowing in manifest dismay.

"Draw out your sword," bellowed Richard, in his most tremendous voice, and heaved his cudgel, as if about to fell an ox. The ireful sound actually made Peter M'Turk spring a yard from the ground, with a sort of backward leap, and when he alighted, it so chanced that his back was toward Richard, and his eye at the same moment catching a glance of one of the impending quivers of the jagged hazel branch, he was seized with *an involuntary and natural feeling of self-preservation*; and as the most obvious way of attaining this, he fell a running with no ordinary degree of speed.

HOGG 2002 [1823]: 96, emphasis mine

Through the buffoon figure of Rickleton, who replaces his omitted sword with a hazel cudgel, Hogg prompts the possibility of a carnivalesque combat which could turn upside down the 'inverted sort of courage' (Ibid.) of 'captain' M'Turk, a supposedly Highland soldier-hero. Yet Hogg does not condemn M'Turk for his not-so-honourable reaction, but rather he tries to justify it as 'an involuntary and natural feeling of self-preservation' (Ibid.), exposing the harsh reality of wars behind the ideology of the Highlander's manly prowess— a reality which, at Hogg's time of writing, had taken the lives of many innocent young men in the Napoleonic Wars. In order to do so, Hogg provides a series of considerations about human fear through the narrative voice, setting the example of one of the most famous military men involved in the defeat of Napoleon, 'Arthur Wellesley [who], in one of the first battles ever he stood in India, fled in a night attack, and left his regiment to be cut up' (Ibid.); but who, subsequently, learnt to combat with honour and to distinguish himself as a true hero.[7] 'Let no man, therefore', the narrator claims, 'flout at Peter M'Turk; for as the old proverb runs, "He may come to a pouchfu' peas before he dies, for all that's come and gone"' (Ibid., p. 97).

Hogg then voices the complexity of human fear through Rickleton himself who, despite having exhibited the utmost performance of brave masculinity by accepting to engage in an unfair duel with M'Turk, admits that he has his own fears too, like every man:

> "You seem to have no sense of danger, nor to know what fear is," said Joseph.
> "Doos I not?" answered he—"I know both of them full well. It is absolute nonsense to talk of any man being void of fear. Joe, wast thou ever in a boggly [ghost-haunted] place in the dark thy lane?—if thou hast, thou knows what fear is."
>
> HOGG 2002 [1823]: 102

Hogg's criticism, though, is even more complex, as while interrogating the ideology of Highlandism exploited in the Napoleonic Wars through the figure of 'captain' M'Turk, he also reveals the classist prejudices on the part of the Lowland middle class through the dialogue between Rickleton and his cousin Joseph. The latter explains the reason why M'Turk is called 'captain', arguing that '[t]he Highlanders are very liberal of their titles [...and e]very commissioned officer, every master of a trading vessel, or even a coal sloop, is captain'

---

7   Arthur Wellesley (1769–1852), who 'after service in India and elsewhere, was created first Duke of Wellington in 1814 after his successful campaigns in the Peninsular War. His greatest triumph came with the defeat of Napoleon at Waterloo in 1815'; see *Perils of Woman*, written by Hogg, ed. by Hasler and Mack, editorial note on pp. 444–45.

(Ibid., p. 98). Cousin Joe, though speaking 'only from hearsay' (Ibid., p. 99), provides a mirror of the Highland clan system and a panoramic view of the entourage of profiting '*gentlemen*' around the Highland chieftains, not all of them as honourable as represented in the collective imagination of the early nineteenth century:

> [S]uch of them as are gentlemen of good families, are the completest gentlemen in the British dominions; polished, benevolent, and high spirited. But then, there is not one of these who has not a sort of satellites, or better kind of gillies, that count kin with their superiors, are sometimes out of courtesy admitted to their tables, and on that ground, *though living in half beggary and starvation*, they set up for gentlemen. *These beings would lick the dust from the feet of their superiors; would follow and support them through danger, and to death; but left to act for themselves, they are nothing, and no real Highland gentleman considers himself accountable for the behaviour of such men.* The cadets of a Highland chief, or the immediate circle of his friends, are generally all gentlemen; but there is not one of these who has not likewise his circle of dependent gentlemen, which last have theirs again, in endless ramifications; so that no one knows where the genteel system ends. None of these latter have any individual character to support; they have only a family one, or the character of a chief, who generally now cares not a farthing about them. *There lies the great difference between these people and our Borderers. With us, every man, from the peer to the meanest peasant, has an individual character of his own to support; and with all their bluntness of manner and address, for honesty, integrity, and loyal principles, shew me the race that will go before them."*
>
> "Ay, shew me the man that will *stand* before us, cousin Joe," cried Richard; "for, rabbit it! We have seen those that can *go* before us already, and that by fair dint of running."
>
> HOGG 2002 [1823]: 99, emphases mine

M'Turk is an exponent of those 'unworthy' 'sort of satellites', continues Joseph Bell, who gravitate towards more honourable Highlanders such as Callum Gun, 'a man of education'. Joseph claims that their difference in social provenance is signalled by their respective Highland and Standard English, which 'always stamps the character with the sterling mark' (Ibid.). It must be remembered, however, that Hogg's use of *heteroglot* voices and Standard English was far more complex than the simple conflation of honour with Englishness and social class. For example, the prostitute Bell Calvert in *Confession of a Justified*

Sinner speaks Standard English, thus showing that women of any social background are exposed to the risk of having to resort to this sad means of survival; while in *The Brownie of Bodsbeck*, the honourable Wat Laidlaw speaks in broad Scots. In the above passage, Hogg has the comments about the conflation of honour with Englishness delivered by a Scottish Lowlander of the middle class—and a student of law. In his volume dedicated to the question of prostitution in nineteenth-century Edinburgh, Dr Tait provides a detailed picture of these debauched students, who were often the fancy men of prostitutes (1840: 56). Joseph's education has not turned him into an honourable and sympathetic gentleman, as he enjoys Rickleton's 'unpolished' manners for the shallow reason of being entertained; while, despite his poor official education, Rickleton is the one who behaves with true honour. In addition, Joseph is blind to the fact that a Highlander of a lower class like M'Turk would 'lick the dust from the feet of [his] superiors' because he may have been reduced to 'half beggary and starvation' by those 'real Highland gentlem[e]n' who, at the time of Hogg's writing, were forcing their tenants to emigrate to Canada or to enrol in the Highland regiments, so as to make room for the more financially convenient grazing of sheep—a new market that Lowlanders of the middle class like Joseph Bell and his father Daniel would exploit at the expense of people like M'Turk. Though Callum Gun is portrayed as having apparently more honourable behaviour, as he does engage in a duel with Rickleton, Hogg de-emphasises such combat with a very short passage, effectively suggesting a critique of the economic issues inherent in the class that Callum Gun represents.

3   Demystifying the Highland Warrior

As argued by Suzanne Gilbert and Peter D. Garside, Hogg's song 'Donald Macdonald' was published numerous times during his life, becoming what nowadays would be considered a successful hit. It first appeared as a song sheet published by John Hamilton in c. 1803; subsequently in Hogg's collection of legendary ballads and songs *The Mountain Bard* (1807); in *The Forest Minstrel* (1810); in *Songs by the Ettrick Shepherd* (1831), as well as in multiple issues of song sheets published, again, by Hamilton (Gilbert 2007: 454–55; Garside 2006).

The positive response to Hogg's song was no doubt excited by its theme, as it met the expectations of its early nineteenth-century British audience. At a time when Britain felt threatened by Napoleon's military campaigns, a song celebrating the indestructible Highland soldier must certainly have conveyed a great sense of safety to British society. According to Garside,

> [w]hat effectively Hogg has achieved in his own 'Donald Macdonald' is to recycle the figure of the self-assertive amorous Highland Donald of the ballad ('I tell ye I am Donald Macdonald/I'll ever be proud of my name') with a comparatively new archetype, at once *emblematic* and *individual*, that of the indestructible French-resisting common Highland infantryman.
>
> 2006: 33, emphases mine

As Gilbert observes, a comparative analysis of the 1803 and 1807 variants of the song shows the validity of Garside's argument. The geographical setting of the 1803 version, in fact, is changed from the more localised: 'My name is Donald Macdonald | I live in Loch-ber sae grand' to 'I live in the Highlands sae grand' in *The Mountain Bard* (1807), thereby suggesting, as Gilbert explains, that '[t]he singer of this song [...] is to be seen as a typical and representative Highlander' (2007: 454) who is, according to Garside, 'at once *emblematic* and *individual*' (2006: 33, emphases mine).

In *The Mountain Bard*, Hogg also anglicises the spelling of some Scots terms of the Hamilton edition. For example, he changes the Scottish generic subject pronoun 'she' into the more affectionate 'laddie' in the third line of the first refrain, possibly to please a wider audience, as shown in the following passage:

> *Brogs* an' *brochen* an' a',
> *Brochen* an' *brogs* an' a',
> An' isna the *laddie* well aff
> Wha has *brogs* an' *brochen* an' a'.
>
> HOGG 2007: 108, ll. 9–12

Gilbert points out that according to his 'Memoirs' in *Altrive Tales* (1832), Hogg composed the song 'Donald Macdonald' either in 1800 or 1803 'on the threatened invasion by Bonaparte' (2007: 454). Further, the *Literary Panorama* in 1807 considered 'Donald Macdonald' as 'a loyal song, which derives an additional interest from the present circumstances of public affairs, to which loyalty is altogether *a propos*' (vol. 2, Aug. 1807: 959).

However, neither current nor nineteenth-century critics appear to have engaged in any degree with 'Donald Macdonald' as a parody of the Highland soldier. Bakhtin conceives of parody as an extremely subtle and, sometimes, hard-to-detect literary technique where two languages cross each other, but where only the parodied language is clearly uttered, while the parodying voice without notice creates and perceives (1981: 41–83). In 'Donald Macdonald', Hogg seems to be imitating the contemporary Romantic trend of Highland lyric songs without exaggerating their stylistic features, hence making it hard to view the song as a parody. However, a careful analysis of the song's lexical content does suggest a burlesque of the myth of the Highland soldier. The following is the series of refrains in Hogg's song:

> *Brogs* an' *brochen* an' a',
> *Brochen* an' *brogs* an' a',
> An' isna the laddie well aff
> Wha has brogs an' brochen an' a'.
>> HOGG 2007: 108, ll. 9–12

[...]

> Guns an' pistols an' a',
> Pistols an' guns an' a';
> He'll quickly see Donald Macdonald
> Wi' guns an' pistols an' a'.
>> Ibid., ll. 21–24

[...]

> Swords an' buckler an' a',
> Buckler and sword an' a';
> For George we'll encounter the devil,
> Wi' sword an' buckler an' a'.
>> Ibid., ll. 33–36

[...]

> Knees an' elbows an' a',
> Elbows an' knees an' a';
> Depend upon Donald Macdonald,
> His knees an' elbows an' a'.
>> Ibid., p. 109, ll. 45–48

[...]

Stanes an' bullets an' a',
Bullets an' stanes an' a';
We'll finish the Corsican callan',
Wi' stanes an' bullets an' a'.
>   Ibid., ll. 57–60

[...]

Brogs an' brochen an' a',
Brochen an' brogs an' a',
An' up wi' the bonny blue bonnet,
The kilt an' the feather, an' a'.
>   Ibid., ll. 69–72, all emphases here and above are mine

The refrains of Hogg's song show 'parallelism'; the four-line refrains at the end of each verse have the same syntactic structure in the first, second and fourth line, though a different lexical content, while the third line shows a change which each time adds some details to the parodic figure of the Highland warrior. In each refrain, Hogg shows a conscious and purposeful replication of lexical items related to the stereotype of Highland masculinity. By repeating them symmetrically in the first two lines, '*Brogs* an' *brochen* an' a', | *Brochen* an' *brogs* an' a'', and then reiterating them in the last line, 'An' isna the *laddie* well aff | Wha has *brogs* an' *brochen* an' a'', Hogg elicits a sympathetic laughter. Each refrain of Hogg's song foregrounds through parallelism the cultural stereotypes of the Highland soldier with a humorous undertone, achieving a comic effect and hence demystifying the heroism of the Highland warrior.

Going beyond a formalist stylistic analysis, which only accounts for the linguistic features of a text, a historical contextualisation of 'Donald Macdonald' exposes the social critique that Hogg implies through his linguistic choices. Though at first glance, the motif of the Highland soldier appears deterministically in line with the historical context of the Napoleonic Wars, as the words 'We'll finish the Corsican callan' (Hogg 2007: 109, l. 59) demonstrate, Hogg is playing humorously and strategically with it to convey a tragic reality. In relation to Hogg's *Poetic Mirror*, Dieter A. Berger argues that 'one can speak of a complete interaction between poets, critics, and parodists [...as t]he interpretation of a parody [...] cannot be preoccupied with the text alone, but must pay attention to cultural, biographical, social, and even political factors' (1988: 43). 'Donald Macdonald' should thus be viewed as a subtle parody through which Hogg exposes the exploitation of young soldiers in the imperial wars at the time when he created this song, hiding himself behind a voice which stereo-typically portrays any Highland soldier.

The third stanza depicts the 1745 Jacobite rising, when Prince Charles Edward Stuart, 'the exiled heir of the deposed Stuart kings', came to Britain from France to regain his throne with the support of the Highland clans that, for this reason, suffered a ferocious reprisal after their defeat in the 1746 battle of Culloden. As Gilbert points out, later in the eighteenth century, the Highland regiments started to play a significant 'role in the British army, in the service of the Hanoverian monarchs who had replaced the deposed Stuarts' (2007: 455). The above-mentioned stanza is as follows,

> What though we befriendit young Charlie?
>   To tell it I dinna think shame;
> Poor lad! He came to us barely,
>   An' reckoned our mountains his hame:
> 'Tis true that our reason forbade us,
>   But tenderness carried the day;
> Had Geordie come friendless amang us,
>   Wi' him we had a' gane away.——
>   *Swords* an' *buckler* an' a',
>   *Buckler* and *sword* an' a';
>   *For George we'll encounter the devil,*
>   Wi' *sword* an' *buckler* an' a'.
>   HOGG 2007: 108, ll. 25–36

As noted by Gilbert, in this stanza 'Hogg registers this remarkable change' of loyalty from the Stuarts to the Hanovers (2007: 455). However, Hogg also parodies the militaristic discourse inherent in the stereotype of the High-land soldier, and this is particularly evident in the interaction between the first eight lines of the stanza and its final refrain, where Donald Macdonald claims that '[f]or George we'll encounter the devil' (Hogg 2007: 108, l. 35). If, on the one hand, Hogg here appears to be re-channeling the Highlanders' militaristic quality of unconditional loyalty to the clan chief into the service of the British king against Napoleon, on the other he also implicitly exposes the ideology of the supposedly blind loyalty of the Highland soldiers who, like 'mad dogs', will encounter even the devil in person for King George III. Hogg's parodying voice seems to be hiding behind this line, as its content alludes to his own essay 'Soldiers' where, some years later, he would criticise the Napo-leonic Wars. In that essay, Hogg interrogates the arbitrary power to which men are exposed in the battles induced by the personal gain of '[p]rinces and great men'(1997 [1834]: 40–47). The members of these privileged strata of society would never experience in person the hardship which a war entails, risking instead the life of their young subjects; those supposedly brave Highland soldiers who, in the collective imagination of early nineteenth-century Britain, and in Hogg's parodic reshaping of it, were viewed as heroes 'up wi' the bonny blue bonnet, | The kilt an' the feather, an' a'' (Hogg 2007: 109, ll. 71–72).

4   Wat o' the Cleuch: A Voracious Scottish Borderer Thief

'Wat o' the Cleuch' is a three-canto parody of Sir Walter Scott's literary style contained in Hogg's collection of poems *The Poetic Mirror* published in 1816. Hogg discusses the genesis of *The Poetic Mirror* in his 'Memoir of the Author's Life' (1832), where he recounts that, being in financial straits, in 1814 he thought of improving his situation by publishing a repository of poems written by the most famous British Romantic figures of the period. Southey, Wordsworth, Wilson, and Byron, among the others, gave their 'good-humoured promise' to contribute a piece; while Scott refused, occasioning a temporary rupture of his friendship with Hogg. According to Hogg, Scott's rejection ruined the project, as he had counted on his literary support. Looking disappointingly over the pieces he received, Hogg comments,

> I fancied that I could write a better poem than any that had been sent to me, and this so completely in the style of each poet, that it should not be known but for his own production. It was this conceit that suggested to me the idea of "The Poetic Mirror."
>
> HOGG 2005 [1832]: 40

Indeed, some of Hogg's contemporary critics, unaware of the real author's identity (as the collection was published anonymously), viewed the poems of *The Poetic Mirror* as serious imitations rather than caricatures. *The Quarterly Review* argued that the works 'do not remind us of any individual passages', while in relation to 'Wat of the Cleuch', it claimed that it could be 'the real though imperfect offspring of the prolific and sometimes hasty pen of Mr. Scott himself' (vol. 15, July 1816: 469, 476). The *Eclectic Review* considered the intentions of the author rather equivocal, and observed that it was not clear whether the poems were 'a serious attempt to catch the manner and spirit of the individual writers, so as to exhibit their intellectual likeness, or that of a broad caricature parody of their more obvious peculiarities'. Yet, the same critic considered 'Wat o' the Cleuch' '[a] very fair parody of Mr. Scott's border-epics' (2nd ser., vol. 6, Nov. 1816: 507, 510).

Twentieth-century critics are likewise divided between those who view all poems of Hogg's *Poetic Mirror* as full parodies and those who consider only some of them as such. Dieter A. Berger, for instance, argues that the collection contains imitations 'notably of Byron and Scott, as well as comic distortions and satirical exaggerations of Southey, Coleridge, and Wordsworth', regarding the 'serious imitations' as pastiche and only the 'comic distortions' as parody 'in the narrow sense' (1988: 45). Antony J. Hasler, on the contrary, considers the 'parodic status' of 'Wat o' the Cleuch' 'apparent at the very outset [... even though] it has been singled out critically as being too close to its original to be a parody' (1988: 83). Hasler takes as evidence the very beginning of the poem, which shows a 'condensation' of Scott's stylistic features:

Wat o' the Cleuch came down through the dale,
In helmet and hauberk of glistening mail;
Full proudly he came on his berry-black steed,
Caparison'd, belted for warrior deed.
O bold was the bearing, and brisk the career,
And broad was the cuirass and long was the spear,
And tall was the plume that waved over the brow
Of that dark reckless borderer, Wat o' the Cleuch.
HOGG 1816: 55

Imitating Scott's poetic style with a series of heroic couplets in anapaestic tetrameters for comic effect, Hogg achieved his little revenge for Scott's refusal to contribute a poem to the collection. Hasler observes that

the "galloping" anapaests from "Bonnie Dundee" (in *The Doom of Devorgoil*) [...] the interpolated song "The Cavalier" in *Rokeby*, [...] the inversions [...] which begin at "bold was the bearing;" the piling up of adjectives ("dark reckless borderer") [...] are exaggerated and concentrated together [...] This concentration and exaggeration is here Hogg's "device of laying bare the devices" of Scott's own verse.
1988: 84, the latter quotation within quotation is an emphasis of Hasler

Indeed, the beginning of 'Wat o' the Cleuch' closely resembles the anapaestic rhythm of Lady Heron's song 'Lochinvar' in Scott's narrative poem *Marmion* (1808):

O, young Lochinvar is come out of the west,
Through all the wide Border his steed was the best;

And save his good broad-sword he weapons had none,
He rode all unarmed, and he rode all alone.
So faithful in love, and so dauntless in war,
There never was knight like the young Lochinvar.

SCOTT 1815 [1808]: 258

Considering again Bakhtin's notion of parody as a double-voiced discourse where only the parodied language is heard, as well as Hogg's well-known strong sense of humour, this section contends that Hogg meant 'Wat o' the Cleuch' to be a parody of Scott's poetic style. Its value, however, should not be viewed per se but, rather, envisioned in the cultural and historical context of Hogg's time of writing. Through Scott's parody, Hogg deconstructs the stereotype of the greedy, middle-class Lowlander by depicting a less idealised version of Scott's Lochinvar, thereby suggesting that the cultural stereotype of the avaricious Scot did not represent the actual condition of all social strata in early nineteenth-century Scotland.

Stephen Cohen points out that recent developments in historicist formalism have tried to overcome 'both the programmatic and the effective exclusion of either form or history that has characterized most formalisms and historicisms' (2007: 3). Yet historical formalism is still too historically deterministic and, for this reason, it offers little space for the agency of both author and reader in creating and co-creating a text. By leaving the parodic status of his works uncertain, Hogg meant to convey a precise point to the reviewers of his time in regard to his ability as a writer. The ambiguous mode of the poems in the *Poetic Mirror* has generated a double interpretation on the part of both nineteenth and twentieth-century critics. Blurring the boundaries between genuine simulations and full parodies, Hogg asserted his own poetic skills implying that he, indeed, 'could write a better poem than any that had been sent to [him]' (Hogg 2005: 40), thus addressing the patronising and condescending attitude that he had suffered by the literary elite until then. Yet, to be fair, Hogg also included a self-parody, 'The Gude Greye Kat', with its exaggerated pseudo-medieval Scots reminiscent of 'Kilmeny' and the 'Witch of Fife' in *The Queen's Wake* (1813).

As mentioned above, a parody must be considered in relation to the socio-historical circumstances in which it originated (see Berger 1988: 43), and which the author may have wished to critique. With 'Wat of the Cleuch' Hogg interrogates the stereotype of the materialistic Lowland Scot, exposing the fact that such a label did not represent all Scottish Lowlanders in the early nineteenth century. As Hogg comments in his article published in the *Quarterly Journal of Agriculture*, the peasantry had been affected rather negatively by the affluence derived from the imperial project (1985 [1831–1832]: 40–51).

'Wat of the Cleuch' narrates the vicissitudes of the eponymous Scottish Borderer moss-trooper[8] who, disguised as a monk, wants to regain the Castle of Roxburgh from the English garrison—a location that Hogg also employs some years later in his long narrative *Perils of Man* (1822) and, likewise, as the site of a contest between English and Scots. In the poem, Wat agrees to yield quite reluctantly his sword, in order to play a more credible role of pious monk and enter, so disguised, into the castle of Roxburgh; but his masquerade triggers instead great laughter among the real monks who are helping him in the enterprise:

> Such rude unhypocritic mien,
> No churchman's eye had ever seen
>
> [...]
>
> No living man the scene could stand,
> Each eye was shaded with the hand[.]
>> HOGG 1816: 74

Wat's boorish and impulsive temperament seems to be even harder to disguise than his appearance. At the Castle of Roxburgh, he can scarcely contain himself when Walsinghame, the English minstrel who is unaware of our monk's true identity, performs a hilarious song to deride Wat, who '[s]toop'd onward with such dire intent | As if each nerve were strain'd and bent' (Ibid., p. 110). Eventually, Wat's page gives the sword back to his master; the latter gladly releases himself from his disguise, kills Walsinghame, and expels the English garrison from the castle of Roxburgh.

Samantha Webb views Wat's sword as a symbol of 'competence and authority' which he loses when disguised as a monk (2002: 27). It may be added that through Wat's regaining of his sword, Hogg also performs a re-appropriation of masculine identity by the Scottish Borderers, which had been damaged by the myth of the Highland soldier. Maureen Martin, for instance, observes that in *Kidnapped* (1886) and *The Master of Ballantrae* (1889), Robert Louis Stevenson represents 'the dilemma of Scottish identity as a dilemma of Lowland

---

8   A moss-trooper was a 'member of any of the marauding gangs which, in the mid 17th cent., carried out raids across the "mosses" of the Scottish Border'; see Oxford English Dictionary online <WWW.OED.com> [accessed 23 April 2013]. They were particularly involved in cattle-raiding.

masculinity' (2009: 13). According to Martin, Lowland Scots suffered from a double feminisation in 'their relation to England' and 'their "coverture" under the Highlands' (2009: 13). If on the one hand, the cultural absorption of the Highland myth into British ideology did not threaten English masculinity, thanks to England's 'secure supremacy within the union', on the other hand, 'Lowland manhood [did] not enjoy any comparable position of objective might from which it [could] safely use the Highland myth to meet its ideological needs' (Martin 2009: 84). In 'Wat o' the Cleuch', Hogg hence re-assumes such 'objective might' through the passionate eponymous protagonist, whose identity cannot be easily contained within his carnivalesque travesty:

> "Hurra!" cried Wat, and onward flew
> Like fire-brand that outwings the view,
> And at Sir Guy he made a blow
> That fairly cleft that Knight in two;
> Then Walsinghame he turn'd upon,
> And pinn'd him through the shoulder-bone
> Against the pavement, and the while,
> Half said, half sung, with grizly smile,
> "Out, songster, with thy chorus true,
> What think ye now of Wat o' the Cleuch?"
> "Ah! ruffian, ah!—for shame! for shame!"
> Were the last words of Walsinghame.
>   HOGG 1816: 112

The series of heroic couplets are now, more conventionally, in iambic tetrameters, as Hogg is conveying a serious message. Wat's disguise fails to turn his identity upside down, while the securing of his sword re-establishes both his male and Borderer identity: a fictional event through which Hogg implies that Lowland Scottishness could not be absorbed into a dominating Englishness so easily, even if under the pretence of an overarching Britishness.

Both Wat's failed masquerade and his strong reaction to the English minstrel represent Hogg's deconstruction of the stereotype of the money-obsessed Lowlander. A close analysis of the lexical level of 'Walsinghame's Song' shows that Wat's robberies in the Borders are motivated by a voracious, carnivorous hunger, a fact that triggers a sympathetic laughter in the reader:

> O heard ye never of Wat o' the Cleuch?
> The lad that has worrying tikes enow,

Whose meat is the moss, and whose drink is the dew,
And that's the cheer of Wat o' the Cleuch.
Wat o' the Cleuch! Wat o' the Cleuch!
Woe's my heart for Wat o' the Cleuch!

Wat o' the Cleuch sat down to dine
With two pint stoups of good red wine;
But when he look'd they both were dry;
O poverty parts good company!
Wat o' the Cleuch! Wat o' the Cleuch!
O for a drink to Wat o' the Cleuch!

Wat o' the Cleuch came down the Tine
To woo a maid both gallant and fine;
But as he came o'er by Dick o' the Side
He smell'd the mutton and left the bride.
Wat o' the Cleuch! Wat o' the Cleuch!
What think ye now of Wat O' the Cleuch?

Wat o' the Cleuch came here to steal,
He wanted milk, and he wanted veal;
But ere he wan o'er the Beetleston brow
He hough'd the calf and eated the cow!
Wat o' the Cleuch! Wat o' the Cleuch!
Well done, doughty Wat o' the Cleuch!

[…]

Wat o' the Cleuch kneel'd down to pray,
He wist not what to do or to say;
But he pray'd for beef, and he pray'd for bree,
A two-hand spoon and a haggies to pree.
Wat o' the Cleuch! Wat o' the Cleuch!
That's the cheer for Wat o' the Cleuch!

[…]

But of all the wights in poor Scotland,
That ever drew bow or Border brand,

That ever drove English bullock or ewe,
There never was thief like Wat o' the Cleuch.
Wat o' the Cleuch! Wat o' the Cleuch!
Down for ever with Wat o' the Cleuch!

                HOGG 1816: 105–108, all emphases here and above are mine

Once again, Hogg makes use of the anapaestic rhythm in heroic couplets to enhance the comic effect of Wat's craving for meat: 'O heard ye never of Wat o' the Cleuch? | [...] Whose meat is the moss, and whose drink is the dew'. Yet behind the depiction of Wat's comical hunger, Hogg also communicates an important social critique. 'Walsinghame's Song' is in intertextual relation with Hogg's short story 'Marion's Jock', a tale that Hogg later embeds in the long narrative *Perils of Man* (1822), where Jock's uncontainable hunger for meat symbolises the fierce exploitation of servants by their master. Ian Duncan— viewing all extreme human drives as tropes of an original urge, the need to fill one's mouth—regards Jock's voracious hunger as the result of a series of privations and his crimes as motivated by extreme poverty, since Jock kills a lamb out of hunger and murders the lamb's vengeful owner to save his life. According to Duncan, through this story Hogg represents a great contest between nature (appetite) and law (property), as well as the paradox of a legal system which, instead of protecting human rights, defends the possessions of self-interested masters. This is why the reader sympathises with Jock, notwithstanding his insatiable hunger (Duncan 1997). The craving for meat is an extended metaphor with which Hogg engages consistently in his *œuvre* when wishing to highlight the exploitation of the poor. Similarly to 'Marion's Jock', Wat o' the Cleuch's raids across the Scottish Borders are determined not by self-interested ends but, rather, by his human drive to survive in a poor world which has exacerbated his craving for meat, a symbol of wealth and prosperity.

    Webb considers 'Wat of the Cleuch' as 'a celebration of spontaneous physicality and moral ambiguity that is found in popular tradition' (2002: 25). Yet Wat also functions as an honest representative of the margins as he reacts with 'spontaneous physicality' to a mere instinct for survival, the extreme poverty that motivates his robberies, a far different reason from the greed to exploit the colonies that characterised the Scottish Lowlanders of the higher classes. Though the poem is set more than a hundred years before the nineteenth century, it mirrors Hogg's socio-historical circumstances. At Hogg's time of writing, the Lowlanders of the higher classes were, in fact, the ones who prospered in the imperial economy; and who, perhaps for this reason in 1707, the time around which 'Wat o' the Cleuch' is set, had bribed the parliament to pass the articles of the Union with England. As Devine points out, one of the prime reasons for the move to unification had been the collapse of the Darien Scheme, Scotland's failed attempt to found a colony on the Isthmus of Panama in the late 1690s. Poor planning, tropical diseases, lack of profitable achievement determined by the Spanish, and English fear of Scotland's economic potential caused the failure of this enterprise, which ruined a great number of Scottish investors (Devine 2004 [2003]: 44–48, 250). Martin observes that the subsequent 'commercial successes of Scotland, as junior partner in the imperial economy [...] contributed to the long-existing notion that, in 1707, Scots had "sold" their own nation' (2009: 110). The Scots' economic competition with the English in the imperial enterprise thus stimulated the satirical representation of the rapacious Lowlander in English popular culture. This caricature, however, did not represent the tragic reality of the Borders peasantry, whom Hogg voiced through the carnivorous 'Wat o' the Cleuch'.

Hogg thus engaged with British masculinities in fascinating ways, showing the limits of, and reasons for, the re-appropriation of Highlandism by the British military discourse, proposing a more honest portrayal of sentimental masculinity through the vigorous character of Rickleton, and portraying the more complex social reality of the Lowlands, thereby deconstructing the stereotype of the greedy Scots.

CHAPTER 4

Women's Sexuality and the Scottish Kirk

This chapter explores *how* and *why*, in some of his texts, Hogg questioned the control that the Scottish Kirk exerted over women's sexuality in the early nineteenth century. It argues that, in so doing, Hogg revealed a different reality of women from the ones depicted in the grand narrative of the national tale and the historical novel, thereby questioning the figure of the primary heroine in these novelistic genres and challenging the assumptions that shaped national and imperial ideologies at his time of writing. As shown in Chapters 1 and 2, early nineteenth-century discourses of empire drew on the notions of sympathy and sensibility to articulate the politics of the marriage plot to support the British union, as well as on Christian values to promote the image of the motherly heroine as national signifier. This chapter shows how Hogg crossed the boundaries of literary genres to articulate his own version of the marriage plot not only in the novel but also in the narrative poem and the short story. It also reveals how Hogg voiced female characters from a wider social spectrum than the one usually depicted in more conventional literature of the time.

The first section of this chapter supplies some historical context about the Scottish Kirk, illegitimate pregnancy, and the issue of infanticide in eighteenth and early nineteenth-century Scotland so as to prepare the ground for analysis of Hogg's long narrative poem *Mador of the Moor* (1816), the short story 'Maria's Tale'(1820), and the character of Bell Calvert in *The Private Memoirs and Confessions of a Justified Sinner* (1824). In these texts, Hogg addresses out-of-wedlock pregnancy, seduction, and prostitution respectively. Contemporary reviewers condemned these works, deeming Hogg's social origins and lack of formal education as responsible for his dealing with such 'indelicate' female issues. Yet this chapter argues that that was a pretext to minimise the challenge that Hogg's writing posed to the ideology of the British empire which the major (and especially Scottish) periodical reviews of the time supported (see Chapter 1).

1   The Authority of the Scottish Kirk

As Mitchison and Leneman explain, according to the Calvinist doctrine of Scottish Presbyterianism, man is sinful in principle and corrupted 'by the taint

© KONINKLIJKE BRILL NV, LEIDEN, 2022 | DOI:10.1163/9789004519992_005

of original sin' (1989: 16). Any form of good work is pointless for salvation, because God has already decreed who will be among the damned and the elect. Calvinism views justification as 'the attribution of righteousness by God, [...] by faith alone and [...] not linked to any action on the part of the justified' (Mitchison and Leneman 1998: 5). That is to say, the individual has neither merit nor virtue apart from that attributed by God himself, who has already chosen who will be part of the true church. Nevertheless, as T. M. Devine (2006b) explains, in Hogg's time the strict observance of moral discipline by any congregation was considered as a sign of being part of the true church and, for this reason, its members were kept under the strictest control; the misbehaviour of one single individual could threaten the elect status of the whole congregation.

This particular brand of church discipline, Callum G. Brown (2006) remarks, had been introduced during the 1560s through the Confession of Faith under the aegis of John Knox, the leading figure of the Scottish Protestant Reformation. A congregation that did not punish breaches of rule threatened its elect status and was likely to attract the wrath of God through famine, plagues, wars or rebellions, 'all signs of divine displeasure' (Mitchison and Leneman 1989: 18).

Discipline was kept by a system of kirk sessions and 'testificats'. The former were special meetings held on a monthly basis by the minister and elders of a parish, with the purpose of exerting a strict moral supervision on the members of the community. As Devine observes, they dealt with cases of 'fornication, adultery, drunkenness, and Sabbath profanation', as well as with 'assault, theft and wife-beating', referring more serious offences to the local civil authority (2006b: 84).

The members of a parish were also controlled by a strict system of 'testificats'. These were certificates of good conduct released by the local minister, without which a person could not move easily to another community and start a new life there. For example, pregnant women were unable to lose their identity in the anonymity of the city; as Leneman's and Mitchison's later research demonstrates, this system was effective not only in rural areas but also in the cities, thanks to an efficient network of parishes on which ministers could depend to obtain information about any member attempting to leave their communities (1998: 1). Pregnant women could therefore not easily escape to another village or city and, without a testificat produced by the minister of their parish attesting their moral character, they could not aspire to a respectable job. R. W. Malcolmson contends that these practices highlight the profound influence of the Scottish Kirk on women's sexuality, compared to the English—though there was a double standard, depending on social class (1997: 197).

This strict moral supervision, Callum G. Brown (2006) points out, was mostly directed against women, particularly from the lower classes, to prevent pregnancy out of wedlock. The social elite, the landowning class, and their servants could easily escape public repentance and thus humiliation before members of lesser status, by writing a persuasive, contrite letter and donating a token payment to the fund for the poor (Devine 2006b: 87). As a consequence, Mitchison and Leneman contend, inability to write, as well as inferior financial power, left peasant and servant women—often pregnant by their master or master's sons—more vulnerable to potential exposure to public shame (1989: 75).

The people who appeared before the congregation were mostly without property, both men and women. Significantly, there are very few cases of upper-class women cited by kirk sessions, and Mitchison and Leneman remark that 'whether such women were more virtuous, better guarded, or less likely to be found out is a moot point' (1989: 155). This is an important aspect to be considered when exploring Hogg's narrative poem *Mador of the Moor*, where a lady of the upper class kills her illegitimate child to avoid public shame. Mitchison and Leneman maintain that the chastity of upper-class women represented an important financial value as 'property could be redistributed by their marriages' (1998: 81). Likewise, Christopher Smout points out that both middle- and upper-class women observed the strictest code of sexual morality before marriage, which was 'a contract by which property was transferred' (1980: 214). To illustrate the significance of premarital chastity for a hereditary system regulated by the system of primogeniture, Smout quotes Samuel Johnson who, considering the importance of women's chastity to society, claims that '[u]pon that all the property in the world depends' (cited in Smout, 1980: 214). An uncertain paternity meant that land and estates could be inherited by an illegitimate child, an issue which Hogg hints at through the figure of Rickleton in *Perils of Woman*, as shown in Chapters 2 and 3.

In this regard, labouring women enjoyed more freedom since, in their case, a pregnancy out of wedlock did not threaten land ownership and, as observed by W. Cramond, having gone through public repentance, they would be considered purged from their sin and could even aspire to marry—as long as they were not promiscuous (1888: 49). It must be argued, however, that even though lower-class women did not transfer land and estates through marriage, an illegitimate pregnancy could cost them their work as their sin would tarnish the façade of respectability of the family for which they worked. As I have discussed elsewhere in regards to Hogg's short story 'Cousin Mattie', at a social level where marriage was not an opportunity open to all, for labouring women their occupation could be their only source of survival (Leonardi 2019a). This chapter illustrates the same issue through Hogg's short story 'Maria's Tale', showing that the patriarchal value of women's chastity was important at all levels of the social spectrum.

As mentioned above, some groups were exempted from public repentance. These included the gentry, and their servants; soldiers; vagrants who did not belong to any specific parish; and, most importantly for the present discussion, those women considered promiscuous and hence not deserving of grace (Devine 2006b: 87; Mitchison and Leneman 1989: 35; Leneman and Mitchison 1993: 24). A woman alleged to be a prostitute was forced to leave the village and could sometimes be physically disciplined by the authority of the town council itself. Mitchison and Leneman report the following historical evidence:

> In February 1701, Rothesay session referred Anna McTimus, a relapse case, to the sheriff depute, who intended to keep her imprisoned and to have her head shaved in the public mercat (i.e. market) place. In one region, Caithness, the sessions themselves used physical sanctions. In March 1716, Christian Machugh, a trilapse case, was ordered by Wattin kirk session to be put in the 'jougs' (i.e. an iron collar) for half an hour before service, and later was ducked, shaved and exiled. Thurso kirk session also used the 'jougs' for several sabbaths on Jannet McKinla in October 1716 for 'notorious prophaneness'. In December 1701, the action there about Barbara McKean was even more drastic. She was to be 'convoyed from the pit by the executioner with a paper hat on her head to the stool, her head to be shaven by the hand of the hangman'. After that she was to be seen out of the town by the hangman and promised a ducking if she appeared again. Here the session made use of the town's officials for the physical treatment. In Wattin, in October 1704, Jean Guna was called 'a vile person unworthy of entertainment in a Christian society' and handed to the baillie for corporal punishment; and in Thurso, in March 1705 and April 1709, Elspeth Murray and Mary Sinclair were handed over to the magistrate for corporal punishment. What was expected was made explicit in October 1724 over Jannet Barrie: the magistrate was recommended to 'scourge her out of town' as a lewd woman.
>
>   MITCHISON AND LENEMAN 1989: 52, 223–24

Yet Mitchison and Leneman remark that the Kirk practiced a dual standard in its treatment of prostitutes since, though considering them 'beyond redemption', it did not take measures against 'well organised and institutionalised sexual services for the upper classes' (1998: 30). As a result of this strict control over women's sexual conduct, a young woman alleged to be promiscuous, forced to leave her village, and with no testificat to guarantee her good reputation had no chance of survival but through organised prostitution in the city. This is the reality that Hogg exposes in the short story 'Maria's Tale' and through the character of Bell Calvert in *The Private Memoirs and Confessions of a Justified Sinner*.

However, in certain cases, Smout contends, sexual intercourse before marriage was practised systematically among the peasant classes, in order to test both partners' fertility, particularly in the Lowlands, where 'the work unit was the family, not the single employee' (1980: 214). The couple would have to go through public repentance for three weeks and would not be allowed to christen their child until they had satisfied this obligation. Mitchison and Leneman remark that though christening was not considered to be 'necessary for salvation' (1989: 33), it bore a strong social significance, as it was a sign of respectability. It also mitigated superstitious beliefs since '[u]nbaptized children were regarded as unlucky, and in north-east Scotland and the Borders they were seen as likely to haunt their parents' (Mitchison and Leneman 1989: 118). In *Mador of the Moor*, Hogg exploits this traditional belief to critique the Scottish Kirk's stigmatisation of children born out of wedlock and their reluctance to christen them.

2 Child Murder and 'The Stool of Repentance'

Stewart Brown (2012) points out that public repentance was not an easy matter. If found guilty, offenders had to pay a fine according to their means and appear before the congregation for a number of Sundays, depending on the sin they had committed (Brown 2012: 80). Devine observes that this could vary from a minimum of three appearances for fornication, six for a relapse, twenty-six for adultery, and a year for incest (2006b: 88). A woman with child by a married man who did not want to reveal his identity would have to go through this terrible humiliation alone for a period of months, staying 'at the pillory—a raised platform or a stool in front of the pulpit, clad in a cloak of sackcloth [...] to be admonished by the minister until he was satisfied of [her] penitence', as Henry Grey Graham vividly depicts (1906: 321). Apparently, these events were a source of great pleasure and spiritual pride for some members of the congregation, who smiled and smirked at their 'neighbours in disgrace' (Graham 1906: 322). Hogg himself, like Robert Burns, had to appear 'with a red face on the Stool of Repentance', as he fathered two daughters out of wedlock (Hogg 2004–08, *Collected Letters*, vol. 1, p. 314; Hughes 2007: 73–80; Hughes 2000b).

As shown by Leneman and Mitchison (1993: 19–39), the system of public repentance was mainly intended to limit extra-marital pregnancies and to control women's sexuality. Unfortunately, in order to avoid standing before the session and 'facing the disgrace and terrible ordeals of the Church'

(Graham 1901: 323), between 1700 and 1706 twenty-one unmarried girls committed child murder and were subsequently hanged in Edinburgh (Graham 1901, note 2, p. 323). The lawyer Hugo Arnot in his *Collection of Criminal Trials in Scotland* (1785) writes that 'four women, condemned to death for child murder on one day, declared that dread of the pillory was the cause of their crime' (1785: 350). Similarly, a letter to the *Scots Magazine* from an 'Anti-Papist' laments public repentance as one of the possible causes of child murder in Scotland, arguing that 'this inhuman practice does not proceed from any natural brutality in my country-women, but from be[ing] exposed on the repenting-stool, to the derision of their neighbours and acquaintance' (9 February 1757, pp. 80–81). Refusal to repent publicly could lead to excommunication which, at a time when social life was primarily organised around religious events, would mean alienation from the community (J. Stewart Brown 2012: 93).

It must be argued, however, that those unfortunate women who concealed their pregnancies did not always commit child murder. Giving birth alone could involuntarily cause the death of their infants—an aspect which, when questioned by the kirk session, was often used as pretext by those women who did kill their child. This is why in 1690 the Scots parliament promulgated the Act Anent (concerning) Child Murder, a statute according to which any woman who concealed their pregnancy, called for no help at birth, and whose child was dead or missing was to be found guilty of child murder and hanged (Symonds 1997: 5). This Act lasted until 1809, when the death penalty was replaced by banning. Hogg may have been hinting at this cruel edict in his short story 'Cousin Mattie', while Walter Scott centred the plot of *The Heart of Midlothian* (1818) on this very law.

Another method of control was through the midwives who, before being allowed to practise, had to sign a commitment to disclose the presence of any stranger woman about to give birth. Leneman and Mitchison point out that this system was abused by those who could afford to pay for the midwives' silence (1993: 25–26). Hogg addresses this issue in his short story 'Maria's Tale', where a young female servant is made pregnant by her master's son and flees from the countryside to the city of Edinburgh to avoid public shame. Hogg, who published this tale for the first time in 1811 in his weekly magazine *The Spy*, was fiercely critiqued for this topic; nevertheless, he republished it unchanged in his 1820 collection *Winter Evening Tales*. A comparison between the tale as it appeared in *The Spy* in 1811 under the title 'Affecting Narrative of a Country Girl—Reflections on the Evils of Seduction' and its later version in the 1820 collection shows no changes of substance (see Hogg 2000 [1810–1811]: 223–30 and Hogg 2004b [1820]: 151–58). Arguably, Hogg was unwilling to accommodate the sense of decorum of his reviewers and keener to expose the sexual exploitation of servant women by their masters.

Fundamental to the rationale that led a woman to commit infanticide were her 'sense of shame and [her] concern for reputation', as Malcolmson remarks (1977: 203). Though Malcolmson's research is related to child murder in England, the dynamics he identifies may certainly be applied to Scotland as well. In England, infanticide was subject to the 1624 Act, likewise focused not on the actual killing, which was difficult to prove, but on concealment. Though active until 1803, this law was never enforced since in England leniency towards women who had killed their child was the general tendency (Malcolmson 1977), probably because its society was not influenced by the strict rules of Calvinism and women were not exposed to public shame. Daniel J. R. Grey likewise points out that '[e]xecutions of English and Welsh women for infanticide during the "long nineteenth century" (1789–1914) were very much an anomaly, not the rule', remarking that '[w]omen accused of killing their infant children were regularly treated with extreme sympathy by both the press and the criminal justice system' (2018: 42).

Malcolmson explains that in the sixty-one cases analysed in the Old Bailey between 1730 and 1774, at least thirty-five involved servants while cases of infanticide by women of the higher classes were rare (1977: 197, 192, 202). Regarding servant women, Malcolmson observes that their financial security depended on their reputation, the loss of which could represent a catastrophe from the social and economic points of view. Abandonment was not an easier option because servants were not allowed to leave the houses for which they worked of their own accord, nor could they risk the baby's cries (Malcolmson 1977: 205).

Malcolmson remarks that it is not possible to estimate exactly how many children were killed in England, because the evidence existent is based upon 'reported cases' and not 'actual instances', as 'reliable statistics simply cannot be compiled' (1977: 191). This assertion contradicts Leneman and Mitchison's thesis, according to which in England were committed more infanticides than in Scotland (1989). They maintain that the statements in the Scottish press concerned with this issue[1] were based on simple impressions rather than quantitative material, arguing that there were more cases of infanticide in England than in Scotland, even considering that 'Scotland has a considerable amount of wild hill country not susceptible of search' (1989: 213). Yet it is arguably impossible to provide statistical evidence of child murder either in Scot-

---

1   See the above-mentioned letter in the *Scots Magazine* of 1757, and also Anon. [A Country Elder], 'Letter to the Author of the *Scots Magazine*', *Scots Magazine*, 19, August 1757, pp. 401–02.

land or England. What can be observed without any doubt is that in England women did not have to repent publicly as in Scotland, and this fact may have made a difference.

Mitchison and Leneman discuss another social issue possibly related to Hogg—who married in his early fifties but who had previously fathered two daughters with two different women—namely, that marriage among the peasant class was restricted to those economically capable of owning a house and supporting a family (1989: 1). These social rules, however, clashed with human sexual drive and its consequences, particularly at a time when the options for birth control were nearly non-existent. Though the Scottish Kirk obliged a father to contribute towards his child maintenance until the latter was grown enough to work, in certain cases an unwanted child could represent another mouth to feed as well as a threat to a servant's working position. On this point, Deborah A. Symonds claims that the 'capitalist transformation of agriculture' had a huge impact upon 'rural women in eighteenth-century Scotland' (1997: 3), arguing that 'the pressures created by population growth and emerging capitalist farming meant that an illegitimate birth could become a matter of life and death, threatening their reputations, their positions as servants, and ultimately their place in the village pecking order' (Symonds 1997: 2). Some women never married and depended upon the generosity of a master for their entire lives.

3   When Discourses Clash: Motherhood and Child Murder

Symonds contends that traditional Scottish ballads of infanticide bluntly mirror the 'hardship of courtship and the difficulties of marriage' (1997: 3), as well as the solutions women had at their disposal to tackle an unwished-for pregnancy out of wedlock. On the other hand, historical sources deal mostly with infanticide by unwed mothers, though E. A. Wrigley and J. D. Chambers 'have speculated on infanticide as a possible form of population control in early modern England' among married couples too (both cited in Wrightson 1975: 10).

Wrightson explains that child murder could take the form of 'studied neglect during nursing', and that unwanted children could be 'abandoned [...] maltreated and frequently killed' (1975: 10). Malcolmson remarks that abortion was generally avoided because it was 'dangerous and often unsuccessful [...] and commonly required that a pregnant girl reveal her condition to at least one other person' (1977: 187–88). Wrightson maintains that strangulation, suffocation, drowning and exposure predominated over more violent methods, the latter usually committed by a mother with a disturbed mental state (1975: 15). Therefore, in the seventeenth, eighteenth, and nineteenth centuries, at a time when abortion was not a safe option for dealing with single motherhood, child murder seems to have been the alternative both in England and in Scotland. Symonds, for instance, affirms that in Scotland 'between 1661 and 1821 some 347 women were indicted or investigated for murdering their children at birth, after attempting to hide their pregnancies' (1997: 2).

Traditional culture engaged with this social issue in the ballads of infanticide as, for instance, in 'The Cruel Mother', which depicts in all its brutality how some women dealt with illegitimate pregnancy (see ballad in Child 1957, vol. 1, p. 218, 20B). Jean R. Freedman points out that particularly the Scottish ballads portray a merciless reality 'of murder and rape and revenge, of war and abduction and broken promises, of thwarted love and malicious cruelty', which made such conflicts more acceptable by 'changing them from reality to representation' (1991: 4). David Atkinson adds that the ballads of infanticide functioned as a healing remedy to exorcise an unsettling social issue among the lower classes (1992: 376).

Interestingly, however, there is a strand of these ballads in which the protagonists are upper-class women such as, for instance, 'Mary Hamilton' (Child 173), 'Lamkin' (Child 93), and 'Lady Maisry' (Child 65). Freedman contends that the latter ballad especially reflects the economic value of women's chastity, portraying the struggle to control a woman's sexual behaviour, whose choice of partner bears important consequences for her family (1991: 13). Lady Maisry has rejected a series of Scottish dukes because she is in love with an English lord. Her pregnancy cannot be amended by marriage because, as Freedman explains, such union 'would simply mean that her dowry [...] would be in the control of the enemy' (1991: 13). The dialogue between Maisry and her brother well illustrates this point:

> 'O pardon me, my brother dear,
> An the truth I'll tell to thee;
> My bairn it is to Lord William,
> An he is betrothed to me.'

> 'O coud na ye gotten dukes, or lords,
> Intill your ain country,
> That ye draw up wi an English dog,
> To bring this shame on me?'
>
> CHILD 1957, vol. 2, p. 114, 65A

Maisry's family will condemn and kill her. As I have previously argued (Leonardi 2016b), Hogg questions women's value as a commodity in his play *The Profligate Princes* through the character of Elenor—a woman from the upper class—who is made pregnant and abandoned by Badenoch, a prince in disguise. Elenor's father wants to punish his daughter for having threatened the family's economic security by losing her chastity and by making it evident through her pregnancy (Leonardi 2016b). Hogg touches on the same theme in *Mador of the Moor*, drawing on the ballad 'The Cruel Mother' in the encounter between the protagonist Ila Moore—an unwed pregnant woman who decides to keep her child—and the Palmer, whose previous lover Matilda, on the contrary, killed her baby in order to avoid threatening the economic value of her chastity, as she was promised in marriage to another wealthy man.

Folklore in Hogg's time depicted a very different woman from the delicate and motherly heroine of elite culture—the carrier of British values—as represented in the grand narratives of the national tale and historical novel. Freedman holds that the female protagonist of the ballad played an active role, even though sometimes she might be victimised, as in 'Eppie Morrie' (Child 223), or depicted as cruel, as in 'The Mother's Malison' (Child 216) (1991: 8). Even so, the ballad heroine showed a freedom and autonomy inconceivable for the typical heroine of contemporary established fiction. Hogg mirrors the proactive ballad heroine in the female protagonist of his long narrative *Mador of the Moor*. Made pregnant by the King of Scotland in disguise, Ila Moore takes action and goes in search for her child's father, defying both human and supernatural powers, and hence proving to be in command of both her life and body. Hogg's character, like a ballad heroine, behaves against the norms of feminine manners as described in conduct books such as, for example, in Dr Gregory's *A Father's Legacy to His Daughters* (1781), where young women's self-control is urged 'as a means of protecting them from seduction' (cited in Symonds 1997: 51).

When studying the impact of rural transformation on peasant women in eighteenth-century Scotland, Symonds found at least fifty cases of women hanged for child murder, many more trials, and hundreds of investigations. However, though this topic tended to reappear in the ballads, it was contained in more official discourses. Symonds explains that '[b]etween 1762 and 1817, doctors, lawyers, jurors, and the writer Walter Scott all scrambled to unravel the dismal story that the court cases presented, by arguing that women did not really kill their children' (1997: 8). The possibility of infanticide is an important plot element in both Scott's *The Heart of Midlothian* (1818) and George Eliot's *Adam Bede* (1859); however, as Malcolmson remarks, they both set their stories in a period previous to their own time of writing, thereby diminishing the impact of their criticism on contemporary cases of child murder (1977: 189).

As observed by Symonds, Walter Scott in his novel re-adapted the true story of Isobell Walker—who in 1736 had committed infanticide in Cluden, a village near Dumfries—by 'blaming a vagabond' for her child's death (1997: 5, 9). Scott addresses the issues of infanticide and concealed pregnancy through Effie Deans, his own version of Isobell Walker, who would never kill her baby. Scott was more willing to convey the proper model of a motherly woman, capable of deep feelings and not endangering the familial nucleus, the fundamental unit of the British nation.

Ann Wierda Rowland (2004) maintains that though some collectors of ballads published them without omitting any brutality or sexual graphic details, they managed to use them as national symbols of traditional lore that belonged to the past. Walter Scott, for example, in his collection *Minstrelsy of the Scottish Border*, included 'Lady Anne' and 'The Cruel Mother' 'with no apologies for their sordid content', privileging the ballad form 'as a vehicle of national cultural transmission'(Rowland 2004: 226). Rowland admits that this was a tactic that allowed antiquarians to exploit traditional lore and to publish the ballads of infanticide without alteration by invoking their status as the so-called primitive practice and superstition of a remote past. In this way, nineteenth-century readers could be amused by traditional folklore as long as they kept a 'critical [...] historical distance from the violence of the primitive past' (p. 227). Likewise, James Hogg set *Mador of the Moor* and *The Profligate Princes* in the past. Yet he also shaped the fictional worlds of these texts on contemporary social issues—a fact that rendered these works highly controversial.

4   *Mador of the Moor* and the Fairies' Abduction of Unchristened Children

Hogg's outstanding imaginative power was fuelled by his traditional background of ballads, songs, and supernatural folk tales from the Scottish Borders; his mother was a tradition bearer and he re-articulated these traditions in his works for both critical and creative purposes. In the narrative poem *Mador of the Moor* (1816), Hogg re-appropriates the tradition of the ballads of infanticide, focusing on Ila Moore, a deserted young woman from the 'woodland', the daughter of a tenant, who is seduced and then abandoned with child by the King of Scotland who has disguised himself as a courtier hunting the deer in the Highlands. Ila's condition is highly stigmatised, resulting in her loss of the chance to marry Albert of the Glen, her father's landlord, and thus to improve her family's social status.

Contemporary English reviewers of *Mador*, though acknowledging Hogg's poetic power, were not pleased with his violation of some of the literary norms of the time. For example, the *Champion* received Hogg's use of the supernatural rather negatively (9 June 1816, p. 182). The *British Lady's Magazine* considered '[a] whole band of courtiers murdered for disrespect to fairies' to be exaggerated and irrelevant to the development of the plot (October 1816, p. 253); while the *Antijacobin Review* critiqued the passages in the Scots language, contending that Hogg lacked 'the knowledge of what is pleasing to an English ear' (June 1817, p. 329). However, Hogg's use of the supernatural dimension with the fairy plot, the supposedly unnecessary murder of the courtiers, and his use of obscure expressions in the pseudo-medieval Scots passages are strategies with remarkable implications. In *Mador*, Hogg exploits the supernatural motif of the fairies' abduction of unchristened children to enhance Ila Moore's psychological torment, in order to question the social stigmatisation of unmarried mothers and the strict morality of the Scottish Kirk that would not christen children born out of wedlock if both parents had not repented publicly.

In the first canto, the King and his courtiers pass some pleasurable time hunting the deer in the forest. One night, the minstrel Gilbert of Sheil recites 'The Harper's Song' in ancient Scots, depicting traditional beliefs in the fairies' abduction of unchristened children. The courtiers start deriding 'superstition's spell' and uttering 'words [...] unfitting bard to tell' (Hogg 2005 [1816]: 27). Outraged by the courtiers' disrespect of folk tradition, the fairies take revenge and

> That night was done, by the supreme decree,
> A deed that story scarce may dare to own!
> By what unearthy hand, to all mankind unknown!
> At midnight, strange disturbing sounds awoke
> The drowsy slumberers on the tented heath.
> HOGG 2005 [1816]: 28

The following morning the corpses of the six courtiers are found horribly mutilated:

> With wonder, woe, and death so fully fraught!
> So far beyond the pale of bounded mortal thought!
> [...]
> Knight, page, and hound, lay scatter'd far around,
> Deform'd by many a stain, and deep unseemly wound.
> HOGG 2005 [1816]: 29

Though the *British Lady's Magazine* (October 1816), as mentioned above, considered the courtiers' murder not relevant to plot construction, this violent episode highlights the incredible supernatural power of the fairies and, consequently, Ila's plight at having an unchristened child as a result of the Sottish Kirk's strict rules.

As argued by Douglas Gifford, Hogg's writing was characterised by a 'directness of expression' which at first attracted some patrons such as Walter Scott, only to embarrass them later for the indelicate issues he addressed (1976: 23). Hogg's depiction of an unmarried, pregnant woman threatened the norms of politeness practised among literary reviewers, thereby contributing to the negative reception of *Mador*. Hogg's female protagonist—based on the proactive heroine of the Scottish ballads—was destined to clash with the discursive significance of the more submissive heroine of contemporary literature, particularly when considering a genre of such high prestige as the long narrative poem. The *Scots Magazine* noted that '[t]he heroine is reduced [...] to too low a state of humiliation; an incident which, though suited to the ballad style, is not in harmony with a more elevated and regular composition' (June 1816, p. 449).

According to James Barcus, through *Mador* Hogg entered into dialogue with Scott's *The Lady of the Lake* (1810)—as both poems begin with a deer hunt—in order 'to question the value system Scott espoused' and his 'elitist agenda', proposing instead 'a new social order in which forgiveness is practised and innate goodness and nobility are recognized' (2005: xxiv, xxvii, xxxvii). Barcus (2005) remarks that Hogg's *Mador* would be likely to receive a more positive reception by contemporary critics for his outstanding deconstruction of feminine and masculine stereotypes. Uncommonly for that time, the strong female character of Ila Moore is certainly more in line with the ideals of both feminist and post-feminist readers, as Ila's unpleasant situation and her proactive reaction to it highlight issues that have been of profound significance to women's fight for gender equality.

Notably, in a previous article, Barcus admits that if one considers 'the role that literature has played in reinforcing stereotypes', a text like *Mador* was innovative in depicting firstly a world replete with masculine values such as 'men obsessed with females as objects', 'a reduced and helpless woman; a callous nobleman; an enraged father; and a strong but conniving mother', only to interrogate those very patriarchal values (1995: 35–36, 39). Yet, the *Literary Panorama* (August 1816, p. 738), the *Antijacobin Review* (June 1817, p. 330), and the *Critical Review* (August 1816, p. 142) seem to have inferred only the first layer of Hogg's message. The *Critical Review* judged Hogg's depiction of Ila's mother rather negatively, arguing that 'from his general reflections upon women dispersed in various parts of this work, he [Hogg] entertains no high admiration for the sex' (August 1816, p. 142).

These reviewers concur that only later does Hogg 'redeem himself in the daughter of this wrangling pair, who is described blooming as the flowers around her, pure as the dews in which they are bathed, and playful as the lamb that sports among them' (*Literary Panorama*, August 1816, p. 734). Arguably, these commentators welcomed the latter description because it aligned more decidedly with the stereotype of the delicate heroine of polite and official literature.

Furthermore, a woman who challenges social stigmatisation by deciding to reveal her pregnant status and to keep her child—contrary to another secondary character in the poem, the Palmer's upper-class lover who kills her baby—questioned early nineteenth-century British discourses of motherhood and mother country. Josephine McDonagh notices that in the eighteenth and nineteenth centuries,

> the inclusion of child murder in a text is a moment of puncturing that deflates the even contours of meaning and narrative, and the chronology on which they depend. The historical memory borne by the figure of child murder therefore complicates the conventional teleology of historical narrative, and opens the possibility of counter-histories that question the authority of conventional, progressive accounts.
>
> 2003: 12

In *Mador*, Hogg wished to portray a more complex 'counter-history'. Yet contemporary British reviewers reacted rather fiercely to Hogg's audacity. As I have argued in my introduction to *Intersection of Gender, Class and Race in the Long Nineteenth Century and Beyond*, at the time when Hogg was writing, 'perceptions of womanhood and motherhood were the core around which all gender expectations were defined' and 'the white, heterosexual family was the fundamental unit of the British nation' (Leonardi 2018a: 1). The depiction of healthy motherhood in literary texts was thus pivotal, as the heroine mirrored the values of middle-class women who controlled the moral health of the nation and who preserved 'its continuation through motherhood' (Ibid.). Hogg's evocation of a lady who kills her child thus clashed tremendously with the political aims which British reviewers wished to promote.

Though in *Mador* the King of Scotland in disguise is a conflation of two Scosttish historical figures—the fourteenth-century King Robert II and the sixteenth-century James V, who lived before the Protestant Reformation—the poem shows the profound influence of the Calvinist tenets that informed the Presbyterian religious discourse of Hogg's time. In Hogg's poem, in fact, Ila Moore, pregnant and forsaken, has endured public repentance, as shown in the following passage:

Sweet Ila Moore had borne the world's revile
With meekness, and with warm repentant tears;
At church-anathemas she well could smile,
And silent oft of faithless man she hears.
But now a kind misjudging parent's fears
Opprest her heart—her father too would sigh
O'er the unrighteous babe, whose early years
Excluded were from saints' society!
Disown'd by God and man, an heathen he might die!

HOGG 2005 [1816]: 56, ll. 199–207

Having made amends, Ila is now a candidate for grace; however, she cannot christen her child because the father still has to repent before the congregation.

In 'Canto Fourth', Barcus observes that Hogg echoes the ballad of 'Tam Lin' (Child 39), particularly the passage 'Janet has kilted her green kirtle | A little aboon her knee' (see Hogg 2005 [1816], editorial note, p. 119). Drawing on this traditional ballad where the protagonist Janet is pregnant with illegitimate child, in *Mador* Hogg portrays a courageous heroine who does not bear her fate of abandoned single mother passively but who, rather, dressed like a fairy '[w]ith robe of green, upfolded to her knee', goes in search for her neglectful lover. Freedman maintains that 'Tam Lin' is an 'inversion ballad' with a reversed Calvinist world where the protagonist, rather than facing public shame and accepting a life of poverty and marginalisation, is proactive and 'controls the course of the story. No brothers appear to condemn or to save her, as they do in other ballads; no fathers bar her way. She goes where she pleases and takes responsibility for her actions' (1991: 10). Contrary to Janet in 'Tam Lin', in Hogg's *Mador* Ila repents publicly. Yet what Ila inherits from the ballad's heroine is her proactiveness as she takes action and embarks in the search for her child's father in order for him to repent, allow their child's christening, and protect the latter from the nefarious action of the fairies.

As mentioned above, contemporary reviewers were rather sceptical of both Hogg's use of the supernatural and pseudo-medieval Scots language. The *British Lady's Magazine* claimed that the scene with the 'fairies visibly and bodily attempting to seize a child [...] astounds our southern apprehensions' (1816: 253); while the *Antijacobin Review* critiqued Hogg's use of the Scots language by arguing that 'we know nothing of [...] the uncouth jargon of the harpers' and fairies' songs [...] as there is no Glossary to which we can have recourse' (1817: 329–30). Nevertheless, the apparent lack of relevance in the courtiers' murder, the depiction of a non-rationalised supernatural, and the unintelligible Scots passage of the fairies' song suggest an important, indirect critique which

Hogg intended to convey to the readership of his time. By portraying the fairies' apparently irrelevant and violent action, conflating the supernatural with the real world, and code-switching from English to Scots, Hogg subtly highlights the strength of the fairies' magical power, thereby questioning the strict rules that the Scottish Kirk demanded with respect to illegitimate children. The fairies' extraordinary power emphasises Ila's forsaken predicament at having an unchristened child, thereby exposing the flaws of Hogg's contemporary religious practices for not observing the Christian values of acceptance and mercy, and for not acknowledging that 'illegitimate children [...] were always primarily children', as Gillian Hughes points out in her article 'James Hogg and the "Bastard Brood"'(2000b: 66), when discussing Hogg's personal experience of fathering two illegitimate daughters.

Though recognising Hogg's exceptional creative skills, the anonymous reviewer of the *British Lady's Magazine* (Oct 1816, p. 252) preferred to dismiss the value of Hogg's poem by invoking his lack of official education. The *Critical Review* rejected Hogg's use of the Spenserian stanza which, at the time, was regarded as one of the most difficult and prestigious forms, only attempted by a few poets such as Lord Byron in *Childe Harold's Pilgrimage* (1812). It must be argued, however, that as David Hill Radcliffe explains, when such measure came into vogue between 1770 and 1833, a line of self-taught Scottish authors such as James Beattie (1735–1803) emerged, skilfully engaging in Spenserian poems. Nonetheless, the writer of the *Critical Review* argued that 'as a native of Scotland, probably not very well acquainted with our literature, he [Hogg] could not be supposed to possess that wide and perfect knowledge of the language which such a reduplication of sounds requires' (August 1816: 143). Remarkably, Barcus contends that Hogg made a conscious choice of this prestigious rhyming scheme as he 'probably realised that his stanzaic pattern would provide him with a golden opportunity to raise the profile of folk culture, and to assert the potential worth of self-educated writers' (2005: xxxii). Hogg himself, in his 'Memoir of the Author's Life', remarks that the Spenserian stanza is for *Mador*

> the finest verse in the world [...] it rolls off with such majesty and grandeur. What an effect it will have in the description of mountains, cataracts, and storms!
>
> I had also another motive for adopting it. I was fond of the Spenserian measure; but there was something in the best models that always offended my ear. It was owing to this. I thought it so formed, that every verse ought to be a structure of itself, resembling an arch, of which the two meeting rhymes in the middle should represent the key-stone, and on these all the strength and flow of the verse should rest. On beginning

this poem, therefore, I had the vanity to believe that I was going to give the world a new specimen of this stanza in its proper harmony. It was under these feelings that my poem of "Mador of the Moor" was begun, and in a very short time completed.

2005 [1832]: 35

Hogg's comments show a writer highly educated in the poetic forms of the period, even though such education had not been acquired in the formal setting of Oxford, Cambridge or Edinburgh University, unlike the famous Romantic poets of the period. Nevertheless, Hogg encountered strong prejudice: the *Eclectic Review* considered Hogg a fine writer as long as he limited himself to the ballad, condemning him when he attempted more prestigious genres (February 1817, p. 175); while the *Monthly Review* judged Hogg's writing vulgar, lacking 'invention', and with a certain 'rudeness of versification' (December 1816, p. 439).

On the other hand, the *Literary Panorama* published one of the most positive reviews of Hogg's poem, deeming Hogg's versification 'easy and polished', and the story 'told with a rapidity which carries the reader along with it' (August 1816: 731). This anonymous reviewer, contrary to his colleagues, praised particularly 'The Song of the Fairies', of which the following is an extract:

SING AYDEN! AYDEN! LILLELU!

Bonnye bairne, we sing to you!   (Bonnye bairne = beautiful child)

Up to the Quhyte, and doune the Blak,   (Quhyte = white magic; Blak = black)

No ane leuer, no ane lak,   (leuer = gleam, ray; lak = flow)
No ane shado at ouir bak;   (shado = shadow; bak = back)
No ane stokyng, no ane schue,
No ane bendit blever blue,   (blever blue = the Scottish blue-bell)

No ane traissel in the dewe!   (traissel = a track left by footsteps)

Bonnye bairn, we sing to you,
AYDEN! AYDEN! LILLELU! &c.

HOGG 2005 [1816]: 24, ll. 324–34[2]

2 Hogg wrote the 'Song of the Fairies' in what he called his 'ancient style', 'a combination of ballad phraseology, the rhetoric of late medieval Scottish "makars," such as Robert Henryson, and more modern idiomatic expression'; see Peter D. Garside, 'Introduction', in *A Queer*

Though slightly condemning the unintelligible song 'in the mountain dialect of Scotland', the above-mentioned reviewer positively remarked that Hogg's song

> must have been taught our poet by the fairies themselves: except by the Bard of Avon, never before were their characteristic offices and feelings so exquisitely expressed. Unfortunately, its beauties can only be guessed at by the "Southrons"; who will vainly endeavour to find out the meaning of such poetry.
>
> *Literary Panorama* 1816, p. 731

Arguably, among all contemporary reviewers, the one above came closest to inferring the critique that Hogg appears to communicate through the fairies' unintelligible language. The supernatural creates an uncanny, eerie, and mysterious atmosphere, while Hogg's code switching in 'The Song of the Fairies' to medieval-sounding Scots adds a sense of awe to traditional beliefs, foreshadowing the plight that Ila experiences later in the story. In Hogg's poem, the fairies' unintelligible language endows the supernatural with an aura which goes beyond the grasp of human understanding, the beauties of which 'can only be guessed at', as the reviewer of the *Literary Panorama* admits, and not always explained. Barcus points out that this passage (contained in 'The Harper's Song' of Canto I) was excised in the 1822 edition of Hogg's *Poetical Works*, with the result that Hogg's intentions were greatly misunderstood and the poem 'seriously weakened' (2005: 105).

To further expose the female protagonist's emotional plight, Hogg also drew on contemporary Gothic themes related to supernatural popular beliefs. When leaving her village in search for her child's father and heading to Stirling castle, where she hopes to find him as a court's minstrel, Ila meets a mysterious Palmer (a pilgrim) of whom she is wary, as she believes him to be an evil spirit who might kidnap her unchristened child. The stormy weather, the 'darksome' hut where the Palmer gives her shelter, the cold hearth, the sound of carnivorous animals with 'fiend-like eye and fetid breath' (p. 64, l. 100), the fairies that looked 'from every crevice of the wall' (p. 66, l. 172) are all elements from traditional lore, in addition to reflecting contemporary Gothic themes and tropes; these have the effect of remarkably emphasising Ila's frightening condition. In a meaningful address to the reader, the narrator declares,

---

Book, written by James Hogg, ed. by Peter D. Garside (Edinburgh: Edinburgh University Press, 1995), pp. xi–xxxvii (p. xxv). This song is contained in 'The Harper's Song' within Canto I, and '[un]like the rest of *Mador of the Moor*, [...] is not in Spenserian stanza'; see James E. Barcus, editorial note, in *Mador of the Moor*, ed. by Barcus, p. 104.

> O ye, who mock religion's faded sway,
> And flout the mind that bows to Heaven's decree,
> Think of the fortitude of that fair May,
> Her simple youth, in such a place to be,
> In such a night, and in such company, —
> With guest she ween'd not man of woman born,
> A babe unblest upon her youthful knee!
> Had she not cause to deem her case forlorn?
> No! Trusting to her God, she calmly waited morn.
>
> HOGG 2005 [1816]: 65, ll. 136–44

This passage shows one of Hogg's 'ethics of address', namely what Roger Sell explains as 'a writer's way of entering into human relationships' (Sell 2011: 4, 6) with the readership of his time. Significantly, in this passage Hogg negotiates the clash between traditional beliefs and Christian values as Ila's profound faith in God enables her to resist the exceptionally powerful and supernatural strength of the fairies. In addition, Hogg is able to balance the clash between supernatural beliefs and post-Enlightenment ideals of reason and knowledge by directing the readers' sympathy towards Ila's forlorn condition.

Furthermore, the proactiveness of Ila Moore's character interrogates Hogg's contemporary discourses of motherhood and mother country, as mentioned at the beginning of this section. Namely, Hogg's alternative heroine questions the progressive assumptions inherent in the maternal discourse that British ideology invoked through the primary heroine. As argued in the Introduction, ideas about infanticide as a feature of uncivilised societies contained in Adam Smith's *Theory of Moral Sentiments* (1759) had been exploited by the supporters of the British empire to endorse economic expansion under the ethos of civilisation. In *Mador*, by comparing the reaction of two women of different social background to illegitimate motherhood, Hogg shows that infanticide did not occur just among backwards societies, thereby exposing the lucrative reasons of the imperial expansion under the cover of civilisation.

The encounter between Ila Moore and the Palmer has a meaningful communicative function as Hogg exploits it to share an important Scottish oral tradition—the ballads of infanticide—with readers of his time, thereby showing that infanticide did occur in Scotland and, notably, across the entire social scale. In *Mador*, The Palmer reveals to Ila that he fathered a child out of wedlock with a Lady of the upper class who, having being promised in marriage to another Lord, decided to kill her child in order to avoid tarnishing her family's name and losing the marital contract. This secondary episode significantly contrasts the ideal of British civilisation promoted through the figure of the nurturing mother.

Analysis of the stanzas where the Palmer delivers his story shows important intertextual relations with 'The Cruel Mother', an oral ballad which was very popular in nineteenth-century Scotland, as the following extract shows:

> She's taen out her little pen-knife,
> And twinnd the sweet babe o its life.
>
> She's howket a grave by the light o the   (howket = dug out)
>   moon,
> And there she's buried her sweet babe in.
>
> As she was going to the church,
> She saw a sweet babe in the porch.
>
> 'O sweet babe, and thou were mine,
> I wad cleed thee in the silk so fine.'
>
> 'O mother dear, when I was thine,
> You did na prove to me sae kind.'
>   CHILD 1957, vol. 1, p. 220, 20B

Suggestively, in *Mador* the Palmer leads Matilda to church as 'chiefest guest' on the day of her wedding; but as they proceed towards the altar, a row of children stop them and Matilda, allured by this unusual juvenile congregation, approaches one of them as follows:

> "'Sweet babe,' she simper'd, with affected mien,
> 'Thou art a lovely boy; if thou wert mine,
> I'd deck thee in the gold and diamonds sheen,
> And daily bathe thee in the rosy wine;
>
> [...]
>
> "'O lady, of the proud unfeeling soul,
> 'Tis not three little months since I was thine;
> And thou did'st deck me in the grave-cloth foul,
> And bathe me in the blood—that blood was mine!
>   HOGG 2005 [1816]: 69–70, ll. 304–15

Although the anonymous reviewer of the *British Lady's Magazine* felt 'astounded' by '[the] row of infant ghosts stopping a marriage procession, and one of them making a formal speech, like the head of a deputation' (1816: 253), Hogg's allusion to this ballad of infanticide carries a crucial message. Since a group of these ballads depicts a 'cruel mother' from the upper class, Hogg's use of this traditional motif suggestively compares Lady Matilda, who murdered her illegitimate child, to Ila Moore, the daughter of a tenant from the High-lands who, conversely, decides to keep her child and to face public repentance. Hogg's noticeable comparison exposes the artificiality of the maternal dis-course that characterised the heroine of contemporary texts. The Palmer him-self admits, 'Fair dame, thy crime is purity to mine!' (p. 70, l. 339), presenting Ila Moore as a genuine and honourable character who accepts the consequences of her mistake instead of committing a crime and, though only the daughter of a country tenant, decidedly deserves to marry the King of Scotland in order to become a genuine model of moral values for the nation.

In this poem, Hogg realises the wedding between Ila and the King of Scot-land by drawing on a series of both traditional and social conventions. Hogg exploits the folk motif of recognition by the ring that the King gave Ila, and the fact that the Scottish law accepted a form of marriage called *verba de futuro*, 'a promise of marriage in the future, followed by sexual intercourse', as Mitchison and Leneman explain (1989: 99). Leah Leneman's research dem-onstrates that if a woman had been seduced with this subterfuge, she 'was entitled to damages for seduction' (1999: 39). The union between Ila and the King might have appeared rather extravagant to Hogg's contemporary readers; in nineteenth-century Britain there was no social mobility and, as Leneman remarks, 'a woman could not expect a man to marry her if she was not [...] his equal in rank' (1999: 40). Nevertheless, in *Mador* Hogg uses a stratagem by having the Abbot of Dunfermline play a trick upon the King who, informed of the plight of a young girl, utters in front of the courtiers: '[T]he knight that so hath done | [s]hall reparation make, or quit the land' (p. 80, ll. 174–75). Upon discovering that the forlorn girl is his beloved Ila, the King feels morally obliged to marry her and, eventually, he abdicates, abandons the corrupted court, and moves to the Highlands where the couple live happily.

Though it is highly improbable that such a union could occur in the real world, through this marriage Hogg reveals that class division is a cultural con-struct, while real nobility lies in the soul, thereby articulating the vision of a more humane society and providing an alternative Scotland that defies eth-nic and class stereotypes. Furthermore, as Barcus notably remarks, in Hogg's new version of society, women have a prominent role, as Ila becomes not 'an appendage to a royal husband [but rather] a partner with her husband in a new environment outside the confines and hierarchy of the court' (Barcus 2005: xxxvii). In addition, the union between Ila and the King bears important class, ethnic, national, and imperial implications. Although it unites the Lowlands and the Highlands in a peaceful and promising Scotland, it joins two characters from opposite ends of the social scale, thereby presenting a new version of the marriage plot within a more socially dynamic portrayal of Scottish national identity. At the level of imperial discourse, the marriage between Ila and the King further interrogates the British discourse of motherhood and mother country usually invoked by a virtuous heroine, giving credit instead to the mother of an illegitimate child of humble origins who, despite the strict morality of the Scottish Kirk and the loss of her chastity's economic value, well deserves to become the Queen of Scotland on account of her genuine, high moral values.

5   'Maria's Tale' and the Evils of Female Servants' Seduction

Hogg published 'Maria's Tale' for the first time in the 22nd number of his periodical *The Spy*, which appeared in Edinburgh on Saturday, 11th January 1811, under the title of 'Affecting Narrative of a Country Girl—Reflection on the Evils of Seduction' (pp. 223–30). As Ian Duncan has noticed in his editorial note to this tale (2004b: 564), Hogg re-published the same story under the title of 'Maria's Tale' completely unchanged in his 1820 collection *Winter Evening Tales* and in his second edition of the same two years later, again, without any substantial variation. Hogg's editorial decision had an important critical purpose.

    This short tale relates in an uncompromisingly forthright manner the poignant story of a female servant who is seduced, impregnated, and abandoned by the son of her master, a student of medicine in Edinburgh who, during a summer visit to his parental house in the rural area of the same city, takes away Maria's innocence, enchanting and deceiving her with very little effort, as he was 'a handsome young man, of easy engaging manners, insinuating in his address, and extremely affable to his inferiors' (Hogg 2004b: 152). Transgressing one of his most typical aesthetic rules, according to which an author has 'always to leave something to *the imagination of the reader*' (see *The Spy*, Hogg 2000 [1810–1811]: 28, emphasis original), in this tale Hogg leaves very little indeed to be guessed at by his contemporary readership. Nor does he adjust its content in subsequent editions to align 'Maria's Tale' with early nineteenth-century principles of literary decorum, thereby failing to appease his contemporary reviewers and provoking the negative review of the *British Critic* which included it among those stories 'containing no matter either of edification or amusement, but a good deal which is quite the contrary of either' (1820: 623).

Hogg's decision to publish 'Maria's Tale' uncompromisingly unchanged is a strategy that resembles what Duncan argues about the 'Clifford Mackay plot' in 'Basil Lee' (Duncan 2004b: 533), where Hogg offers his own version of the marriage plot through the union between the eponymous Lowland character and Clifford, a prostitute from the Highlands. Hogg included this novella in the same collection of *Winter Evening Tales*, where 'Maria's Tale' and 'Cousin Mattie' appeared, without changing his peculiar revisitation of this plot's conventions. Likewise, with 'Maria's Tale', Hogg seemed to be more interested in showing the hardship of female servants than concern for the principles of politeness that contemporary reviewers would expect, justifying his choice with the following address—possibly to such reviewers—by the titular character:

> SIR,—You have manifested your desire of rendering yourself a useful member of society, by ridiculing the foibles, and branding the crimes of your fellow-citizens. Amidst your ingenious and engaging speculations, can you listen to the voice of the wretched? Even in your endeavours to please, you have hitherto appeared anxious to instruct and to reform; to you, therefore, as the friend of virtue and of man, I beg leave to address the following narrative. It contains nothing wonderful, but it is *true*; and may in some degree serve to warn others against the arts by which I was deceived; it is the relation of a perfidy of which myself was the victim.
>
> HOGG 2004b [1820]: 151, emphasis original

'Maria's Tale' is written in the autobiographical mode with a first-person narrator, the protagonist herself, who denounces the common and deplorable practice of the upper- and middle-class masters of the time, who would seduce young female servants through their flattering and 'insinuating' manners, which an inexperienced young woman of a lower status might have found quite hard to resist. Hogg invokes 'Maria's Tale' as a form of both advice to and prevention of harm for young female servants.

Notably, the 'Sir' at the beginning of the tale marks a 'social deixis', namely it points out the social distance between Maria—the narrator of this tale—and the implied reader of her story. This strategy alerts the reader that the story will discuss issues concerned with class and gender relations of the period when the tale is set, which is also contemporary to Hogg's own time, as the social issues addressed in the story suggest.

The 'person deixis' expressed by the noun phrase 'you [...] yourself a *useful member of society*' (emphasis added) situates the topic under discussion in an ironic relation to a male representative of the dominant class, while voicing at the same time 'the wretched' Maria, an abused and abandoned female servant. Social deixis is an important linguistic tool which, as Roger Sell explains, 'models relationships within the communicative triangle [the writer, the text, and the reader] from the point of view of politeness' (2001: 152). In Hogg's tale, the politeness conveyed by the form of address 'Sir' has the effect of mocking deference when such form of respect is established only by social status rather than through high moral values.

Through such deference, Maria invokes both the reviewers who would read and judge her story and the male exponents of the upper and middle classes who, similarly to the master's son who disgraced her, may 'decoy' other young female servants and lead them 'to folly and ruin' (p. 156). Though 'Maria's Tale' did not meet the expectations of propriety of early nineteenth-century British reviewers, Hogg wished to draw the attention of his contemporary readers towards the reality of a community at the margins of Scottish society and to voice the hardships of young female servants through a story which, though containing 'nothing wonderful, [...] is *true*' (p. 151, emphasis original).

Maria cannot stand '[t]he shame of acknowledging that [she] had so long persisted in a falsehood, together with the necessity of giving that satisfaction which the church would demand' (pp. 154–55). This social circumstance positions the tale's temporal setting close to the moment at which the story was actually composed, as Hogg himself had faced public repentance for the same reason. It also alerts the reader that Maria's reluctance to undergo public repentance might lead her to further perils: if Maria abandons her parish without a testificat that guarantees her good conduct, she will not be able to find a respectable job. As mentioned at the beginning of this chapter, the options for women with illegitimate children in Edinburgh without a testificat to guarantee their character to any possible employer would have been non-existent; their only remaining resource for survival would have been prostitution.

A maid servant like Maria could not certainly afford to provide financial support for the poor to avoid public humiliation, and her illegitimate pregnancy would have involved the loss of her reputation and of her position as servant within her master's family. Her work as a servant was probably her only financial support at a time when social mobility was inconceivable and when she could not expect to be married to someone like the 'Sir' whom she addresses in the tale. Compelled to disappear from her parish without a reference, Maria would probably have followed the same path as one of those pitiful cases which Dr Tait indicates as the major causes of prostitution in nineteenth-century Edinburgh (Tait 1840: 97–98). That is to say, had her little child survived and her family not forgiven her, Maria could have become a prostitute as she was 'without a friend, and without a home; without money and unable to work' (p. 155), and the only place where she found asylum in the city was 'a house, which I supposed was the haunt of debauchery and vice; for this appeared to be the only abode to which I was entitled now, and the only one where I was likely to be admitted' (p. 155).

Nevertheless, Hogg presents 'Maria's Tale' as a boisterous critique of how male members of the privileged strata of society took advantage of young female servants, thereby showing little concern for the norms of politeness that British reviewers demanded with regard to what was appropriate for publication. Hogg's supposed lack of propriety in addressing Maria's situation defied the discursive dichotomy between delicate heroine and fallen angel. As Clair Wills explains, the freely circulating body of the working-class woman represented a threat and an antithesis to the restricted figure of the lady contained within the familial domestic arena, as promoted by middle-class ideology (2001: 94). Jane Gallop (1985) remarks that the strong sexual desire for the servant girl on the part of the male bourgeoisie symbolised a tool for controlling a threatening figure who could circulate between the domestic and the extra-familial space and who, for this very reason, had to be both seduced (assimilated) and abandoned (expelled). Even more crucially, Gallop (1985) points out, in the male mind of this social class not only were the prostitute and the female servant equalled, but there was an even more subtle equation between the prostitute and the lady, as both were on the market for the husband's physical and financial gain.

The master's son who seduces and abandons Maria, in addition to being a member of the gentry who will never marry her, may also have been one of those university students mentioned by Dr Tait, whom brothel keepers supported (1840: 56). Maria relates that her family eventually found her, and that they 'conducted [her] to the house of a relation, a few miles from Edinburgh, where ill health' seriously affected her (p. 157). Maria's illness could have possibly been a venereal disease which she may have contracted from her seducer and which may also have been responsible for the premature death of her child.

Rather than accommodating the *status quo* by adopting a more elusive strategy, as Massimiliano Morini explains with regard to Jane Austen's narrative techniques (2009: 76; see Chapter 1), in 'Maria's Tale' Hogg disregarded such a tactic. On the contrary, when shaping his story, Hogg chose to adhere to his own 'ideal social autonomy', as Mao would call it (see Mao 1994: 451, 472). In so doing, Hogg distanced himself from a centripetal force towards adherence to norms of propriety, challenging early nineteenth-century expectations of literary politeness. No wonder the *British Critic* viewed Hogg's tale as 'containing no matter [...] of edification or amusement' (1820: 623). Hogg rather appeared to have been more interested in exposing the reality of contemporary female servants' lives and in telling the truth about their risks, following the very piece of advice that he once gave in a letter to his daughter Elizabeth, whom he had fathered out of wedlock. What really matters, Hogg declared in his letter, is '[t]ell[ing] always the downright simple truth although it should appear to be against you it will ultimately turn out to be in your favours [sic]' (see Hogg 2004–08, Collected Letters, vol. 3, p. 167). In 'Maria's Tale', Hogg had a specific critical goal: to raise his readers' attention to a different reality from the one represented in the literature supported by the reviewers of the big periodicals. Yet in doing so, Hogg's tale also exposed the ideological significance of the domestic angel and her profound relation to the more marginalised figures of the prostitute and the female servant in the early nineteenth century, thereby triggering reflection on the subtle entanglement of gender with class and power at his time of writing.

6   Bell Calvert and the Tragic World of 'Women of Ill Fame'

During Hogg's lifetime (1770–1835), Edinburgh was one of the most sophisticated cultural centres of Europe. In *The Private Memoirs and Confessions of a Justified Sinner* (1824), Hogg—self-educated and labouring-class—opposes the city's elitism, insisting on the greater value of marginal voices, among them a prostitute: Bell Calvert. This character questions the reliability of the official discourse of Hogg's time which, in the novel, is represented by the Editor, the third-person narrator of the first part of the novel. The prominence that Hogg conferred on a prostitute from the margins clashed, once again, with the bourgeois ideal of delicate heroine. The figure of Bell Calvert questioned the ideology represented by this female emblem of British progress in both the national tale and historical novel because it exposed an unsettling social reality in the Northern part of the British empire: prostitution in Edinburgh. I argue that this is one of the aspects that might have contributed to the reviewers' lack of enthusiasm at the time when Hogg's novel was first published.

By contrast, and for the same reason, twentieth-century scholars, such as Douglas Mack, have judged Hogg's *Confessions* as one of the most significant Scottish novels of any time for the authority that Hogg bestowed on the character of a fallen woman. One of the strategies that Hogg uses to voice the margins, and contrast them with a supposedly more authoritative voice of the period, is telling the same story from two different perspectives—a strategy that has fascinated twentieth-century scholars because Hogg, in 1824, made use of a narrative structure that would be at the core of postmodern fiction. Postmodern scholars have found appealing the fact that in Hogg's *Confessions* no voice is given prime status of reliability, while much responsibility for the construction of textual meaning is left to the reader. Peter D. Garside maintains that post-colonial critics have been fascinated by the novel's challenge mounted by marginal voices in Scots language against the dominant English culture; Douglas Mack has remarked that Hogg's message in the novel is that 'well-educated people might sometimes be in error' while people from the margins—such as the prostitute Bell Calvert—might have 'a valuable story to tell' (2006: 57). The following section explains the structure of Hogg's novel before engaging in an overview of its reception by contemporary reviewers; it then explores the significance of Bell Calvert's voice in the context of early nineteenth-century discourse of British progress.

Hogg's *Confessions* is divided into two main narratives. The first part is narrated by the post-Enlightenment Editor, a contemporary of Hogg, who offers a third-person account of the life of Robert Wringhim, the Justified Sinner, a religious fanatic who lived between 1687 and 1712. The second part is Robert Wringhim's autobiographical narrative, interrupted by an embedded supernatural tale. Hogg then concludes the novel with the Editor's account of how he and his friends discovered Robert's manuscript in a grave of Ettrick Forest more than a hundred years after the narrated events.

The plot shows the negative consequences of Robert's religious fanaticism and his adherence to antinomianism, an extreme faction of Calvinism. According to Calvinism, though God has already predestined the elect, they still have to observe the strictest moral behaviour in order to confirm their predestined status. On the other hand, antinomianism releases the elect from the obligation of observing the moral law as they have been predestined by God without restrictions. As a consequence, Robert feels justified to commit any crime in order to destroy God's enemies and those who take pleasure in life.

In the *Confessions*, Hogg interrogates the blind reliance on authoritative discourses by using the voices of characters from subaltern classes which question both the Editor's biased rationality and the Justified Sinner's antinomian enthusiasm. Hogg's idea of voicing the margins to question the authorities anticipate the ideas of French philosopher Michel Foucault who, in the twentieth century, would contend that modern society is characterised by a particular system of institutionalised values at the expense of other knowledge (1990: 18). Hogg also seems to align with Bakhtin's ideas of *heteroglossia*, the social dimension of fictional voices according to which the verbal ideological centre is questioned by other centrifugal levels of language varieties (1981: 41–83). Likewise, in the *Confessions* Hogg voices prostitution, one of the dark sides of nineteenth-century Edinburgh, which the reviewers of the periodical press would have rather kept hidden as it disturbed the ideals of Englishness, politeness, progress and civilisation promoted by the British nation. Though Robert Wringhim's narrative is set more than one hundred years before the 1820s, it mirrors this disturbing contemporary reality.

Preoccupied with the negative reception of his previous two novels, *Perils of Man* (1822) and *Perils of Woman* (1823), and possibly also influenced by the success of The Great Unknown's (Walter Scott's) series of Waverley Novels, Hogg decided to publish the *Confessions* anonymously. Despite these precautions, contemporary reviewers suspected that Hogg was the author of this extravagant novel and expressed their concerns. The unenthusiastic reception of the *Confessions*, Gillian Hughes explains, 'could not have been for the want of Hogg's name', as six out of the ten anonymous reviewers attributed the novel to him, using as evidence his style, 'an incongruous mixture of the strongest powers with the strongest absurdities' (1982: 11, 12). With the only exception of the *Monthly Critical Gazette*, which praised highly Hogg's satire of extremist Calvinism (1824: 437), the main objections 'were made to what are now taken to be the deliberate ambiguities of the novel' (Hughes 1982: 12). Some reviewers condemned Hogg's ambiguous portrayal of the devil as either real or as the product of the Justified Sinner's imagination, arguing that such uncertainty was doomed to cause great confusion in the reader as to who the responsible for the crimes committed in the novel is. The *London Literary Gazette* admitted his 'ignorance of Mr. Hogg's precise drift [...] as regards his incoherent machinery' (17 July 1824, p. 451); while the *Westminster Review* remarked that 'if an author [...] introduce[s] supernatural beings, he is at least bound to invent plausible motives for their interference in human concerns'(1824: 561). Apparently, theses reviewers did not appreciate Hogg's choice to leave the reader free to decide where the truth of the novel lies.

In addition, the double narrative—a feature that would appeal to postmodern scholars in the twentieth century—raised some concerns among the reviewers of the nineteenth-century periodical press, as 'the author has managed the tale very clumsily, having made two distinct narratives of the same events' (*Westminster Review* 1824: 560–61). The *New Monthly Magazine* argued that 'it is altogether unfair to treat the reader with two versions of such extraordinary trash' (1824: 506); while *The Ladies' Monthly Museum* viewed the *Confessions* as exhibiting 'the characteristic ingenuity and extravagance of the highly-gifted, but eccentric writer' (1824: 106). In general, as Hughes points out, Hogg's 'tremendous power over the human imagination' (1982: 13) was acknowledged, though not always in positive terms. Significantly, contemporary reviewers made no comments whatsoever on Bell Calvert opposing the reliability of the Editor's voice in the first part of the novel. Only the *British Critic* defined this secondary female character rather mockingly as 'a genuine melodramatic heroine, who with the exception of the minor feminine virtues of chastity and honesty, was endowed with every quality which might entitle her to canonization' (July 1824, p. 70).

Keeping in mind the contentious reception of the *Confessions*, the following section argues that Hogg's lack of inhibition in giving a prominent role to a prostitute may have been one of the unstated reasons for the negative reception of the novel. Concerning Hogg's treatment of prostitution in *Perils of Woman* (1823), Groves remarks that, in a period when even the depiction of a pregnant woman would violate the principles of literary politeness and thus affect negatively the reception of a text, Hogg went far beyond the limit (1987: 129). The year before the publication of the *Confessions*, Hogg's *Perils of Woman* had elicited great consternation among British reviewers by addressing the tragic reality of prostitution for some women in the city of Edinburgh. Raising such a disturbing issue and making bourgeois female readers aware of it was perceived as subversive; such a portrayal of Edinburgh complicated the progressive narratives of the national tale and the historical novel. Bell Calvert supports herself by 'the most degrading of all means' (Hogg 2002 [1824]: 49); nevertheless, though her reality would have embarrassed or shocked a middle- and upper-class female readership, Hogg was keen on emphasising that Bell Calvert was from the same social background of these ladies, as her beautiful English suggests.

Dr Tate has shown (1840) that 'unprotected' women from all social strata were threatened by the risk of resorting to prostitution. Hogg's suggestion that Bell Calvert was of high social origins was quite problematic because, in so doing, he merged the figures of the lady and the prostitute in the same character. Bell pronounces,

> My name is Arabella Calvert [...] Miss, mistress, or widow, as you chuse, for I have been all the three, and that not once nor twice only [...] There have been days, madam [...] when I *was* to be seen, and when there were few to be seen like me. But since that time there have indeed been days on which I was not to be seen.
>
>   HOGG 2002 [1824]: 43, emphasis original

Hogg makes strategic use of a voice clash that Jacob May defines as 'voice trash' (2000: 198–202) and which occurs when the speech of a character mismatches their status in the world. By featuring a prostitute whose Englishness clashes with her current social status, Hogg can therefore be seen to question the dynamics of power, class, and politeness of his time. Interestingly, though the women that Dr Tait treated for venereal diseases belonged for the greater part to the lower classes, he also cured three upper-class women who had resorted to prostitution in reduced circumstances, and twelve middle class women for 'misplaced affection' (Tait 1840: 27). Bell Calvert's character bears out Bennett and Royle's re-interpretation of Bakhtin's *heteroglossia*, as they contend that 'there is difference and multiplicity *within* every voice [...] not only the kind of socio-literary polyphony that Bakhtin describes, [...] But in addition to this, and more fundamentally, any one voice is in fact made up of multiple voices' (1999: 78). Bell Calvert is a polyphony of social strata; through her tragic story, Hogg seeks to give voice to an unsettling reality that could threaten women from all social backgrounds. Yet, in so doing, Hogg also threatened the moral role of middle-class women, the 'mothers of the nation', and the soundness of the progressive assumptions of the British empire.

Bell Calvert recounts an episode already narrated by the Editor, providing an eye-witness account of the killing of young George, the Justified Sinner's brother. The Editor, on the other hand, assumes that George has been murdered by his friend Drummond, basing his account on the general impression of George's friends who, at the moment of the homicide, were in a brothel: 'Not one of them could swear that it was Drummond who came to the door, and desired to speak with the deceased, but the general impression on the minds of them all, was to that effect' (p. 38). On the other hand Bell Calvert, though unable to work out what she actually saw on the night of the crime, does know that Drummond cannot be guilty:

> I had only lost sight of Drummond [...] for the short space of time we [Bell and a client] took in running up one pair of short stairs; [...] and, *at the same time*, I saw the two men [Robert Wringhim and Gil-Martin] coming down the bank on the opposite side of the loch, [...b]oth he and they were distinctly in my view, and never within speech of each other, [...] so that it was quite clear he neither could be one of them, nor have any communication with them.
> HOGG 2002 [1824]: 51, emphasis original

Doctor Tait, the surgeon who treated the prostitutes working in Edinburgh, observes that these unfortunate women were considered to be consistent liars and hence unreliable 'as witnesses before a public court' (1840: 39). This is a point that Hogg challenges in the *Confessions* by presenting Bell Calvert's testimony in an Edinburgh public court as more reliable than the evidence provided by the post-Enlightenment Editor. However, by deconstructing a notion of power based on class and apparent decorum, Hogg destabilises his contemporary social order.

Remarkably, besides questioning the authority of the Editor's narrative, Bell's tale, as Mack points out, makes the reader reconsider the Editor's jovial portrayal of George's friends, as she describes a group of drunken men who, on the night of the murder, were contracting sexual favours with her while she was suffering from hunger (1999: 5). Such outrageous episodes, however, reveal the disturbing reality of Edinburgh's margins which women of the middle and upper social strata—who comprised part of Hogg's readership—were not supposed to know. As mentioned in the Introduction, Sinha (2004: 188) and Wilson (2004: 20–21) contend that nineteenth-century bourgeois women represented the moral authority of the imperial project. As I have argued elsewhere (Leonardi 2018b), in their role model status as mothers of the nation, middle-class women represented the moral soundness of Britain and preserved future generations through their civilising motherhood. Yet the reality of marginal social existence in Edinburgh, which Bell Calvert foregrounds in the *Confessions*, was rather distant from the picture of such supposedly sound morality. Bell Calvert's unfortunate condition reveals that the margins were certainly not enjoying prosperity in the Northern territory of the British empire, thereby questioning the progressive assumptions of the British Union.

In general, Hogg's lack of inhibition in dealing with these matters provoked great aversion among contemporary reviewers who, for this reason, censored his texts. The *Confessions*, too, may have been critiqued for the same reason, though it is never explicitly mentioned by the reviewers cited above. When discussing politeness in Charles Dickens's *Dombey and Son* (1846–48), Roger Sell points out that the novel's success at its time of writing was due to Dickens's skilfully balanced 'endorsement and subversion of a homogenizing bourgeois decorum' (2001: 165), similarly to what Morini argues for Jane Austen (2009: 76), and to what Mao contends when describing the internal struggle of those individuals who wish to adhere to social norms but who also want to maintain the freedom to express themselves (1994). As Sell explains, Dickens's fluctuation between traditional values and their subversion mirrors a 'tension between the social and the individual' which Dickens 'powerfully' co-adapted (2001: 168–69). A total subversion, in fact, may have been 'too intoxicating for a middle-of-the-road Victorian reader' (Sell 2001: 181). This is probably the balance that Hogg was unable to strike in the *Confessions*: instead of placing Bell Calvert in the background, he made her one of the most prominent characters of the novel.

In conclusion, Hogg challenged the ideal of 'the pure lady' that was promoted in early nineteenth-century canonical literature as the bearer of British moral values and the epitome of British progress, providing instead the portrait of a more realistic and diverse heroine; though she may have 'fallen' from a 'pure' status—according to the ideology of Englishness and mother country— she goes through redemption and forgiveness, and therefore well deserves to become a symbol of the nation. In *Mador of the Moor*, the heroine Ila Moore does not hide her guilt; while, on the contrary, Lady Matilda kills her child in order to preserve the chance to marry the lord that her family intends for her. Honesty for Hogg was an important value, so much so that he kept publishing 'Maria's Tale' without variation from his short-lived weekly magazine, *The Spy*, in both editions of his collection of *Winter Evening Tales*: what mattered to Hogg was providing advice to women of any social sphere. This is borne out in *Confessions of a Justified Sinner*, where the Englishness of the prostitute Bell Calvert signals that in the nineteenth century, women from all social backgrounds were at risk of falling and losing what was considered the ideal of purity by contemporary social conventions.

CHAPTER 5

Unconventional Heroines

1   Introduction: When Primary and Secondary Heroines Merge

In her book *Secondary Heroines in Nineteenth-Century British and American Novels* (2010), Jennifer Camden points out that some secondary female characters destabilise the marriage plot, as the hero's repressed attraction towards this more rebellious character poses a threat to his union with the primary heroine and, as a consequence, to the stability of the nation that the main couple symbolises. Camden remarks that the hero's repressed feelings for the secondary heroine return like a Freudian 'uncanny' to 'destabilize' and 'complicate' the 'national ideals' that the primary heroine represents, contending that the hero's hidden feelings for the secondary female character point out to 'national anxieties' deriving from 'the instability of national identity' (2010: 2, 6, 5).

Camden draws on Benedict Anderson's and Katie Trumpener's models of nationhood to shape a paradigm for the tension between primary and secondary heroines. Anderson's view of the nation as an 'imagined community' defined by a 'majority' which 'excludes the "other" in the interests of group cohesion' supplies Camden with a theory for conceptualising the role of the primary heroine, whose marriage with the hero represents 'the basic unit on which the larger nation is constructed' (Anderson 2006 [1983]). Katie Trumpener's idea of nationalism as located on the borders provides a model for the 'rebel, outcast, or merely forgotten' secondary heroine who 'pulls readers' attention to the margins' (Camden 2010: 3; see Trumpener 1997). Regarding the British novel, Camden discusses Walter Scott's *Waverley* (1814) and *Ivanhoe* (1820) where the secondary heroines, Flora and Rebecca respectively, 'complicate the incipient nationalism these novels appear to endorse', as they both 'narrate a sort of last stand against an already-changed world order, and in each novel the secondary heroine registers the cost of that shift' (Camden 2010: 15, 60).

This chapter argues that in the short story 'Tibby Hyslop's Dream' (2002 [1829]), Hogg fuses the tension between primary and secondary heroines in a unique character symbolic of the Scottish margins—a new heroine who does not engage in any courtship with the hero—thereby suggesting that the grievances of Scotland's less socially privileged groups cannot find an easy resolution in the political union with England. In other works, Hogg engages with the conventional dialectics between primary and secondary heroines (for example, in *Perils of Woman* (see Chapter 2) where Cherry's death signals the cost of the marriage between Gatty and M'Ion), but in 'Tibby Hyslop's Dream' Hogg gives birth to a new prototype of heroine where the traits of both female characters merge, thereby articulating a heterodox solution to contemporary Scottish national dilemmas.

In 'Tibby Hyslop's Dream', Hogg's eponymous heroine does not engage in any love affair that may result in marriage. This was not a new narrative strategy in Hogg's work. As I have argued elsewhere (Leonardi 2016a), in *The Brownie of Bodsbeck* the hero Daniel Roy Macpherson—a Highlander who could potentially realise the marriage plot with the Lowlander Katharine Laidlaw—is already married. According to the reviewer of the *Clydesdale Magazine* (vol. 1, May 1818), the female readers of Hogg's *Brownie* would 'feel much disappointed at the perusal; no love scene is to be traced here—Katharine Laidlaw has no lover. The happy winding up of a long and interrupted courtship, is not to be found in the conclusion' (p. 25). In *The Brownie of Bodsbeck* there is no ideological marriage to solve the political issues between the Scottish Highlands and Lowlands. Instead, Hogg engages in a resolution through the loyal friendship between Walter Laidlaw, the heroine's Lowland father, and Daniel Roy Macpherson, a Highland soldier.

When the story contains anti-heroes whose only purpose is to take advantage of the female protagonist's body, as in 'Tibby Hyslop's Dream', then the heroine chooses spinsterhood, because '[t]here is neither sin nor shame in being unwedded, but there may be baith in joining yourself to an unbeliever'—Tibby's grandmother warns her granddaughter (Hogg 2002 [1829]: 155). Through this *heteroglot* voice, Hogg demystifies the marriage plot and its familial microcosm as ideological tools in shaping the identity of the British nation. The family metaphor, as Anne McClintock explains (1995: 43–45), based on the dependency of wife and children on the father, shaped British relations between the margins and the centre, articulating perceptions of class, gender, and ethnic diversity as normal and natural (see Chapter 2). On the other hand, in 'Tibby's Hyslop's Dream' Hogg voices spinsterhood as a solution to the reality of labouring women, thereby providing a more realistic representation of the social margins in the early nineteenth-century Scottish Borders.

As explained in Chapter 1, when Hogg was writing and publishing Scotland had been going through a major economic transformation for a variety of reasons (Devine 2004 [2003]: 326). The agricultural improvements based on capitalistic notions of progress had penalised the labouring classes who did not own any land, as they were exploited without any sense of humanity or support from their master (Mack 2006: 58–62). This was a very different way of treating servants from the past, when masters did take care of their subalterns.

In his article 'On the Changes in the Habits, Amusements and Condition of the Scottish Peasantry' (1985 [1831–1832]: 40–51), Hogg lamented this deteriorated condition among the servants, suggesting that what the ruling classes considered to be outstanding progress in agricultural innovation did not equal improvement in the life of these servants, as the tale of 'Tibby Hyslop's Dream' illustrates. Mr Forret, Tibby Hyslop's abusive master, though not directly involved in colonial trade himself, was a very successful, capitalist-oriented farmer who may indeed have rented land from ex-colonial traders not interested in dealing directly with the farming business. Seemingly, Mr Forret was one of those agricultural innovators who abused the land he did not own—and young female servants like Tibby—for his own personal profit. Hogg's tale portrays the hard working-conditions of those labouring women at this time: Tibby's trials of life and her master's attempts to violate her body expose the tragic reality of such women in the Scottish Borders during this period of imperial growth and agricultural innovation.

In relation to the character construction of both Katharine Laidlaw and Tibby Hyslop, in *The Brownie of Bodsbeck* and 'Tibby Hyslop's Dream' respectively, Hogg does not present what Camden defines as 'Western stereotypes of femininity' of 'beauty and dependence' (2010: 7). Meaningfully, in both texts Hogg portrays alternative, self-determining heroines, with strong and genuine moral values, while providing minimal physical description. In *The Brownie*, Katharine shows 'the strength of mind, and energy of the bravest of men, blent with all the softness, delicacy, and tenderness of femeninity [*sic*]', an innovative primary heroine that Hogg contrasts with the 'poor shilly-shally milk-an'-water' ladies of early nineteenth-century Edinburgh, as defined by the *heteroglot* voice of the heroine's father (Hogg 1976: 164, 163).

This chapter concludes by exploring Hogg's mock-epic *Queen Hynde* (1824), where he engages with a slightly more conventional portrayal of primary and secondary heroines. Perhaps disappointed with the negative role that the Edinburgh blue-stockings had played in Robert Miller's refusal to publish *The Pilgrims of the Sun* (1815),[1] in *The Brownie* Hogg initiates a literary dialogue with these ladies through Walter Laidlaw's voice, the heroine's father, which achieves its final apotheosis in *Queen Hynde* with the hilarious exophoric address of the narrator to the 'Maid of Dunedin', a prototype of the Edinburgh

---

1 Hogg was not completely displeased with Miller's refusal, however, as he was expecting to get his poem published by John Murray's more prestigious London firm. See Gillian Hughes, 'Essay on the Genesis of the Text', in *Midsummer Night Dreams and Related Poems*, written by Hogg, ed. by Rubenstein and others, pp. xiii–xliii (pp. xviii–xx). See also James Hogg, 'Memoir of the Author's Life', in *Altrive Tales*, written by Hogg, ed. by Hughes, pp. 11–52 (pp. 36–39).

lady of his time. In this long narrative poem, Hogg declares his intellectual freedom and poetic independence, subverting contemporary constructions of delicacy as epitomised by the primary heroine, the eponymous Queen Hynde, whom he sets in intra-textual relation with the Queen's maid of honour—the rebellious and insubordinate Wicked Wene, the secondary heroine. Douglas Mack maintains that Wene represents the 'fairy' nature of Hogg's poetry and that Hogg hides a serious purpose behind her 'mischief-making' behaviour (2009: 143). Indeed, Wene bears a *double* serious purpose, because in addition to representing Hogg's independence from nineteenth-century literary conventions, she also symbolises middle-class women's freedom from the role of national signifiers.

2   'There Is Neither Sin Nor Shame in Being Unwedded, but
       There May Be Baith in Joining Yourself to an Unbeliever':
       Choosing Spinsterhood When There Are No Heroes

In the early nineteenth century, female peasants and labourers of the Scottish Borders had to come to terms with a far more tragic reality than the one experienced by upper- and middle-class women living in the safety of their domestic microcosm. In 'Tibby Hislop's Dream', Hogg depicts the hardships of women from the countryside, merging magic and realism and, as Jason Mark Harris explains, 'posing folk beliefs against élite conventions of rationality' (2008: 33). Harris observes that 'works of the literary fantastic use aspects of supernatural folklore [...to] present voices and perspectives of unofficial culture [...] that contradict the mindset of rational, religious, and imperial power' (2008: 34). Likewise, in 'Tibby Hyslop's Dreams' Hogg makes use of supernatural beliefs to denounce the harsh situation of female labourers in the Scottish Borders.

   On the surface Tibby's character seems to perform the role of Bakhtinian fool, as her innocence emphasises the opportunism of the anti-heroes who court her—her master Gilbert Forret, who attempts to rape her, and John Jardine, a calculating man famous for having neglected his previous wife, who wishes to make Tibby his new spouse. Yet Hogg invests this female character with a far more important function. Significantly, not only does Tibby expose the problems that afflicted labouring women at the time of agricultural improvement, standing as a symbol of exploited land, as Mack has argued (2006: 62); but Hogg also portrays Tibby as a 'respectable spinster', and spinsterhood as a valuable choice, thereby countering the traditional ending with the marriage plot.

In 'Tibby Hyslop's Dream', which Hogg sets towards the end of the eighteenth century, Gilbert Forret leases a farm in the Scottish Borders. Forret is a man without fear of God: though married and with a large family of his own, he leers at young, pretty women whom he hires as dairy maids and then seduces. The Presbyterian elders of his parish have admonished him several times for his debauched behaviour—though not publicly as, being a rich master, he probably has always managed to pay a token for the poor (see Chapter 4). As T. M. Devine reminds us, '[i]t became much more common for kirk sessions to demand a monetary fine rather than the public appearance of the sinner before the congregation' (2006b: 88), particularly when the case involved a prosperous master like Gilbert Forret, who could afford to support the church financially.

Hogg published this tale for the first time in *Blackwood's Edinburgh Magazine* in June 1827 and, shortly after, in his collection of tales *The Shepherd's Calendar* in 1829. The 1829 tale, however, is a toned-down version excised of any sexual innuendoes thanks to the intervention of James Hogg's nephew, Robert Hogg, who accommodated it to the dominant nineteenth-century sense of decorum. Douglas S. Mack remarks that Robert Hogg was 'anxious to tone down his uncle's indelicacy in writing about [Gilbert Forret's] sexual pursuit of Tibby', though these 'extensive revisions remove much of the vigour and vitality of "Tibby Hyslop's Dream"' (1988: 29–30).[2] As mentioned above, Forret is also a usurper of the Scottish land, as his improper cultivation without rotating crops threatens the fertility of the farm he has leased. Mack contends that '[j]ust as he sought to rape Tibby, so he seeks to rape the farmland on which he is tenant' (Mack 2006: 62). Hogg denounced the harsh conditions endured by the peasantry in the Scottish Borders after the Napoleonic Wars, lamenting that the relationship between master and servants had considerably deteriorated. The new capitalist mindset in agricultural innovation had distanced masters from their servants and resulted in a loss of familial communion (Hogg 1985 [1831–1832]). In light of this, the excision of the sexual allusions in 'Tibby Hyslop's Dream' acquires a new significance.

The revision of the tales for a collection was important because it would reach a wider female readership than a magazine. In a letter to Hogg of 28 May 1828, Thomas Pringle laments that a poem he received for the annual *Friendship's Offering* was

---

2   For a detailed account of the variants in 'Tibby Hyslop's Dream' between the version in *Black-wood's Edinburgh Magazine* (1827) and *The Shepherd Calendar* (1829) see Douglas S. Mack, 'Editing James Hogg' (unpublished doctoral thesis, University of Stirling, 1984), pp. 126–40.

too strange & droll, & 'high-kilted' for the very 'gentie' publication now under my charge: were it for a Magazine or some such work I should not feel so particular but for these "douce" and delicate publications the annuals I think it rather inappropriate [...] I think it ought to be a rule [...] to admit not a single expression which would call up a blush in the Cheek of the most delicate female if reading aloud to a mixt company.

National Library of Scotland, MS 2245, ff. 122–23; qtd. in Mack 1988: 28

Notably, as Thomas C. Richardson points out, the annuals and gift-books were collections of works by contemporary authors which 'normally appeared late in the year to serve the Christmas market and usually were directed towards a female or genteel audience' (2009: 193). Yet the removal of the sexual suggestions in the 1829 edition of 'Tibby Hyslop's Dream' not only excises the tale of anything that could threaten a blush in the cheek of young privileged ladies, but it also deprives the story of the pointed social critique that Hogg conveys through Forret's simultaneous threats to Tibby and the Scottish land. Hogg conferred the cultural role of a regional allegory on this female character, in order to expose contemporary issues of gender and class exploitation on the part of those 'agricultural innovators', as Mack defines them (2006: 65), like Gilbert Forret. If Forret's attempt to violate Tibby's body is toned down, then the negative effects of Scotland's internal colonisation are also blurred. On the other hand, Forret's sexual threat reveals the harsh conditions of the female labourers in the Scottish Borders, voicing a reality that was not part of the elite, and presenting Tibby as a heroine who does not fall thanks to her genuine Christian values and traditional beliefs.

Hogg shapes the plot of his tale with a succession of dreams, prophesying Tibby's future happiness—in her socially respected spinsterhood—and her master's punishment through death. Hogg's suspension between divine judgment and supernatural divination conveys an extraordinary sense of mystery to the tale; while tradition, once again, symbolises an important cultural value: not only does God convey his message through dreams so as to relieve the poor from the hardships of life but, most importantly, Hogg presents Tibby as a socially respected 'spinster', thereby distancing his tale from the conventional closure with the heroine's marriage to the hero.

Forret offers generous wages to Tibby, wishing to enjoy the pleasure of her physical beauty; but his hopes are dashed when the young girl, though inexperienced and innocent, rebukes Forret with an exceptional, moral strength derived from her strong Christian faith. After having escaped her master's attempt to rape her, Forret reduces Tibby to destitution. Nonetheless, Tibby is called soon after as a witness in court and, unwittingly, provides evidence against her master for exploiting the land through improper cultivation. Hogg shows the fantastic element of the tale through Tibby's dream about her master:

> A great number of rooks and hooded crows were making free with his person;—some picking out his eyes, some his tongue, and some tearing out his bowels. But in place of being distressed by their voracity, he appeared much delighted, encouraging them on all that he could[.] [...] In the midst of this horrible feast, down came a majestic raven [...which] opened the breast of his victim [...] and after preying on his vitals for some time, at last picked out his heart, and devoured it[.]
>
> HOGG 2002 [1829]: 152

During her testimony in court, Tibby is shocked when she recognises 'her master's counsel and the Dumfries writers and notaries [...] as the birds that she saw, in her dream, devouring her master' (Hogg 2002 [1829]: 157). Meaningfully, at the end of the tale Forret commits suicide in a secluded area and Tibby finds his corpse 'woefully defaced by these voracious birds of prey' (Ibid., p. 161).

Magdalene Redekop views Tibby Hyslop as 'Hogg's version of the idiot or the fool who acts as a vessel for an oracular truth', adding that though 'Mr Forret's efforts are foiled, [...] his actions start a chain of events that bring down on him a horrible vengeance for having sought to defile the pure' (1988: 35). Undoubtedly, in Hogg's tale Tibby plays the role of Bakhtinian fool, as her innocence exposes her master's unscrupulous nature. However, Bakhtin's static notion of the fool figure does not do justice to Tibby's evolution as a character within Hogg's tale. The narrator describes her as unearthly, claiming that 'there was something in her manner and deportment different from other people—*a sort of innocent simplicity, bordering on silliness, together with an instability of thought, that, in the eyes of many, approached to abstraction*' (Hogg 2002 [1829]: 142, emphasis mine). Yet Tibby grows aware of the world, since when talking to John Jardine, the local cooper who 'knew every man, and every man's affair—every woman, and every woman's failings' (Hogg 2002 [1829]: 153), she admits rather tragically that 'life's naething but a fight [...] frae beginning to end' (Ibid.).

Tibby's character is an extraordinary mixture of innocence and common sense, arising from her extensive knowledge of the Bible. Though 'in the eyes of many' her simplicity 'border[ed] on silliness, [...] then Tibby could repeat the book of the Evangelist Luke by heart, and many favourite chapters both of the Old and New Testaments' (Hogg 2002 [1829]: 142). When Forret is about to rape her, the voice of Tibby's grandmother rescues her from such threat as,

after an ominous dream, old Aunt Douglas sent her sister to Mr Forret's farm.
The narrative voice of the Ettrick Shepherd then informs the readers that

> Mr Forret, alias Gledging Gibby, had borne the brunt of incensed kirk-
> sessions before that time, and also the unlicensed tongues of mothers,
> roused into vehemence by the degradation of beloved daughters; but
> never in his life did he bear such a rebuke as he did that day from the
> tongue of one he had always viewed as a mere simpleton. It was a lesson
> to him—a warning of the most sublime and terrible description, couched
> in the pure and emphatic language of Scripture.
>
> HOGG 2002 [1829]: 147–48

Hogg therefore presents Tibby as a character that goes beyond the typical
Bakhtinian fool since, in addition to revealing her master's flaws, she reacts
with impressive strength to his attempt to rape her. Tibby's non-violated body
thus becomes a symbol of how the inhabitants of the Scottish Borders in the
early nineteenth century could find relief from the harshness of their working
conditions in both God and tradition—two important values for rural society
which did not clash with each other because God could convey his message
through dreams. In Hogg's tale 'Cousin Mattie', Flora's mother claims that 'the
Almighty [...] made nothing in vain, and if dreams had been of no import to
man, they would not have been given to him' (Hogg 2004a [1820]: 437).

In 'Tibby Hyslop's Dream', issues of class, gender, nation, and empire are
closely entangled: Tibby voices the negative consequences of Scotland's internal colonisation of the land at a time when the upper and middle classes were
thriving thanks to their investments in agricultural innovation. Hogg exploits
the threat of Tibby's rape as a social metaphor to denounce the abuse of the
lower classes in such growth, and her innocence to highlight that such agricultural progress was made at the expense of marginal communities:

> When he [Forret] would snatch a kiss or two, Tibby did not in the least
> comprehend the drift of this; but, convinced in her heart that it could
> mean something *holy, and good, and kind,* she tried not further to reflect
> on it, for she could not; but she blessed him in her heart, *and was content
> to remain in her ignorance of human life.*
>
> HOGG 2002 [1829]: 146, emphases mine

Through free indirect discourse, Hogg incorporates Tibby's thoughts within
the narrative voice: 'holy, and good, and kind' are adjectives that Tibby herself
would have pronounced to describe her master. However, at this early stage of

the tale, Tibby's innocence also exposes the rhetorical dynamics of modern progress in the internal colonisation of Scotland, showing through this character the blind acceptance of marginal peoples of their harsh conditions.

Tibby's state of 'ignorance of human life' renders her similar to another of Hogg's female characters: Kilmeny in *The Queen's Wake* (1813). Douglas S. Mack has suggested that 'as the sinless woman who couldna remain, Kilmeny is a marvellous poetic symbol; but by her nature she has only a limited capacity to be a role model for mortal women' (1990: 70). Similarly, when considering Forret's intentions, Tibby's prophetic aunt exclaims: 'Poor Tibby!—as lang as the heart disna gang wrang, we maun [must] excuse the head, for it'll never aince [once] gang [go] right. *I hope they were baith made for a better warld, for nane o' them were made for this*' (Hogg 2002 [1829]: 145, emphasis mine). Nonetheless, though endowed with the same purity of Kilmeny, Tibby becomes an exemplary role model for mortal women, because she manages to maintain her integrity in the real world. This aspect renders Tibby similar to another of Hogg's female characters: Mary Lee in *Pilgrims of the Sun*, who comes back from fairy Heaven for 'she must also learn to play her full part in the life of "this world of sorrow and pain"—the world that Kilmeny left behind her' (Mack 1992: 70)—the world where, according to Tibby, 'life's naething but a fight [...] frae beginning to end' (Hogg 2002 [1829]: 153).

Mack observes that Hogg sets Kilmeny as a prototype of the Blessed Virgin (1992: 68–75). It could be argued that Hogg views Tibby in similar terms, juxtaposing her to the hypocritical conceptualisation of the morally blessed heroine of the national tale. While Kilmeny is moved to fairyland since no worldly man deserves to become her husband—'It wasna her hame, and she couldna remain; | She left this world of sorrow and pain, | And returned to the land of thought again' (Hogg 2005 [1813]: 296)—Hogg leaves Tibby unmarried in the earthly world, defying the conventional closure with the marriage plot.

As mentioned at the beginning of this chapter, through the *heteroglot* voice of Tibby's grandmother, Hogg claims that 'there is neither sin nor shame in being unwedded, but there may be baith in joining yourself to an unbeliever' (Hogg 2002 [1829]: 155). Considering what Murray G. H. Pittock writes in relation to 'the voice of the rural peasantry of Scotland in Hogg' as 'the voice of common sense', particularly 'when it is represented in direct speech' (2003b: 35), it can be argued that through Tibby's grandmother, Hogg suggests a different solution to the idealised marriage of the national tale, implying that the financial gains derived from the British Union did not necessarily reflect an equal economic growth among the lower classes. Chapter 4 details how difficult it was for a couple from a low background to achieve the financial security necessary to support a family of their own. Even when such circumstance was achieved, marriage did not necessarily represent a wise choice for women. In 'Tibby Hyslop's Dream', Mr Forret's wife lives a life of shame and humiliation and, perhaps, of destitution after her husband's suicide; while according to Tibby's grandmother, John Jardine 'is not the man to lead a Christian life with [...] it is weel kend how sair he neglected his first wife' (Hogg 2002 [1829]: 155). Spinsterhood thus becomes a far more promising choice than marriage when there are no heroes, and Tibby ends up circulating freely in the public space of the North British Empire as a highly respected single woman.

Nevertheless, as a symbol of the Scottish land, Tibby's unmarried condition signals a threat to the Scottish nation, as Scotland is left without progeny for the future. Even so, the absence of Tibby's offspring portrays a far more realistic picture of Hogg's rural Scotland. The marriage plot promoted in contemporary progressive novels looked for political reconciliation between England and Scotland promoting, as Mack explains, 'adjustment to English cultural and linguistic norms', which was certainly embraced by 'members of the Scottish élite', who could benefit from the wealth derived from the colonies; but 'the poor and dispossessed of subaltern Scotland', of whom Tibby is a representative, had 'very little direct access to the material rewards of Empire' (Mack 2006: 6–7). As Mack remarks, 'Tibby Hyslop's Dream' raises

> searching questions about the values and assumptions of the powerful people in the North British society of his day. [...T]he economic and social changes that took place in rural Scotland around the time of the Napoleonic Wars do not necessarily add to Progress. These changes may well have been good news for "a fine gentleman" (a farmer or a landowner), but they can be seen as very bad news indeed for a "menial" like Tibby, who has ceased to be "a member of a community," and has become "a slave; a servant of servants, a mere tool of labour." [...] In 'Tibby Hyslop's Dream' this exploration of a contrast between an older and a more modern set of values is very far from asserting that this move from old to new amounts to the Progress so valued by the North British elite of the early nineteenth century. [...] Gibby, the exploiter, is detached from any sense of community, and from any sense of religion. [...] Gibby and Tibby, then, embody a contrast between the new ways and the old; but in presenting this contrast, Hogg's story unexpectedly subverts some of the assumptions of the new North Britain about the nature of progress and social change.
>
> 2006: 58–62

In such a culture of exploitation, Tibby's spinsterhood thus performs the voice of the counter culture, pulling against the idealised matrimonial resolution of the national tale. Hogg's merging of realism and the fantastic helped to question constructions of Scottish nationhood in the early nineteenth century, revealing how they were strictly entangled with structures of power and wealth, where cultural assumptions about class, gender, and ethnicity played an important role for the benefit of the higher classes. Tim Killick contends that '[i]n his tales, Hogg articulated the values of a section of society that did not necessarily share the ideals of urban Scotland' (2004: 29), while Mack remarks that in the tales of *The Shepherd Calendar* 'the narrative voice is that of the Ettrick Shepherd speaking as a representative of the Ettrick community (2006: 57). This might explain why though in a letter to William Blackwood of 28 May 1827 Hogg hoped that 'Tibby Hyslop will be accounted a good tale', its sales turned out to be rather poor (Hogg 2004–08, *Collected Letters*, vol. 2, p. 266). A letter to Hogg from Blackwood claims, 'The Shepherd's Calend [*sic*] which I hoped would by this time have enabled me to make you a payment, has not yet I am sorry to say nearly paid the expenses'.[3] Unfortunately for Hogg, the ruling-class readers were not ready to come to terms with the negative impact of agricultural progress on the margins of rural Scotland.

3   'Maid of Dunedin, I'm the King o' the Mountain and Fairy School'

The final section of this chapter focuses on Hogg's most ambitious work: his epic poem *Queen Hynde* published in January 1825, soon after the release of his famous novel *The Private Memoirs and Confessions of a Justified Sinner*. Choosing a literary genre associated with Virgil and Homer, as well as entering in competition with Macpherson's *Ossian Poems*, was certainly an ambitious project. Noticeably, Mack remarks that Hogg's work 'sets out, audaciously, to offer a shepherd-bard's modern reinvention of the venerable epic genre' (2009: 141).

As argued in Chapter 4, Hogg's *Confessions* had been received unenthusiastically by contemporary reviewers for its double narrative and the value bestowed on marginal voices. Disappointed, Hogg resumed his modern epic *Queen Hynde* as a platform from which to defend himself against charges of indelicacy, attacking contemporary critics and mocking Edinburgh's bourgeois women for hiding their hypocrisy behind a mask of politeness. As Gilbert and

---

3   See Blackwood's undated letter to Hogg in NLS, MS 30,311, p. 402, qtd. in an Editorial Note of Hogg's *Collected Letters*, vol. 2, p. 342.

Mack point out, *Queen Hynde* was written in two stages: in 1817 up to line 1071 of Book Third; and in 1824, when the poem was completed just before its publication (1998a: xiv). The address to bad reviewers in the concluding lines of Book Fifth is dated just after the negative reception of Hogg's *Confessions*.

Unfortunately for Hogg, *Queen Hynde* did not meet the approval of all contemporary reviewers. The *Lady's Magazine* (n.s., vol. 6, 1825), though admitting that 'Mr. Hogg is unquestionably a man of considerable talent', contested that 'when he displays vigour, it is destitute of elegance; and his attempts to reach sublimity have sometimes a ludicrous air (p. 97). The *Literary Gazette* (no. 414, 1824) lamented that '[t]here is as much to censure as to praise. Though the story is interesting, it is made tiresomely long; and such is the manner of the author, that, at the end of it, it defies our penetration to tell whether he means to be serious or burlesque' (p. 817). The same reviewer added that 'the work [is] of unquestionable talent, but miserably deformed by want of taste and judgement' (Ibid.), finally concluding with 'we are prone to believe that his errors proceed from want of just perception and cultivation of mind, and not from a desire to outrage decorum by his familiar coarseness' (Ibid., p. 819).

The writer of the *Westminster Review* (vol. 3, 1825) was certainly the most critical of all, professing that *Queen Hynde* must 'have been inspired by insolence and whisky-punch [...] as an experiment intended to ascertain how far the English public will allow itself to be insulted' (p. 531); to which the reviewer of the *Philomatic Journal* (3, 1825) replied in Hogg's defence, viewing *Queen Hynde* as a 'wildly-beautiful and very original poem [...] highly deserving the warmest welcome, and the most cordial support', while condemning the criticism of the *Westminster Review* as an 'unfeeling article [..] for its want of candour, and utter insensibility to the poor poetic merits of the piece' (p. 161). Gillian Hughes remarks that, in general, *Queen Hynde* 'was described as incongruous in tone and characterisation, and even impious and irreverent', and that 'six months after publication more than a thousand of the fifteen hundred copies printed remained unsold and most of the edition was eventually remaindered' (2007: 195). Hogg did not expect such failure and, in a letter to William Blackwood of 24 February 1827, he claimed, 'I am grieved as well as disappointed that *Queen Hynde* should stick still. I cannot believe that she does not deserve notice and think some expedient should be fallen on to draw notice to her' (Hogg 2004–08, *Collected Letters*, vol. 2, p. 258).

Queen Hynde again demonstrates how Hogg challenged accepted ideas about literature, culture, and society in early nineteenth-century Britain, engaging with gender in sophisticated (though often contentious) ways. Hogg's transgression of conventional norms of literary politeness and delicacy, his skilful mixture of the serious and the burlesque, his overlapping of

literary genres, and his unconventional rewriting of the marriage plot contributed enormously to the subversiveness of *Queen Hynde*. The anonymous com-
mentator of the *Literary Gazette* (no. 414, 1824, p. 817), for example, was unsure
'whether [Hogg] mean[t] to be serious or burlesque' and, probably, viewed
him as failing to satisfy the expectations of the post-Enlightenment readership. This reviewer considered Hogg's poem to be 'the work of unquestionable
talent, but miserably deformed by want of taste and judgment' (p. 817). In her
study on the relationship between class and perceptions of politeness, Sarah
Mills contends that 'utterances which are judged to be impolite are an indi-
cation [...] of [...] the perception of status difference, of the participants in
relation to one another' (Mills 2009: 1049). This is what probably affected the
above-mentioned reviewers who failed—or probably pretended not—to recognise the critique that Hogg, through *Queen Hynde*, was making of class prejudices, the role of middle-class women as carriers of British moral values, and
of contemporary norms of propriety based on hypocritical principles of politeness which emerged in Britain during imperial expansion (see Chapter 1).

Chapters 2 and 4 have demonstrated how the openness with which Hogg
addressed prostitution and unwed motherhood clashed with bourgeois norms
of decorum, as his lack of inhibition in dealing with such matters was perceived
as particularly inappropriate for middle-class women, in their role of moral
educators of the British nation. It is thus no wonder that Hogg was accused
by *Blackwood's Edinburgh Magazine* of being 'too fond of calling some things
by their plain names, which would be better expressed by circumlocution'
('[Review of] *Winter Evening Tales*', vol. 7, 1820, p. 154). Regardless, in *Queen
Hynde*, Hogg declares his intellectual freedom from contemporary norms of
propriety, exploiting the conventions that guided the construction of primary
and secondary heroines in the national tale.

Hogg conveys his declaration of independence in two different ways. Firstly,
through the narrator's exophoric address to his implied readers, where Hogg's
linguistic acts range from extreme impoliteness, when addressing bad reviewers, to mock impoliteness, when teasing bourgeois ladies for their prudery.
In *Queen Hynde*, the narrator threatens both groups, with no regard for their
social status and power; yet Hogg conveys such threats with great irony, showing a degree of human respect for these ladies, as he alternates between 'leer-
ing gallantry and heavy-handed chaffing', as Ian Duncan remarks (1998: 138).

Additionally, Hogg communicates his poetic independence at a more
implicit level by setting the eponymous Queen Hynde, a textual representation of Edinburgh's middle-class ladies, in intra-textual relation with her maid
of honour: the unruly Wene. Mack contends that Wene mirrors the supernatural aspects of Hogg's poetry, performing an important aesthetic function

in addition to being a 'mischief-making' player (2009: 143). Hogg describes Wene's charm in the same 'witchery' terms as when depicting the Queen of the Fairies, his poetic muse, soon after his attack to bad reviewers. The passage devoted to the Queen of the Fairies exhibits noun and adjectival phrases reminiscent of mischievous Wene, whom Hogg sets as a symbol of both women's freedom from middle-class cultural constraints and as a representative of his own independence from literary conventions of delicacy.

The epic poem *Queen Hynde* has to be read against a cultural context where Hogg failed to observe not only the polite norms of literary decorum, but also the expectations surrounding the literary transaction between author and reader, having engaged in a literary genre which was considered too sophisticated for a self-educated shepherd. Hogg's writing of ballads and songs was received favourably because it embraced the Romantic ideal of the self-tutored peasant poet; but Hogg's commitment to a more prestigious genre such as the epic was destined to meet a rather prejudiced reception.

New research on labouring-class poets and their engagement with the epic genre has shown that Hogg was not the only self-tutored author who, during the Romantic period, went beyond the folk tradition of ballads and songs. For example, Scott McEathron (2012) remarks that there are long epics such as John Nicholson's *Airedale in Ancient Times* (1825), 'a chronicle of the natural and human history of the Aire River valley in Yorkshire'; and James Bird's *The Vale of Slaughden* (1819), 'a story of the ninth-century invasion of Britain by the Danes' (2012: 745). Both works are written in heroic couplets, like Hogg's *Queen Hynde*, thus breaking with the blank verse 'employed concurrently in Wordsworth's *Excursion* (1814), Shelley's *Alastor* (1816), and Keats's *Hyperion* (1820), [...] more traditionally associated with the epic legacy of Romanticism' (McEathron 2012: 745), and hence showing the poets' willingness to present themselves as intellectually capable of engaging with more sophisticated genres than ballads and songs, notwithstanding their social origins. Yet, even though 'these self-taught writers' could plausibly be assumed to be 'authoritative' voices, as they described local history and legends, they were still 'more artistically successful when [...] scal[ing] back their ambitions and wr[iting] in shorter forms' (McEathron 2012: 745). As Kirstie Blair notes, these authors were subjected to the influence of contemporary 'critics in constructing the figure of the labouring-class poet and defining traditions of labouring-class poetics' (2013: 11), in a way very similar to Hogg.

In *Queen Hynde*, Hogg references and demystifies the melancholy of James Macpherson's *Ossian* poems, *Fingal* (1761) and *Temora* (1763), so much celebrated in the Romantic period. In line with Macpherson's epic, Mack explains, *Queen Hynde* describes the victory of Scotland 'over an invading Scandinavian army' (2009: 140); but while the action of Macpherson's poems 'is interwoven with tales of broken love and premature death' in an 'elegiac' tone (Fiona Stafford, cited in Mack 2009: 140–41), Hogg presents a burlesque modern epic, which 'celebrates energy, liberation, hope and new beginning' (Mack 2009: 141). As Mack points out, Hogg's narrative strategy is also radically different from Macpherson's who '[f]amously and controversially, [...] had asserted that *Fingal* was a direct translation from the Gaelic poetry of Ossian, a third-century Scottish warrior bard' (2009: 141). On the contrary, *Queen Hynde* is presented as 'a modern performance by a nineteenth-century Scottish shepherd-bard, James Hogg', who addresses 'an equally modern poetry-reading audience', the 'Maid of Dunedin', where Dunedin is the old Gaelic name for Edinburgh (Mack 2009: 141).

The narrative voice, personifying the Ettrick Shepherd's himself, declares his intellectual freedom, 'mak[ing] no pretence of politeness', Duncan points out, and presenting a 'literary impression' of 'a raucous oral performance' (Duncan 1998: 139), as the following extract shows:

Maid of Dunedin, thou may'st see,
Though long I strove to pleasure thee,
That now I've changed my timid tone,
And sing to please myself alone;
[...]
Then leave to all his fancies wild
Nature's own rude untutored child,
And should he forfeit that fond claim
Pity his loss but do not blame.

HOGG 1998 [1825]: 30–31, ll. 1060–63, 1104–07

Hogg then engages in a teasing, flirtatious, and playful address to his implied female reader, the Maid of Dunedin, declaring that

Have I not seen thy deep distress,
Thy tears for disregarded dress?
Thy flush of pride, thy wrath intense,
For slight and casual precedence?
And I have heard thy tongue confess
Most high offence and bitterness!
Yet sooth thou still art dear to me,
These very faults I love for thee,
Then, why not all my freaks allow?
I have a few and so hast thou.

HOGG 1998 [1825]: 18, ll. 542–51

In these two passages Hogg exhibits, once again, the tension between a centripetal force towards social recognition and a centrifugal one towards his own wish for independence. However, Hogg manages to celebrate his freedom without becoming an outsider thanks to his mocking and playful tone, thereby striking the balance between his own individuality and the social and literary conventions of his time. Though some contemporary reviewers found Hogg's engagement with the epic genre rather ambitious for a self-tutored shepherd (Gilbert and Mack 1998a: xi), and did not approve Hogg's mixture of the serious and the burlesque, the *Monthly Critical Gazette* judged Hogg's declaration of intellectual freedom as a passage of 'unequalled beauty in its kind; [...which] for tenderness, simplicity, and genuine feeling, cannot be excelled' (vol. 2, 1825, p. 345).

In *Queen Hynde*, Hogg re-shapes the conventions that, in the early nineteenth century, would guide the construction of the primary and secondary heroine in the national tale by juxtaposing Queen Hynde with her maid of honour, the wayward Wene, without punishing the latter with death for her socially defiant behaviour; instead, Hogg rewards Wene with the title of Queen of Scandinavia. Additionally, Hogg endows this secondary heroine with a double critical function, as her character symbolises both Hogg's intellectual freedom and middle-class women's emancipation from hypocritical norms of propriety.

After a dream foretelling the Scandinavian invasion, where Queen Hynde is attacked by a 'roaring and foaming monster' (Hogg 1998 [1825]: 14)—a dream that Elaine E. Petrie (1998) considers to be reminiscent of the Scottish folktale 'The Black Bull of Norroway'—the Queen and her train of maids depart for the isle of Iona in search of Saint Columba's advice who lives there in a monastery. Here, Hogg sets one of the most hilarious passages of his epic, where the 'petul[a]nt and pesterous' Wene (Hogg 1998 [1825]: 27), who teases the friars of the community, is introduced as follows:

> There was one maiden of the train
> Known by the name of wicked Wene;
> A lovely thing, of slender make,
> Who mischief wrought for mischief's sake,
> And never was her heart so pleased
> As when a man she vexed or teased.
> By few at court she was approved,
> And yet by all too well beloved;
> So dark, so powerful was her eye,
> Her *mein so witching* and so sly,   [mein = mien, appearance]
> That every youth, as she inclined,
> Was mortified, reserved, or kind,

This day would curse her in disdain,
And next would sigh for wicked Wene.
No sooner had this *fairy* eyed
The looks demure on either side,
Than all her spirits 'gan to play
With keen desire to work deray.
Whene'er a face she could espy
Of more than meet solemnity,
Then would she tramp his crumpled toes,
Or with sharp fillip on the nose,
Make the poor brother start and stare,
With watery eyes and bristling hair.
And yet this wayward *elf* the while
Inflicted all with such a smile,
That every monk, for all his pain,
Looked as he wished it done again.

HOGG 1998 [1825]: 22–23, ll. 722–49, emphases mine

In this extract, Hogg presents Wene as endowed with extraordinary magic power, a 'witching fairy', whose enchanting nature nobody can resist. Yet a comparison between Hogg's own manuscript and the first edition of *Queen Hynde* shows that the passages where Wene plays her mocking tricks were deleted. Gilbert and Mack, editors of the 1998 Stirling/South Carolina edition of *Queen Hynde*, argue that though Hogg may have self-censored himself before delivering his manuscript to the publisher for the increasingly prudish climate of the 1820s, it is more probable that such deletions were the result of the alert activity of Ballantyne's copy-editors, who might have removed what they considered indelicate (1998b: 224). One such omission (not attributable to Hogg) describes Wene's delight at teasing the monks of Iona: 'O how the elf enjoyed the strife, | It was to her the balm of life; | But when her laugh could not be drowned, | She said 'twas thro' her sleep, and moaned!' (Hogg 1998 [1825]: 30). Since Hogg places this passage just before his own declaration of intellectual freedom—'Maid of Dunedin, thou may'st see, | Though long I strove to pleasure thee, | That now I've changed my timid tone, | And sing to please myself alone' (Ibid.)—its deletion in the first edition enormously decreases Wene's symbolic freedom blurring, as a result, Hogg's implicit critique of his contemporary national discourse which saw middle-class women as the carriers of British propriety and moral values.

At a more explicit level of literary communication, Hogg engages in another exophoric address where the narrator, voicing the Ettrick Shepherd, attacks contemporary unfavourable reviewers and gently mocks Edinburgh women, as the following extract reveals:

> He next debars all those who dare,
> Whether with proud and pompous air,
> With simpering frown, or nose elate,
> To name the word INDELICATE!
> [...]
> Such word or term should never be
> In maiden's mind of modesty.
> [...]
> But yet, for all thy airs and whims,
> [...]
> I must acknowledge in the end
> To 've found thee still the poet's friend,
> [...]
> Ah, how unlike art thou to those
> Warm friends profest, yet covert foes!
>
> HOGG 1998 [1825]: 177, ll. 2260–63, 2268–69, 2276, 2278–79, 2286–87

Once again, this challenging performative act reveals the tension between Hogg's desire to depict women free from the hypocritical constraints of false delicacy and his own wish to be accepted and acknowledged as a writer of value, perfectly capable of engaging in high-level poetic genres such as the epic. At a more implicit level, Hogg demanded that his literary circle of supposed friends not judge him as indelicate for the social issues he was seeking to critique, perhaps nodding at Wilson's outrageous review of Hogg's novel *The Three Perils of Woman* published in *Blackwood's Edinburgh Magazine* two years before (see vol. 14, 1823, pp. 427–37).

Significantly, Hogg's defence from accusations of indelicacy in his exophoric address to adverse reviewers is followed by his address to the Queen of the Fairies, his poetic muse and symbol of the Scottish Borders' tradition—a narrative strategy that implicitly reinforces his freedom from cultural conventions. At a textual level, the charming portrayal of the Queen of the Fairies is reminiscent of Wicked Wene:

> Thou lovely queen of beauty, most bright,
> And of everlasting new delight,
> Of foible, of freak, of gambol and glee,   [freak = whim]

> *Of all that pleases,*
> *And all that teases;*
> All that we fret at, yet love to see!
> In *petulance*, pity, and love refined,
> Thou emblem extreme of the female mind!
> [...]
> O well I know the *enchanting mein*
> Of my loved muse, my Fairy Queen!
> [...]
> *Her smile where a thousand witcheries play,*
> *And her eye that steals the soul away*[.]
>
> HOGG 1998 [1825]: 179–80, ll. 25–32, 43–44, 47–48, emphases mine

The depiction of the alluring effect of the Queen of the Fairies upon the Ettrick Shepherd invokes the same adjectival, noun, and verbal phrases with which the narrator describes the mesmerising effect of Wene on the monks of Iona— an aspect that bears out what Mack argues in relation to Wene as a symbol of the 'fairy' nature of Hogg's poetry. As a result, Hogg not only presents himself as the King of the 'mountain and fairy school', free from post-Enlightenment empiricist cultural conventions, as Mack explains (2009: 147), but he also places this rebellious maid as the symbol of middle-class women's emancipation from contemporary conventions of fake politeness.

Emphatically, Hogg announces his autonomy from contemporary, non-genuine norms of propriety by declaring that in *Queen Hynde*, he will portray women as they are, with all their flaws and qualities, rather than as they should be:

> Now I've called a patriot queen,
> Of generous soul and courtly mein;
> *And I've upraised an unruly elf*
> *With faults and foibles like thyself.*
> And these as women thou shalt see
> More as they are, than they should be.
>
> HOGG 1998 [1825]: 56, ll. 1016–21, emphasis mine

To the dominant/centripetal model of primary heroine, based on the Maid of Dunedin, Hogg opposes the subversive/centrifugal secondary character of Wene, placing the latter as both a symbol of women's liberation from contemporary stereotypes of feminine propriety and as a metaphor for Hogg's own independence from nineteenth-century norms of literary decorum.

In *Queen Hynde*, both the primary and the secondary heroine embark on a conventional marriage plot conducive to the political union between Ireland, Scotland, and Scandinavia. Nevertheless, Hogg defies the discursive significance of the marriage plot in the way through which the two heroines achieve such unions. Wene is a sassy, outrageous secondary heroine, reminiscent of ballad fairies, who manipulates the events of the story as she pleases in order to marry the man she loves. Cross-dressed as Queen Hynde, and thus manipulating social hierarchies, Wene introduces herself to Prince Haco who falls madly in love with her and who thus transforms Wene into the Queen of Scandinavia through marriage. Wene's extraordinary proactive behaviour has the effect of advancing her position on the social ladder, showing an uncommon female power for that period and thus setting an example to the Maid of Dunedin, not to be forced into unhappy marriages for the financial gains of their families. At a more symbolic level, the union between Wene and Prince Haco defied the class boundaries of the marriage plot in the national tale.

Hogg also defies class and ethnic boundaries through the marriage between the primary heroine, Queen Hynde, and M'Houston. Though later on, M'Houston is revealed to be King Eiden of Ireland in disguise as a Scots peasant, Queen Hynde decides to marry him before this revelation:

> The queen descended to the green
> With lightsome step, but solemn mein;
> And passing Ross and Sutherland,
> She took M'Houston by the hand,
> And with a firm unaltered voice,
> Said, "Here I make my maiden choice.
> Since thou hast come without a meed
> To save me in my utmost need;
> And since, *though humbly born, thou art*
> *A prince and hero at the heart,*
> *So, next my saviour that's above,*
> *Hence thee I'll honour, bless, and love."*
> > HOGG 1998 [1825]: 201–02, ll. 951–62, emphasis mine

Invoking the conventions of the national tale, in *Queen Hynde* Hogg joins Ireland and Scotland through the marriage of its main characters. Yet in Hogg's text, the political significance of such a union is only revealed at the end. Before M'Houston's real identity as the King of Ireland is disclosed, Hogg emphasises that M‚Houston's sense of honour is what really leads to his marriage with Queen Hynde. Notably, when disguised as a Scots peasant, M‚Houston is the only warrior who offers to fight with the invader of Scotland, Norse King Eric, while the noble (by birth) warriors of Scotland lack the necessary bravery and valour to be able to challenge King Eric in single combat:

> The evening came, and still no knight
> Had proffered life for Scotia's right.
> The morning rose in shroud of gray
> That ushered in the pregnant day,
> Big with the germs of future fame,
> Of Albyn's glory or her shame!
> *And still no champion made demand*
> *Of fighting for his sovereign hand!*
>   HOGG 1998 [1825]: 188, ll. 374–81, emphasis mine

The Scots aristocrats, who 'made' no 'demand | Of fighting for his sovereign hand', do not accept M‚Houston as their king because of his humble origins. Only when his real identity is revealed, do they acknowledge him as their superior. Through this episode, Hogg exposes the cultural construction of social hierarchies: Queen Hynde respects M'Houston and chooses him as her husband for his nobility of the heart, while the Scots aristocrats only value his social rank.

The class prejudices against M'Houston mirror the snobbery that Hogg suffered on the part of the Edinburgh literary elite, as Mack (2009: 151–53) and Gilbert and Mack (1998a: xlv) have remarked. Likewise, Sharon Alker and Holly Faith Nelson maintain that Hogg's humble social origins 'caus[ed] him to question the political conservatism and inflexibility' of the Edinburgh literati (2001: 26). Alker and Nelson suggest that though Hogg was not a supporter of French revolutionary ideas, he did endorse the possibility of a flexible social order based on honourable values, showing that 'merit and heroism could and did exist outside the upper classes (2001: 27). In *Queen Hynde*, Hogg debunks the conventions of the marriage plot to challenge the class prejudice of the Scottish reviewers. Hogg then reshapes the conventional dynamics between primary and secondary heroines, promoting a proactive female character who enjoys the pleasures of life without any sense of shame originating from hypocritical norms of politeness and who, for this reason, is able to control her life and to advance her social position to the rank of 'Scandinavia's queen' with the man she loves: Prince Haco who married and 'loved her to his latest day' (p. 216). Last but not least, Wene's advancement in the social scale also symbolises Hogg's own freedom from literary conventions of propriety and his wish to situate himself at the top of the list of the most renowned British poets of his time and as the 'king o' the mountain and fairy school' (Hogg 2004 [1834]: 9).

In conclusion, Hogg's engagement with, and reinterpretation of, the marriage plot was subversive in relation to early nineteenth-century social and cultural norms. Through 'Tibby Hyslop's Dream', he portrays the reality of labouring women at the time of agricultural innovation, when supposedly progressive developments in Scottish agriculture did not equal a better lifestyle for the less privileged, and particularly women, for whom marriage was not always the best choice. Tibby's unmarried condition threatened the political significance of the matrimonial conclusion in more conventional literature of the period, where the final marriage of the two protagonists was meant to support the political reconciliation between England and Scotland. In addition, Tibby's non-reproductive condition threatened the continuation of the Scottish nation. Yet this was the reality of Scotland at the time of Hogg's writing, where agricultural innovators such as Mr Forret were more inclined to enjoy instant financial gains but risking, in the long run, the fertility of the land.

Hogg subverts the marriage plot in the more socially privileged setting of *Queen Hynde* too, this time by portraying an apparently cross-class union between the eponymous protagonist and M'Houston, who only later turns out to be a character of noble origins. Though this union would not have been conceivable in the early nineteenth century, Hogg's argument is that Queen Hynde's choice is determined by the fact that M'Houston is a person of noble principles—a far more important quality than being of noble origin.

CHAPTER 6

James Hogg and the North American Literary Market

1   Networking with the United States

This final chapter explores Hogg's presence in the North American periodical press and the more positive reception of his works in this area, highlighting how the particular political circumstances of the United States during the first half of the nineteenth century allowed him to feel more free to re-engage with the marriage plot in unconventional ways.

Hogg's letters show that he was aware of his popularity in the American literary market, as his most important works had been pirated and published there. For example, Hogg's novel *The Brownie of Bodsbeck, and other Tales* was first published in Edinburgh by William Blackwood in 1818, reprinted in New York by Charles Wiley the same year; in Philadelphia by T. W. Ulstick and in Pittsburgh by Robert Dunlop in 1833. *The Forest Minstrel; A Selection of Songs* was first published in Edinburgh by Constable in 1810, reprinted in Philadelphia by Carey and sold in Boston by Wells & Lilly in 1816. The long poem *Mador of the Moor* was first published in Edinburgh by William Blackwood in 1816 and reprinted in Philadelphia by Moses Thomas the same year. *The Queen's Wake; A Legendary Poem*, first published in Edinburgh by George Goldie and in London by Longman in 1813, was Hogg's most successful work during his lifetime. It was reprinted in six successive editions in the UK, the fourth of which, published in Edinburgh by William Blackwood and in London by John Murray in 1815, was pirated in the United States, appearing in Baltimore, Boston and Philadelphia in 1815, and in New York in 1818 (see Stephanie Anderson-Currie 1993).

Unfortunately, Hogg did not receive any money for the republication of his works in North America because, as argued by the reviewer of Hogg's *Familiar Anecdotes of Sir Walter Scott* (1834), the copyright system of the United States 'shut out the productions of foreign writers' and there was discrimination in the law 'between the productions of foreigners and native citizens' (*New York Spectator*, 26 May 1834). Likewise, the writer of 'The New Copyright Law' in *The American Monthly Magazine* remarked that 'if the work of a British author is brought to the United States it may be appropriated by any resident here, and republished without any consideration or compensation whatever being made to the author' (February 1838, p. 107). This writer maintained that '[a]n international copyright law would at once elevate the cause of letters in this country, and give to our literature a better station in Great Britain' (Ibid.). *Familiar Anecdotes of Sir Walter Scott*, first published in New York by Harper & Brothers in 1834, with a 'Sketch of the Life of Hogg' by Simeon De Witt Bloodgood, was the only work for which Hogg was paid. It was subsequently pirated and published in Glasgow, Edinburgh, and London.

Conscious of his popularity in the United States, Hogg worked incessantly during the winter of 1833–34 with the double purpose of improving his financial situation and helping a few American periodicals in their infancy to grow. As Frank Luther Mott explains, 'in the years immediately following 1825 there was an extraordinary outburst of magazine activity which paralleled the expansion in many other lines of development' (1957: 340–41). On 25 January 1834, Hogg sent a tale and two ballads with a letter to Simeon De Witt Bloodgood, who had invited him to contribute to the *New York Mirror*. Gillian Hughes points out that 'Hogg's letters reveal that he sent several pieces of work to the United States in 1834, but was for the most part left in total ignorance of their fate' (2006: xxvii). On 5 February 1834, Hogg wrote to Wilson that he had been 'very busy all winter though to little purpose mostly writing for the American press' (Ibid.). In a letter dated 5 September 1835 to Robert Shelton Mackenzie, a British correspondent for the American press, Hogg laments that 'I find my literary correspondence with the United States so completely uncertain that I have resolved to drop it altogether' (*Hogg's Letters*, vol. 3, p. 284). In spite of this, the writings that Hogg produced in that winter would see the light in a few American journals, as Janette Currie's research has revealed (2002–2004).[1] Hogg's texts would subsequently penetrate the most remote areas of the United States through their republication in local newspapers, as the consultation of several digital platforms hosting historical newspapers has disclosed.[2]

---

1   The Arts and Humanities Research Board has funded the project 'James Hogg and/in the Nineteenth-Century American Periodical Press' carried out by Janette Currie at Stirling University from 2002 to 2004.

2   The Arts and Humanities Research Council has generously funded the project 'James Hogg's Publications in International Periodicals' based at Stirling University from 2014 to 2017 with Dr Suzanne Gilbert as Principal Investigator, Adrian Hunter as Co-Investigator, and the present writer as Research Assistant who, in April 2015 visited the following archives on the East coast of the United States: The Library of Congress, Washington D.C.; The Library Company of Philadelphia; The New Historical Society of Pennsylvania in Philadelphia; The New York Public Library; The New York Historical Society; The New York State Library in Albany; The Boston Public Library; and Boston Athenaeum. I then implemented my research with the following digital collections: *American Periodical Series Online* (ProQuest); *Historical Newspapers & Periodicals* (ProQuest); *American Antiquarian Society* (AAS); *Historical Periodical*

Mott has noticed that during the period of expansion of American periodicals between 1825 and 1850,

> [o]wnership of magazine contents was not very well defined. [...] Reprinting magazine poems, tales, and articles in the newspapers was a very general practice. [...] Magazines ordinarily liked to be clipped by the newspapers, providing credit was given: it was considered good advertising.
>
> 1957: 502–503

This is how Hogg's poems, songs, tales, and essays reached the most remote areas of the United States.[3]

Andrew Hook's research on the transatlantic literary connections between Scotland and America has highlighted the significant presence of Hogg in the United States (1975: 152–53). Hook remarks that '[t]he great majority of Hogg's works, prose and poetry, were reprinted; and transatlantic critics and reviewers of the day were disposed to find much to admire in them' (1999: 128). Starting from Hook's insights, Janette Currie has traced Hogg's works in nineteenth-century American periodicals 'published between 1807 and 1911' (2009b: 220). According to Currie's *A Listing of Hogg Items in the American Periodical Press*, Hogg appeared in 104 journals in the form of new works published exclusively in American journals; reviews of his works; republications; and literary articles which mention Hogg. The places of publication of these periodicals were twenty-one towns clustered on the east coast of the United States, with Albany, Boston, New York, and Philadelphia as the most thriving publishing centres of the period, where Hogg appeared respectively in five, fourteen, thirty-two, and seventeen periodicals various times.

Recent digital research has revealed an outstanding spread of Hogg's works across American periodicals and newspapers, with more than 350 republications of poems, short stories, essays and letters not only in the journals of the major publishing hubs on the east coast, but also in more local newspapers

---

Collections (Ebsco); *Gale News Vault; 19th Century US Newspapers* (Gale); *America's Historical Newspapers*; *Newspapers.com*; *Collection Hathi Trust Digital Library*; *Google Books*; *Internet Archive*; and *JSTOR Early Journal Content* (a selection of journal materials published prior to 1923 in the United States and prior to 1870 elsewhere).

3 For a detailed list of Hogg's reprints in North America, see 'Reprintings of Hogg's Works Overseas', compiled by Barbara Leonardi, in *James Hogg's Publications to English, Irish, and American Periodicals*, written by James Hogg, ed. by Adrian Hunter with Barbara Leonardi (Edinburgh: Edinburgh University Press, 2020), pp. 187–201.

in the south and midwest regions.[4] At the time, the debate about slavery had brought a period of political turmoil to the United States and Hogg's works appeared in a plethora of publishing venues that embraced the full spectrum of political trends: from abolitionism to emancipation, including those that advocated pro-slavery ideals. What follows is a short overview of where Hogg's works and reviews appeared, before focusing on two specific texts, the ballad 'Bruce and the Spider' and the short story 'Tales of Fathers and Daughters', which Hogg wrote especially for the American periodical press. The latter work, as we shall see, provides a fascinating transatlantic coda to this book in regards to Hogg's rewriting of the marriage plot.

2   The Ettrick Shepherd in the American Periodical Press

American journals put great emphasis on Hogg's self-education and on his outstandingly successful literary achievements. When writing 'Sketch of the Life of Hogg' for the American publication of Hogg's *Familiar Anecdotes of Sir Walter Scott*, Simeon De Witt Bloodgood commented that

> The American reader of Blackwood must have noticed in the celebrated articles called The Noctes, that the Shepherd has often appeared there as a very singular character, and we have not a single doubt that his boldness of opinion has often been distorted into whimsicality, and indifference to propriety.
>
> p. 101

While Scottish reviewers tended to emphasise Hogg's social origin as the cause of his supposed lack of delicacy, American reviewers, particularly those

---

4   Ten years in the digital age have added possibilities to archival investigation that were not available when Currie developed her project between 2002–04. She took as a starting point Jayne K. Kribbs's annotated bibliography *American Literary Periodicals, 1741–1850* (1977) and browsed the *American Periodical Series* (APS) part II, from 1799 to 1850 (Currie 2009a: 144). The APS is a microfilm project sponsored by the University of Michigan in 1941, which gathers a collection of early American periodicals from 1741 to 1935. ProQuest has now digitised the APS and made it cross-searchable with *ProQuest Historical Newspapers* database. In 2013 Ebsco has also launched the *American Antiquarian Society* (AAS) *Historical Periodical Collections*, a digital platform collecting material held at the eponymous archive in Worcester, near Boston. Other valuable digital archives are Gale's *19th Century US Newspapers*, Readex's *America's Historical Newspapers* and *Newspapers.com* which, all together, have remarkably increased the capacity of archival research across North American historical newspapers.

writing for abolitionist periodicals, were inclined to emphasise Hogg's 'literary achievement [...] from obscurity and to set his self-education as an example of democracy to former Afro-American slaves, for whom education would make a difference in finding a path in their newly emancipated condition' (Leonardi 2019b: 200). For example, the *Minerva* focused on Hogg 'winning his way with the firm step of genius' (New York, 20 Aug 1825, p. 315); while the *Atheneum; or Spirit of the English Magazine* republished an article on 'The Ettrick Shepherd' from the *London Literary Gazette* of 1st January 1831 (pp. 5–6): 'We respect the energy that has made its own way, — the industry that has done the best with material in its power' (*Atheneum*, Boston, 1 March 1831, p. 513). Contesting Hogg's boisterous image arising from *Blackwood*'s 'Noctes', it argues that the volume of Hogg's *Songs* would 'greatly raise the poet in the estimation of the public, who are too apt to mistake him for a Noctesian roister, and, though imaginative, a sometimes coarse prose writer' (Ibid., p. 516).

The *American Monthly Magazine & Critical Review* of New York published a twenty-page review of the American edition of Hogg's *The Brownie of Bodsbeck*, commenting that '[t]he whole volume [...] does infinite credit to Mr. Hogg, and we cannot close without expressing our most earnest wish that we will not be long before he presents us with some more of his attractive and beautiful stories' (1st September 1818, p. 354). *The Critic*, a short-lived weekly founded in New York by William Leggett in November 1828, published a review of the American edition of Hogg's *The Shepherd's Calendar*, remarking that '[t]he volumes before us are agreeable evidences [...] of the excellence of the Ettrick Shepherd in this kind of composition. These tales will at least sustain, and, we are inclined to believe, advance, the previous reputation of their author' (16 May 1829, p. 31).

The Albion, A Journal of News, Politics and Literature (New York), an eclectic weekly that 'kept American readers abreast of the latest English writers' (Mott 1957: 397), published eleven items related to Hogg, gathering some of his poems, songs, reviews from English magazines and adverts of his American editions. A few of these were 'Scotland', Song [O, weel befa' the maiden gay]' (26 August 1826, p. 84); 'Verses to the Comet' (6 February 1836, p. 41), from the *Scots Magazine* of July 1819 (p. 30); a biography of Hogg (19 March 1836, p. 89); a review of '*Sermons* by the Ettrick Shepherd', from the *London Literary Gazette* of 26 April 1934, where the writer, rather patronisingly, reported that '[t]he holy Chesterfield of Altrive [namely Hogg] treats of politeness in ladies and gentlemen; of belles and beaux, and not of ewes and rams'. This shows the typical class-prejudiced attitude of British reviewers, though also observing how Hogg 'assuredly deserves all that a liberal and grateful public can do for one whose natural genius has lifted him into high and just distinction' (*The Albion*, 19 July

1834, p. 228). *The Albion* also republished a review of 'Songs by Mr. Hogg', from the *London Literary Gazette* of 1 January 1831, remarking that '[o]f such a man a country may be proud' (*Albion*, 19 February 1831, p. 292), and 'Some Particulars Relative to the Ettrick Shepherd', noting that 'we remember him as a man of natural and vigorous genius' (19 March 1836, p. 89).

The Rover of New York republished Hogg's poems 'The Broken Heart' (5 February 1844, p. 80), 'The Moon Was A-Waning' [Dirge] (15 February, 1845, p. 338), and 'A Tale of an Old Highlander' (vol. 1, 1843, pp. 314–17). One of the most important quarterly, *The North American Review*, published two long articles on Hogg's American editions: one on *The Queen's Wake*, remarking that '[t]hat the author of this poem was a *common* shepherd, which is asserted by the editor in a preface of his own personal knowledge, is the most extraordinary circumstance about the work' (1st November 1815, p. 103, emphasis original). Another comprehensive review of Hogg's American republications of *The Queen's Wake*, *Pilgrims of the Sun*, *Mador of the Moor*, and *The Brownie of Bodsbeck* emphasised the remarkable effort of Hogg's self-education, pointing out that

> his works, with much simplicity, bear no marks of an illiterate mind. He seems well acquainted with Scottish history and tradition, and manages them for the purpose of poetry with sufficient dexterity and familiarity. Mr Hogg [...] has acquired considerable information, familiarity with language, and even good taste without the usual helps; this is undoubtedly evidence of some superiority, for no man can overcome his condition without it.
>
> *The North American Review*, 1 June 1819, p. 2.

Of the same opinion was the reviewer of Hogg's *Altrive Tales* in *The Journal of Belles Lettres*, who argued that '[t]he contemplation of genius struggling against, and finally overcoming difficulties, which, to the less enthusiastic, would have appeared insurmountable, is always interesting, gratifying, and instructive' (8 April 1834, p. 1). *The Journal of Belles Lettres* was a supplement to the *Select Circulating Library* edited by Adam Waldie, a Scottish emigrant who became the successful editor of some of the most important American magazines of the period, among which the above-mentioned *Museum of Foreign Literature*. In her essay 'Hogg in the Zodiac', Currie explains that Waldie treated Hogg with 'affection and genuine concern', proposing a scheme to publish a selection of his works in America in 'a review of *Altrive Tales* that appeared in the *Journal of Belles Letters* of 22 April 1834' (http://www.jameshogg.stir.ac.uk).

Other North American periodicals that substantially republished Hogg's works are the weekly *New-England Galaxy* of Boston, which reprinted 'An

Awful Leeing-Like Story' (3 December 1831, p. 1), from *Blackwood's Magazine*; 'Emigration' (27 June 1835, p. 4), from *Chamber's Edinburgh Magazine* of 18 May 1833, a tale where Hogg reflects on his own personal experience, as two of his brothers had emigrated to America in 1830 (see Claude Howard 1986). In this tale, the narrator points out, 'I know of nothing so distressing as the last sight of a fine industrious independent peasantry taking the last look of their native country, never to behold it more' (*New-England Galaxy*, 27 June 1835, p. 4), thus emphasising the sense of displacement that Scottish emigrants must have experienced at the time. The same magazine republished Hogg's 'Ode on the Death of Lord Byron' (29 June 1827, p. 3); 'The Palmer's Hymn' (1st February 1828, p. 1), from *Mador of the Moor*, which portrays the story of a pilgrim who repents for having conceived a child out of wedlock that was murdered by his lady (see Chapter 4) and which, similarly to the extract 'Epitome of War' from Hogg's essay 'Soldier' in *Lay Sermons*, was republished by a large number of American periodicals. The *New-England Galaxy* also republished 'The Witch of the Gray Thorn' (18 January 1828, p. 4), from *Blackwood's Magazine* of June 1825 (pp. 714–16), and announced 'Hogg's brother's arrival to America' (16 August 1834, p. 2).

The Museum of Foreign Literature and Science of Philadelphia and New York likewise reprinted Hogg's poems, songs and reviews, among which: 'I Hae Nae-body Now' (1st July 1831, p. 35), from *Fraser's Magazine*; 'Love's Legacy', in three subsequent issues of January, February and March in 1835, from *Fraser's Magazine*; 'Maggy O'Buccleuch. AIR: Days of Yore' (December 1831, p. 640); 'Random Reminiscences of Sir Walter Scott, of the Ettrick Shepherd, Sir Henry Raeburn, &c. &c.' (1st December 1843, pp. 563–72), from *Tait's Magazine*; 'Song: O, weel befa' the maiden gay' (1st June 1831, p. 511), from *Blackwood's Magazine*; a review of *Altrive Tales* (1st August 1832, pp. 97–106), from the *Monthly Review*; a review of the 1831 Edinburgh edition of 'The Songs of James Hogg, the Ettrick Shep-herd' (1st April 1831, pp. 351–53), from London's *Athenaeum* which, as typical of British reviewers, remarked rather condescendingly that the songs 'have no affinity whatever to those polished and pretty verses which pass for songs in the polite world, but resemble the spontaneous lyrics of the pastoral muse of old Scotland' (p. 352). Notably, the collection of *Songs by the Ettrick Shep-herd* would be pirated and printed in New York the following year by William Stodart.

The Museum of Foreign Literature and Science also published a review of *The Wars of Montrose* under 'A Decade of Novels and Novelettes' (1st July 1835, pp. 91–106), from *Fraser's Magazine*, a collection of tales that would be pirated and printed in Philadelphia the following year by E. L. Carey & Hart; and a celebra-tory article on the death of 'James Hogg, the Ettrick Shepherd: "Sweet poet of the woods! A long adieu!'", from the London's *Annual Biography*. This article highlights Hogg's effort to become a self-made literary figure:

> With the sole exception of Burns, Mr. Hogg stands forth as our greatest Scottish poet; and when we consider the early struggles of the man, his obscure birth and want of education, and look at the triumphant manner in which, by the mere force of his natural abilities, he overcame them all, and placed himself in the first rank of modern poets, we cannot sufficiently do honour, where so much is due.
>
> *Museum of Foreign Literature*, 1st December 1836, p. 394

Hogg's works appeared consistently in the *Philadelphia Album*, a weekly designed for women (Mott 1957: 354) which republished, among other texts, an extract entitled 'Fortune' (26 July 1834, p. 239), from Hogg's *Lay Sermons*; a 'Jacobite Ballad' (24 August 1833, p. 272), from *Fraser's Magazine*; 'Song' [O, weel befa' the maiden gay]' (25 June 1831, p. 208), from *Blackwood's Magazine*; a review of Hogg's *Altrive Tales* (2 June 1832, pp. 170–71); and an article on 'The Ettrick Shepherd' (10 May 1834, p. 149) which, though slightly condescending, emphasised that '[f]ew poets who have risen from the humble ranks of life have enjoyed, during their lifetime, a name of greater celebrity than James Hogg' (p. 149).

The *Philadelphia Album* also published an announcement about the Ettrick Shepherd in London (17 March 17 1832, p. 85); a review entitled 'A Roland for an Oliver' on Hogg's Fullarton edition of the works of Robert Burns (13 Sept 1834, p. 294); a review of 'Songs by Mr Hogg' (5 March 1831, p. 74), from the above-mentioned *Albion*; and an article entitled 'A visit to Hogg, the Ettrick Shepherd', from *The American Monthly Magazine* of 1 April 1834 (p. 85). This reports the meeting between Hogg and an American tourist who describes 'his manners' as 'very agreeable', adding that 'without apparent effort, he made each feel at home' (*Philadelphia Album*, 23 Aug 1834, p. 270). This is a remarkable comment that shifts Hogg onto the positive side of the politeness spectrum as conceived in the American culture of the period. The writer of the the article entitled 'Politeness' in *The Album, and Ladies' Weekly Gazette*, for example, maintains that '[t]here are a hundred different sorts of ceremony, all of which go by the name of politeness; but how few persons are there who possess that real politeness—the will and power to make all happy around them?' (1826–1827, p. 5). Another article, likewise entitled 'Politeness', published in the *New-York State Journal*, points out that '[b]y politeness I do not mean a great deal of unnecessary bowing and courtesying, but that delicate attention to the comfort of those around us that springs from a kind generous heart' (3 February 1836, p. 161). Evidently, the American tourist of the *Philadelphia Album* seemed far more willing to emphasise that no matter Hogg's background, his self-education had certainly taught him how to converse and behave with good manners, in sharp contrast to the class-prejudiced portrayal of the roistering Ettrick Shepherd in *Blackwood*'s 'Noctes'. The article 'A visit to Hogg, the Ettrick Shepherd' also appeared in the *Cincinnati Mirror, and Western Gazette of Literature, Science, and the Arts* (17 May 1834, p. 242).

Hogg was consistently republished in *Atkinson's Casket* from 1828 to 1836, the antecedent of *Graham's Magazine* according to Mott (1957: 544), which reprinted 'The Brownie of the Black Haggs' (December 1828, p. 558), from *Blackwood's* for October; 'The Palmer's Hymn' (March 1834, p. 111), from *Mador of the Moor*; 'A Scots Luve Sang' (September 1834, p. 432); 'A Tale of an Old Highlander' (September 1832, p. 390–93); a poem 'To the Ettrick Shepherd' signed by C. H. W. (January 1833, p. 24); and another song to Hogg by Robert Gilfillan in a section entitled 'The Ettrick Shepherd', with a mock response by Hogg that, though imitating the raucous voice of the Ettrick Shepherd in *Blackwood's* 'Noctes', it also highlights Hogg's incredible effort to pursue a literary career: 'Mr Wilson can tell ye that I have fought very hard for my literary fame, but I have got it at last' (March 1835, p. 130).

The Friend: A Religious and Literary Journal republished Hogg's tale 'Emigration' (22 August 1835, p. 363). This was a Quaker weekly published in Philadelphia and devoted to 'various "concerns" of the Friends' which included 'peace, temperance, antimasonry, antislavery and colonization, and Indian education' (Mott 1957: 563). *The Friend* would grow particularly concerned with the education of African-Americans in later years, publishing a few articles on the 'slavery conditions during the progress of the dispute' (Ibid., p. 564) in the 1850s.

The renowned American editor Nathaniel Parker Willis published 'The Ettrick Shepherd and Other Scotch Poets' in the *American Monthly Magazine*, arguing that although the English publisher of the *Queen's Wake* points out that since Hogg went to service at the age of seven he received no education, this probably means 'no academical or public education, a very different thing, as we shall endeavor to show, from none at all' (November 1829, p. 522); this highlights once again attention to Hogg's effort to improve himself. Willis also reprinted a few of Hogg's poems and songs in his *Youth's Companion* of Boston, a juvenile that he edited for thirty years from 1827; these are Hogg's 'A Child's Prayer', which appeared on 27 January 1830, 21 July 1830 and 6 November 1833; and 'A Boy's Song', published on 27 April 1831. Interestingly, Willis supported emancipation and hired the escaped slave Harriet Jacobs, the author of *Incidents in the Life of a Slave Girl* (1861), as a nurse for his daughter when she moved to New York. When Jacob witnessed the condition of the poor in England reported in her autobiography, she was there with Willis and his daughter. In her memoir, she explains that 'the most ignorant and the most destitute of these peasants was a thousand fold better off than the most pampered American slave' (p. 170). After denouncing the systematic sexual abuse of black female slaves by their masters, she refers to the situation of impoverished English families: '[t]he father, when he closed his cottage door, felt safe with his family around him. No master or overseer could come and take from him his wife, or his daughter', neither was there a 'law forbidding them to learn to read and write' (Ibid.). Education was in fact an important tool for the emancipation of African Americans. Na'im Akbar explains that after 'the legal emancipation of the slaves in 1865, [...] It was recognized that education was a key tool for freedom' and 'enthusiastically pursued by the newly freed population' (2009: 23). This explains why a self-taught writer like James Hogg appealed to the collective imagination of both abolitionists and emancipationists of North America.

Hogg's works reached the American states of the West too. In this area, during the period of magazine expansion, Cincinnati was the chief centre, 'not behind New York, Boston, and Philadelphia in the variety of periodicals produced' (Mott 1957: 389). *The Cincinnati Mirror*, a weekly miscellany edited by William D. Gallagher, Thomas H. Shreve and James H. Perkins (Kribbs 1977: 38), reprinted an extract from Hogg's *Lay Sermons*, 'Language of Animals' (6 June 1835, p. 254); a few reviews about Hogg such as 'Biographical Sketches. The Ettrick Shepherd' (19 March 1836, pp. 57–58), remarking that '[t]he careers of great men—particularly of self-made men—are always interesting. Hogg was one of this class' (p. 57); 'James Hogg, the Ettrick Shepherd', from the London's *Athenaeum* of 5 December, which highlighted that 'Hogg was, undoubtedly, a man of fine original genius' (27 February 1836, p. 34); and a reprint of Allan Cunningham's 'The Ettrick Shepherd' (26 April 1834, p. 218–19). The *Western Christian Advocate* of Cincinnati, 'established in 1834 by the Methodists' and still current when Mott published his *History of American Magazines* in 1957 (Mott 1957: 389), reprinted the 'Language of Animals' (2nd October 1835, p. 92) and Hogg's tale 'Emigration' (16 October 1835, p. 97).

In the context of the slave debate, it is important to distinguish between abolitionism and emancipation, as the former movement was considered too extreme in Northern and Southern states alike. As Mott explains, 'abolitionism had been so bitterly opposed by such large faction in the North that it was not easy to make it acceptable to all' (1957: 612). The majority of Northern periodicals supported gradual emancipation rather than instant abolition of slavery: in an article entitled 'Slavery', *The American Magazine of Useful and Entertaining Knowledge* states that '[w]ithout doing anything to uphold slavery, or to justify it, we must say, that we disapprove of the conduct and proceedings of those who are urging the immediate abolition of slavery at every hazard' (September 1835, p. 23, cited in Mott 1957: 459). As Mott remarks, in the Northern states only a few periodicals were openly abolitionist. The weekly *Liberator* of Boston, founded in 1831 by William Lloyd Garrison—which republished six of Hogg's works—is historically the most important abolitionist magazine. In Boston, Mott explains, only the *Zion's Herald* and the *New England Spectator* 'stood by the *Liberator* and its editor in this crisis'; the abolitionists were attacked and 'the excitement culminated in the mobbing of Garrison and the destruction of the *Liberator*'s press' in 1835 (Ibid., p. 460).

Nonetheless, a few abolitionist periodicals took an interest in the figure of a self-made man like Hogg and republished some of his works. *The Independent* of New York, which opposed slave holding, republished Hogg's 'The Covenant's Scaffold Song' (13 February 1868, p. 2) and 'The Palmer's Hymn' (11 May 1857, p. 11). The *Zion's Herald*, likewise an 'opponent of slaveholding' (Mott 1955: 458), republished extracts from Hogg's *Lay Sermons* (1 April 1835, p. 52; 16 October 1850, p. 1) and from *The Three Perils of Woman* (19 January 1848, p. 12), 'On Carmel's Brow. A Hebrew Melody' (16 January 1823, p. 8), and an article on the Ettrick Shepherd with the poem 'To the Sky Lark', citing a few lines from the preface of Hogg's American edition of *Songs* to point out that the writer's 'history exhibits a triumph of genius and perseverance over the difficulties of original situation in life, and defective education, such as is seldom exhibited in the annals of literature' (*Zion's Herald*, 15 April 1835, p. 59). Significantly, this therefore constructs Hogg as an outstanding model for newly freed slaves. This journal also published a tribute on Hogg's death, entitled 'The Ettrick Shepherd Gone!' (13 January 1836, p. 7). In addition, the *Harbinger* of Boston, later based in New York, succeeded the *Dial* as 'a vehicle for the writings of transcendentalists' and condemned 'the evils of slavery' (Mott 1957: 366, 458); it republished Hogg's 'The Sky-lark' (23 August 1845, p. 165) and the above-mentioned article on 'The Ettrick Shepherd' by Allan Cunningham (29 May 1834, p. 149).

In Southern states, periodicals were careful not to take extreme sides with regard to the slavery debate, as they did not want to lose Northern subscribers. For example, James E. Heath, the editor of the *Southern Literary Messenger* of Richmond, Virginia, was himself against slavery, even though his magazine published pro-slavery articles. In his 'Editorial Remarks' he took the opportunity to say that

> we must be permitted to dissent from the opinion that it [slavery] is either a moral or a political benefit. We regard it, on the contrary, as a great evil, which society sooner or later will find it not only to its interest to remove or mitigate, but will seek its gradual abolition, or amelioration, under the influence of those high obligations imposed by an egalitarian Christian morality'
>
> vol. 1, January 1835, p. 254; cited in MOTT 1957: 632

In the same volume, the *Southern Literary Messenger* published one of Hogg's poems, 'There's no Laddie Coming' (vol. 1, January 1835, p. 200).

The *Southern Literary Gazette*, edited by Gilmore Simm, published a review of the American edition of Hogg's *The Shepherd's Calendar*, arguing that

> [t]here is a bewitching simplicity, a something of nature about all the fiction that is wonderfully touching; [...] the existence of these wanton creatures, gives a coloring to the national character which, while we smile at what we consider an absurd fondness for the idlesse [*sic*] of superstition, nevertheless, goes very far towards raising them in our esteem.
>
> 15 June 1829, p. 52

On the other hand, the *Southern Literary Journal*—which in its pages recorded 'the progress and achievement of southern culture, defended slavery, and encouraged southern authors' (Mott 1957: 664)—published Hogg's song 'Birnieboeuzle' (vol. 2, no. 4, June 1836, p. 258), a different version, as Currie explains (see *A Listing of Hogg Items in the American Periodical Press*), from the one Hogg had previously published in *The Forest Minstrel* (1811) and in *Songs by the Ettrick Shepherd* (1831); it was perhaps rewritten in the winter of 1833–34, when Hogg was proactively working for the American periodical press.

Interestingly, Hogg is mentioned in an article signed 'J. G. W.' and entitled 'The Slave Poet of North Carolina' in *The Western Literary Messenger*, discussing the poet 'George, a slave of James Horton, of Chatham county, North Carolina [...] and the publication of a "pamphlet" [...] containing several short compositions' (vol. 12, 1849, p. 114). The article reports a sketch written by the Rt. Rev. Bishop Hawkes of Missouri who, 'when a student at the University of North Carolina, was well acquainted with the poet slave George'; he remarks that '[t]he pieces of this little collection indicate genius of no common order. [...] Compared with the earliest productions of the Ettrick Shepherd, which are in print, they by no means sink in the reader's estimation' (Ibid.). Again, Hogg was presented as an exemplary model on which African Americans could draw in the struggle to educate and emancipate themselves. Significantly, the pamphlet was advertised in order to increase the number of subscriptions and enabled George to purchase his freedom.

3   'Bruce and the Spider': The Voice of Abolitionism and Independence

Research carried out between 2014 and 2017 has brought to light an original poem entitled 'Bruce and the Spider', which Hogg sent to America and which appeared in a long series of journals and newspapers across the United

States between 1835 and 1844.[5] Adrian Hunter points out that, according to Gillian Hughes, 'Bruce and the Spider' 'may have originally belonged to a set of "Historical Ballads" intended for the London publisher Samuel Chappell' (Hunter 2020b: 241). Nevertheless, in the United States the ballad acquired a new significance and was used to promote abolitionist ideals, setting the example of Robert the Bruce's resilience when fighting for Scotland's freedom in 1314. The *Virginia Free Press* of Charlestown, West Virginia, published it seemingly for the first time on 16 April 1835, with a slightly longer introductory note than the subsequent republications which appeared between 1839 and 1844. This headnote was 'derived from Scott's Tales of a Grandfather', Hunter explains, and 'presumably also supplied by Hogg' (2020b: 241).

The ballad reappeared four years later in various newspapers, with *The Emancipator* of New York—the official organ of the Anti-Slavery Society (Mott 1957: 373)—suggesting that Hogg's incitement in this ballad, 'Try Again', 'may be a motto for abolitionists, and should be often in the minds of our citizens of color, as a preventive of despondency' (11 April 1839, p. 202). Joshua Levitt, the editor of the *Emancipator*, was 'an anti-slavery advocate' who had edited the *Evangelist* from 1832 to 1837, founded 'expressly to promote revivals and missions, temperance, and other reforms' such as 'abolition' (Mott 1957: 373). The same motto was repeated and supported by the *Morning Star* of Limerick (ME), where Hogg's ballad appeared on 1st May 1839 (p. 4) under the title of 'Try Again'. Hogg's ballad was then republished with the same shorter introductory note, but without the abolitionist statement, in the following venues: the *Vermont Chronicle* of Bellows Falls (3 April 1839, p. 4); the *New York Evangelist* (6 April 1839, p. 56); *The Cleveland Observer* of Hudson, Ohio (8 May 1839, p. 196); on the front page of *The Portsmouth Journal of Literature and Politics* (18 May 1839); in the *Hartford Courant*, Connecticut (28 May 1839, p. 2); and, five years later, in *The Cincinnati Weekly Herald and Philanthropist* (16 October 1844, p. 4). Below is the first version of 'Bruce and the Spider' that appeared in the *Virginia Free Press* of 16 April 1835; later republications do not show variations of substance:

> Try again, little weaver,
> Try again, try again!
> Ere you yield hope for ever,
> Try again!
> There's a tide in nature's law

5   AHRC-funded project 'James Hogg's Publications in International Periodicals' based at Stirling University (2014–17) with Dr Suzanne Gilbert as Principal Investigator, Adrian Hunter as Co-Investigator, and the present writer as Research Assistant. I discovered this ballad during a research trip to the United States in April 2015.

Man never, never saw,
An' some blessed breeze may blaw,
Try again, little hero!
Tho' you risk a deadly fa',
Try again!

Do you ken, little hero,
Do you ken, do you ken,
Though a dream or chimera,
Do you ken,
That on your effort good,
There depends a sea of blood,
And a name, that long has stood
Among men! little hero!
In the land of frith and flood,
Dale and glen!

In my dear native land,
Far away, far away,
With my brave little band,
Many a day,
I tried, and tried again,
In sorrow and in pain,
Our freedom to regain!
And, like thee, I'll try again,
If I may!

See! A King is on his knee!
Swing away, swing away,
To pray success for thee,
Swing away!
His monitor to be,
Here, he takes thee solemnly;
Thou art fix'd! and so is he!
So, huzza, little hero,
Now my country shall be free!
So huzza.

The topic of 'Bruce and the Spider' could serve different purposes in the United States of the period. On the one hand, it helped promote the value of resilience for African American slaves, as shown in the lines 'Try again, little weaver, | Try again, try again! | Ere you yield hope for ever, | Try again!', seemingly to incite slaves to escape their condition. On the other hand, the ballad also aligned with the American political spirit, as shown in 'Many a day, | I tried, and tried again, | In sorrow and in pain, | Our freedom to regain!', as the United States had fought for and gained their independence from Britain in 1783 in a way which could be seen as analogous to Scotland which had achieved independence from England in the Battle of Bannockburn led by Robert the Bruce in 1314.

4   'Tales of Fathers and Daughters': Crossing Class Boundaries in the
       Marriage Plot

The final section of this chapter focuses on an important re-interpretation of the marriage plot that characterises many of Hogg's works: the abolition of class boundaries in the union of the two protagonists. As argued in the Introduction, Hogg questioned the ideology inherent in the marriage plot because it promoted a political union of the British nations that only mirrored the privileged layers of society, hiding the moral implications of that union occurring in the lower strata of the social scale. Hogg re-imagined the marriage plot in 'Tales of Fathers and Daughters' which, as mentioned above, appeared in three subsequent issues of *The Zodiac, a Monthly Periodical, Devoted to Science, Literature, and the Arts* in July, August and September 1835, respectively the first, second and third numbers of this very promising magazine, published in Albany, the capital of the state of New York, by Erastus Perry, publisher and owner, who was 'assisted by a number of literary gentlemen' (*The Zodiac*, March 1836, p. 144).[6]

This monthly periodical was an imperial octavo of sixteenth pages, well executed, sold at the price of one dollar per annum and devoted to 'exhibit a faithful and instructive picture of the literary world, passing through all its signs and season' (Ibid.). *The New-York State Journal*, lamenting the short durability of the literary periodicals of the time for lack of confidence in the general cultural attitude, showed some hope for *The Zodiac*, remarking: 'We believe the *Zodiac* will succeed—it has a good deal of the right kind of spirit in its pages' (9 March 1836, p. 204). Unfortunately, *The Zodiac* lasted only two years, from 1835 to 1837, probably succumbing to the same fate of many other magazines

---

6 'Tales of Fathers and Daughters' was discovered by Janette Currie during her research trip to the United States for her project 'James Hogg and/in the Nineteenth-Century American Periodical Press', carried out from 2002 to 2004 at Stirling University.

of the period, caused by their 'non-paying subscribers', as Mott explains (1957: 515), as well as by the high price of magazine postage (Ibid., p. 517).

The reason why Hogg's tale saw the light in the pages of *The Zodiac* must be traced to his American epistolary contact, Simeon De Witt Bloodgood, a lawyer with literary interests based in Albany who, in this monthly, published a series of 'Lectures on American Literature' from August 1835 to May 1836 and who must therefore have passed Hogg's tale to Erastus Perry, the publisher of *The Zodiac*, with the intent to help this American periodical in its infancy.[7]

Douglas and Wilma Mack have discussed the political agenda of this tale, remarking that it 'is forceful in its implied criticism of the Scottish aspect of the British class system, and it may be that writing for an overtly democratic American audience helped Hogg to feel free to explore this topic with especial vigour in this particular story' (2004: 126). On the other hand, in his 'Introduction' to Hogg's *Contribution to English, Irish, and American Periodicals*, Adrian Hunter contends that 'it is desire to convey something of the national complex at home, rather than the wish to appeal to American ideals about a classless democracy, that would appear to be the guiding impulse behind Hogg's story' (2020a: xxxvi), as shown by his focus on the Gaelic voice of the female protagonist's father in the tale. Yet, during the winter between 1833 and 1834, Hogg wrote this tale with a multicultural American audience in mind, as the United States was being populated by a large number of Scottish emigrants, including the family of his brother, as mentioned above. These people had to adjust to a new world which would hopefully offer them a more democratic life than in Scotland.

'Tales of Fathers and Daughters' portrays the story of Mary McFarlane, who leaves her paternal house in the Highlands for Edinburgh to be maid to Lady Manor's three daughters. During her solitary journey to the city, Mary meets Mr Ward, an alluring young student of law from the upper class of an uncertain location in the southern periphery of Britain: 'I think Mr. Ward was an Irishman' (Hogg 2020 [1835]:148), utters the third-person narrator; though Lord Ward, the father, sends a letter from Bangor in Wales, later on in the tale. Be that as it may, Mr Ward junior meets Mary when making his return to Edinburgh, after the shooting season in the Highlands, and feels instantly mesmerised by this gentle Highland maid. It so happens that at Lady Manor's house, Mary encounters

---

7   For a more detailed history of publication of Hogg's 'Tales of Fathers and Daughters' see Adrian Hunter, 'Introduction' and 'Textual and Explanatory Notes', in *James Hogg's Publications to English, Irish, and American Periodicals*, written by James Hogg, ed. by Adrian Hunter with Barbara Leonardi (Edinburgh: Edinburgh University Press, 2020), pp. xi–xliv (pp. xxxvi; xxxix) and pp. 202–47 (pp. 242–43) respectively.

a cold welcome on the part of the old housekeeper, 'a grim, fat, English Kerline' (Hogg 2020 [1835]: 149), as well as Lady Manor's three daughters, who grow jealous at discovering Mr Ward's attachment to Mary. Subsequently the two elope and start living as husband and wife in Mr Ward's apartment, supported by the allowance that the latter's father sponsors for his son's law studies at college. Upon discovering that Mr Ward is neglecting his studies for some obscure reason, his tutor sends a letter to Lord Ward who comes immediately to Edinburgh from his parliamentary duties in London. The father interrupts the idyll, providing some money to Mary who is thus abandoned and left pregnant with illegitimate child. Mary finds support in poor Betty Wier, a kind washerwoman who, unfortunately, dies soon after. Mary's father, Duncan McFarlane, leaves the Highlands in search for his daughter; he finds her and forgives her elopement. In order to try to help Mary, Duncan's nephew William McFarlane, a shrewd lawyer, makes use of a Scottish law called *verba de futuro* (see Chapter 4), according to which a couple who has lived together under the same roof for a certain length of time are considered to be legally married (Mitchison and Leneman 1989: 99). Lord Ward has thus to acknowledge Mary as his son's lawful wife and their son as the heir to his fortune, as per the law of primogeniture.

In this tale, Hogg addresses some of the themes already explored in Chapters 3 and 4 of this book: the stigma that a child born out of wedlock would cause a young maid like Mary; the figure of a forgiving father whose love for his daughter surpasses the unforgiving laws of the Scottish Kirk; issues related to class privilege; the inheritance law of primogeniture; and a re-elaboration of the marriage plot typical of the national tale, which Hogg re-invents for this short story, in order to abolish and question class boundaries in the name of true love.

What Hogg highlights in this tale is that Mr Ward does not seduce Mary with the intent to abandon her, as happens in 'Maria's Tale' (see Chapter 4), where the eponymous protagonist relates a cautionary tale 'to warn others against the arts by which I was deceived', thereby presenting her story as 'the relation of a perfidy of which myself was the victim' (Hogg 2004b [1820]: 151). On the contrary, in 'Tales of Fathers and Daughters', Mr Ward junior appears to be genuinely devoted to Mary as he 'loved her with all his heart' (Hogg 2020 [1835]: 154), and when Lord Ward, his father, arrives at their secret lodging, 'he found the two lovers sitting together on the sofa, in the fondest endearment' (Ibid.). What Hogg questions through this tale are the class barriers that would forbid this couple to pursue a future together. This is shown by the son's reaction: 'Mr. Ward's blood run [*sic*] chill to his heart when he saw it was his father, he could not articulate a word' (Ibid.). It is true that at the start of the tale, Mr Ward's intentions do not seem to be completely honourable. When he discovers that Mary is a lady's maid, he does take some liberties which, had she belonged to a higher status, he would have never dared. When

> Mary's tongue blabbed the fatal secret that she was on her way to Edinburgh, to be maid to Lady Manor's daughters! Mr. Ward's face glowed with a triumphant smile, and Mary had not won to the top of the hill on the south side of the Ferry, until his arm was round Mary's waist'.
>
> HOGG 2020 [1835]: 149

Mr Ward's familiarity with Mary at the start of their encounter signals an issue originating from class privilege at the expense of the female labouring class. Lady Manor explains this point to her daughters, when they remark that had they reached Edinburgh on foot like Mary, they would have accepted a passage on the gig of a handsome gentleman: 'Lady Manor smiled, and said, "I should have found no fault with any of you for it, my girls. Your rank would have protected you from all familiarity. But with a simple country maiden going to service, the case is widely different"' (Ibid., p. 150). Mr Ward, Lady Manor explains to Mary, is 'a young Nobleman, as wild a slip of mischief as ever was born' (Ibid., p. 151).

Nevertheless, Mary's upbringing in the Highlands by a father who, though 'illiterate', was an 'intrepid, honest man, with a great deal of shrewdness of the Scottish character about him' (Ibid., p. 159) seems to have provided her with the right skills to survive the difficult situations of life; so much so that her frugality allows the couple to sustain themselves when Lord Ward cuts his allowance to his son. In contrasts to Mr Ward's excessive ways, 'Mary was exceedingly thrifty, neat and cleanly and as he saw no company there, he actually lived one half cheaper with her than he did at his lodgings' (Ibid., p. 154). Mary, a maid from the Highlands, is the one who civilises the excessive ways of this nobleman from Wales, thereby performing the duties of a true mother of the nation. Ward himself, at the start of the tale, 'took Mary for a country lady, for she had all the appearance of it, and her having been so long in genteel service, gave both her manners and language a genteel turn' (Ibid., p. 148). Mary's nobility of the heart renders her equal to Mr Ward, who recognises her real value from the start. Deeply in love with her, he declares to his father, 'I have been living here with this young lady since the beginning of December, but if you look at her beauty and knew her nature, I think you will forgive me' (Ibid., p. 155). Mr Ward's familiarity with Mary at the start can thus be forgiven, as he was following nature in his uncontrollable attraction towards the Highland maid, while culture would have obliged him to check his natural impulses, had Mary belonged to a higher social status.

Notwithstanding class rules, in this tale Hogg presents his own re-elaboration of the national tale, where his heroine truly deserves to climb the social ladder not because of her physical beauty, as her aunt, 'Mrs. McGlashen, the widow of Sergeant McGlashen, of the Clan Alpine regiment' (Ibid., p. 144), seems to suggest upon discovering her niece's departure for Edinburgh, as she 'was even more delighted with Mary's grand prospects than she was herself, and calculated that she would at last secure a Sergeant of dragoons, which was a very honorable rank in life' (Ibid.). On the contrary, Mary deserves to become a lady in the eyes of society because her error has been dictated by her true love for young Ward, without second ends. As Lady Manor explains at the start, 'Mary McFarlane was far too lovely and too simple to take to Edinburgh' (Ibid.) and, similarly to Mr Ward's Irish tutor who fails to fathom what is going on with his ward (forgive the pun), Mary was 'quite unacquainted with the ways of the world in high life' (Ibid., p. 153).

Mr Ward is aware that his social rank will never allow him to marry the woman he loves. Financially dependent on his father, he has no choice but oblige to Lord Ward's decision. On the other hand, Mary's pregnancy out of wedlock makes her completely unworthy of her father's blessing, which he did not provide to his daughter at the start of the tale because,

> if you get your father's blessing now you have no more to work for, but if you have your father's plessing to earn it will be a motive for you to pe coot, so I'll not pe giving you it when you go away. You know I have nothing else to give you, and it is quite coot that you earn your wages before you receive them.
>
> Ibid., p. 147

Significantly, Hogg has Duncan McFarlane deliver a moral lesson to his daughter in his Gaelic speech.

Disheartened by the prospect of having disappointed his father's expectations and thus not worthy of his 'wages', Mary finds refuge in Betty Wier's house, the washerwoman who though perceiving what Mary is going through, 'yet with a delicacy rare among women of certain age, she never put a question to Mary' (Ibid., p. 157). This is the type of delicacy that Hogg advocates in his tale: the acceptance that Betty Wier shows towards Mary's condition, despite the consequences. '[S]he is going with a genteel family, where no irregularity will be permitted' (Ibid., p. 145), had argued Mary's aunt, Mrs McGlashen, to Duncan McFarlane, who thus replied:

> Shene Cameron tould me [...] tat all the ladies in Edinburgh are pure, and chaste, and good, and nothing is said before tem, tat might not be said before te Angels [...] But though the tear ladies be so pure and so chaste, tere is not one of the lower ranks suffered to be so[.]
>
> Ibid.

Duncan's words question the type of delicacy that the norms of politeness of the period would require in the presence of women of the middle and upper classes. Unfortunately, this was a delicacy that hid the reality of Hogg's contemporary Edinburgh, as shown in Chapter 2 with the discussion of prostitution in Hogg's novel *The Three Perils of Woman*, and in Chapter 4 with the character of Bell Calvert in *The Private Memoirs and Confessions of the Justified Sinner*, a fallen woman from the upper class. Hogg's intention was to show life as it is. In defence of his choice, it could be argued that it was important that young privileged women knew the reality of female life at the other end of the social spectrum, if they wanted to grow into valuable mothers of the nation who would have to protect the children from all walks of life.

Though Mary McFarlane has fallen, she demonstrates a resilience in the face of adversity that renders her worthwhile of her father's forgiveness: 'she is mine own pairn, and I will pe sharing my last penny with her. I knowed my Mary was a good girl at heart. But och! tese mens! tese mens!' (Ibid., p. 161). This is the forgiving father that Hogg had already portrayed in a few of his previous works such as *Mador of the Moor*, *The Profligate Princes*, and *The Three Perils of Woman* (see Chapters 2 and 4), where they accept their daughter's illegitimate pregnancy. Likewise, in 'Tales of Fathers and Daughters', Duncan consider his daughter worthwhile of redemption: 'Then making his daughter to kneel on the carpet, he laid both his hands first on her head and then on her son's, and blessed them both in Gaelic, in the name of the Holy Trinity' (Ibid., p. 163). He hence makes his return to the Highlands, delighted by how events have turned in his daughter's favour, as her union with the Hon. Mr. Ward is recognised as legal by the Scottish law.

As in *Mador of the Moor*, in 'Tales of Fathers and Daughters' Hogg defies a supposedly unproblematic political union by joining two characters from the peripheries of Britain; though belonging to two opposite social backgrounds, they well deserve to be united in lawful marriage:

> The cause was tried before the Court of Session. [...] and four witnesses having deposed that he [Mr Ward] acknowledged her [Mary] as his wife, and lived with her as such, the case scarcely bore a hearing. [...] and the Court Lords agreed unanimously that Mary was Mr. Ward's lawful wedded wife, and his son his legal heir.
>
> Ibid.

Eventually, the union is blessed by Lord Ward too, who appreciates Mary's moral values and is able to sympathise sincerely with her situation for his 'heart had been greatly moved by Mary's beauty and distress, and the wrong she had suffered' (Ibid.). Lord Ward thus accepts Mary McFarlane as the lawful wife to his son—whom she has transformed into a true gentleman—thereby acknowledging this Highland maid as a valuable mother of the British nation.

This chapter has highlighted Hogg's significant presence in the American periodical and newspaper press of the first half of the nineteenth century, exposing how a more lenient perception of norms of politeness moved the reviewers' attention to Hogg's talent as a writer. Hogg's humble origins and incredible writing career assumed an important political agenda in those periodicals that advocated the end of slavery and the emancipation of African American citizens through education. North American democratic ideals also enabled Hogg to re-engage with his own re-interpretation of the marriage plot, promoting true love, forgiveness and redemption through a socially and ethnically diverse society, both in Britain and the growing United States of America.

CHAPTER 7

Conclusion: Reflecting on Hogg's Position in the Literary Canon

This project had two aims: to trace how Hogg challenged stereotypes of gender, class and ethnicity in his work; and to show how new trends in the linguistic field of pragmatics, particularly discursive (im)politeness theory, can be used productively for the analysis of literary works, especially when the author engages with the criticism of social issues outwith the text at the time of writing. In the specific case of Hogg's work, discursive (im)politeness theory contextualised with the support of historical sources has shown theoretically Hogg's strategic use of language and narrative techniques, thereby shedding new light on why he parodied gender stereotypes, and on the ways in which these stereotypes then interacted with norms of class and ethnicity during emerging discourses of empire.

Being a self-educated author of humble origins, Hogg spoke from a position outside the Scottish literary elite. Paradoxically, this aspect allowed him to write more freely about the important issues of his age, including gender politics and Britain's imperial aims, which he revealed by voicing characters from the margins. Chapter 2 has shown that Hogg did not shy away from the Edinburgh prostitution scandal of 1823, nor from critiquing the behaviour of the British elite towards 'subaltern' classes. Indeed, Hogg's characters include some very memorable, proactive women from the margins such as Clifford in 'Basil Lee', Bell Calvert in the *Confessions*, and the title character in 'Tibby Hyslop's Dream'. Yet early critics condemned Hogg's choice of subjects as too 'indelicate' for genteel audiences, and viewed his innovative narrative experiments as outrageous violations of literary decorum. Hogg's diverse texts, however, are remarkable for the alternatives they offered to the writing of the literary establishment of his day, including Walter Scott. Hogg's style was received rather negatively because it infringed the rules of bourgeois readers' expectations; however, his persistence in addressing the same issues over and over again shows that his aim went beyond challenging those expectations.

Hogg voiced a different reality from the one represented in the national tale, thus challenging the assumptions upon which the identity of the middle classes (the emerging classes of the British Empire) was constructed. Today, Hogg's texts are being republished in their unbowdlerised versions to both critical and popular acclaim, and his works have been favourably received on

© KONINKLIJKE BRILL NV, LEIDEN, 2022 | DOI:10.1163/9789004519992_008

the part of postmodern, postcolonial, and posthuman critics because they mirror twentieth- and twenty-first-century critiques of class, gender, and ethnicity. Surprisingly, despite Hogg's engagement with these aspects in his works, with the exception of Alker and Nelson's research on Hogg as working-class author (2009), there has been no substantial study of the interrelation between such aspects in Hogg's works. This book hence contributes to revealing Hogg's sophisticated approach to class, gender, race, and ethnicity in relation to early nineteenth-century discourses of empire, redressing a significant gap in Hogg studies.

This book shows that in Hogg's oeuvre there is a subtle thread that appears and re-appears in most of his works: Hogg's distinctive re-interpretation of the marriage plot that in his contemporary context served to re-affirm the political union of the British nations through the marriage of the central protagonists in the national tale. Hogg provided a more realistic re-interpretation of this narrative tool, addressing the reality of the entire British social spectrum and exposing issues related to class, gender, race, and ethnicity. His proactive female characters questioned the ideology inherent in the conventional heroine portrayed as a symbol of the nation—a politicised female character that invoked the ideology of a civilising mother country, particularly in the dichotomy with the figure of the fallen angel.

Chapter 3 has demonstrated how Hogg questioned the cult of Highland masculinity based on ethnographic conceptualisations of strength and endurance, thereby interrogating the imperial militaristic discourse that caused the death of so many young men in the name of British patriotism during the Napoleonic Wars. On the other hand, Chapters 2, 4, and 5 have revealed how Hogg consistently exploited the motif of rape in order to expose the economic value of women's chastity at all social levels. Chapters 4 and 5 have shown how Hogg played with the two stereotypes of delicate and transgressive heroine, sometimes merging them in one single character, thereby creating unorthodox symbols for the Scottish nation. Chapter 6 closes the book's exploration of the marriage plot in Hogg's oeuvre, with Hogg's reinvention of a politically democratic marriage plot specifically for an American audience.

Going beyond late twentieth-century feminist research into gender performativity, this book has engaged with new insights into the eclectic linguistic field of pragmatics applied to literature, using especially (im)politeness theories and viewing Bakhtin's notions of *heteroglossia* and dialogism as a literary pragmatics in its embryonic phase. Exposing power relations in gender, class, race, and ethnicity through (im)politeness theory, social deixis, and Bakhtin's socio-linguistics, this book has traced how emerging discourses of British Empire contributed to the construction of *heteroglot* voices in Hogg's work, and how Hogg then voiced his own personal view about these power relations in the dominant discourse.

Chapter 2 has shown how in *Perils of Man*, Hogg briefly hints at the celebration of the royal wedding between Princess Margaret and Lord Douglas, while conferring a longer narrative space to the comical performances of the friar's mule infuriated at the vain behaviour of one of the knights. Hogg then counteracts the symbolic significance of the royal wedding through the fantastic marriages between the witches and the devil. The hyperbolic and carnivalesque description of the old wives' terrifying deaths following their wedding dashes any hope of happiness in the royal marriages. It also demonstrates how, in 'Perils Two' and 'Three' of *Perils of Woman*, Hogg goes back to Culloden in 1745, retracing the negative consequences of the battle that determined the collapse of the Highland clans and the beginning of the Scottish Clearances. Hogg depicts a cyclical history which reiterates the same human errors rather than one which evolves in progressive stages, both in the battle of Culloden as well as during the Napoleonic Wars. Hogg shows that Sally Niven's marriage of convenience leads to her death, portraying the negative effects of the battle of Culloden on the neglected corpses of this female protagonist and her little daughter, thus presenting this tragic imagery as a metaphor for a Scottish nation without a promising future—a nation whose social contradictions cannot be healed in political union with England.

Chapter 3 has shown how the song 'Donald Macdonald' (1807) parodies the mystique of the Highlander by displaying a soldier so manipulated by ideological assumptions of loyalty that he would offer his soul to the devil for King George in the Napoleonic Wars. In *Perils of Woman*, Rickleton is an honourable model of sentimental masculinity, evolving from untamed to sensible man, and then truly sympathising with his wife by accepting her son (conceived with a previous lover) as his own. The long poem 'Wat o' the Cleuch', a parody of Walter Scott's poetic style, deconstructs the English stereotype of the avaricious middle-class Scottish Lowlander by exposing the reality of a Lowland Scots from the social margins, whose robberies and fixation on meat symbolise the exploitation of the peasantry by the Lowland upper and middle classes—those who were really prospering in the British Union. In *Perils of Man*, the combat between English and Scots in Roxburgh castle, with the imagery of the pulsating heap of dying warriors evoking the tragic consequences of war, conveys an implicit critique of the Napoleonic Wars: soldiers are manipulated by ideologies of ethnic difference to fight (at the expense of their life) for the economic gain of a few privileged men.

Chapter 4 has argued that, in early nineteenth-century Britain, women's chastity was an important commodity at all levels of society. Among the higher classes, it guaranteed that property was not transferred to an illegitimate child (Mitchison and Leneman 1998: 81); while among female servants, a good reputation was of the utmost importance when looking for employment in a respectable family (Symonds 1997: 2). The value of women's chastity therefore affected both higher- and lower-class women's sexuality: the former were confined within the domestic sphere; while the reputation of the latter was constantly threatened by the sexual desire of the male bourgeoisie, a tool at the latter's disposal for containing the freedom of female servants to move between public and private spheres (Wills 2001: 94). Hogg counteracted the idealised representation of the devoted and loving heroine by exposing the reality of women living in the margins of Lowland Scotland. Here, in the early nineteenth century, birth control was not an option, and women had to deal with more pragmatic solutions. Illegitimate motherhood, infanticide, and prostitution affected the lives of a number of women not just among the lower classes. Hogg's more realistic portrayal, however, questioned the ideology inherent in contemporary representations of the delicate heroine who symbolised the civilising mother of the British nation.

Through analysis of *Mador of the Moor*, Chapter 4 has exposed the reality of two women from different social backgrounds: Ila Moore, the daughter of a poor farm tenant, and Matilda, a lady from the gentry. Both women react in opposite ways to their illegitimate pregnancy: rather than committing a crime, Ila faces public repentance and keeps her child; while Matilda commits infanticide, so as not to tarnish the honour of her family's name and to keep the economic value of her supposed chastity. Hogg's contemporary critics were outraged by Hogg's suggestions. His use of the supernatural dimension to show the power of the fairies; the supposed unnecessary murder of the courtiers for plot development; and the obscure language of the song of the fairies have important functions in Hogg's poem. Hogg wanted to expose the strict morality of the Scottish Kirk through the plight of Ila, while simultaneously questioning the idealised heroine as symbol of a civilising mother country through the reality experienced by Matilda who kills her child. Hogg then presents his own version of the marriage plot, by having Ila Moore, the daughter of a poor farm tenant but a lady at heart, married to the King of Scotland, the father of her child.

'Maria's Tale' blatantly voices the hardships of a female servant who loses her chastity, and hence her employment, after having being seduced and made pregnant by her master's son who later abandons her. During his life, Hogg published this tale three times without revision, despite the negative reception of his contemporary reviewers who felt outraged by the issues he addressed. Nevertheless, Hogg seems to have been more interested in poising Maria's story as a cautionary tale to expose the reality of female servants and not at all concerned about the consequences for not respecting his reviewers' expectations of literary decorum. On the contrary, in 'Maria's Tale' Hogg portrays this female servant freely circulating between domestic and public spheres. Her independence, however, posed a threat to the male bourgeois identity. For this reason, Maria is tamed (seduced) and then expelled (abandoned).

In the *Confessions*, Hogg deconstructs the cultural dichotomy between the fallen angel and the pure heroine symbol of the nation by merging these two stereotypes in one single character: Bell Calvert, a prostitute from the margins whose beautiful English marks a far different social origin. In addition, rather than leaving this controversial heroine in the background, Hogg has her counteract the reliability of the Editor, the narrator of the first part of the book, a prototype of the Edinburgh literary elite of his time.

Chapter 5 has further exposed how Hogg interrogates the marriage plot. In the tale 'Tibby Hyslop's Dream', Hogg sets spinsterhood as a dignified solution to marriage when there are no heroes. The male characters of this short story are only interested in abusing Tibby's body—a metaphor for the Scottish land exploited by selfish masters and a symbol of the gender grievances from which women of the peasant class suffered in the Scottish Borders in the early nineteenth century. Female servants had to defend their chastity to keep their reputation, but could also lose their position if they did not yield to their masters' amorous requests.

In the mock-epic *Queen Hynde*, the narrator in the person of the Ettrick Shepherd (namely Hogg) addresses directly his negative reviewers and bourgeois ladies, presenting Wene (the secondary heroine) as a double symbol for middle-class women's freedom from false assumptions of propriety and as a symbol for Hogg's own intellectual freedom to portray women as they are and not as they should be, thereby refuting the principles of literary decorum established by his contemporary reviewers. Hogg then engages in his own re-elaboration of the marriage plot by having Queen Hynde, the primary heroine, marry the king of Ireland when disguised as a poor peasant because he is the only male character who behaves honourably and heroically, defending the Queen from the Scandinavian invasion, while the male characters of the upper class do not attempt to defy King Eric, the terrible Norse king.

The last chapter of this book portrays the stature of Hogg beyond Scotland, highlighting the profound legacy of the Ettrick Shepherd in North America. It closes the book in a circular way, by contrasting the American far more favourable reception of Hogg with British reviewers and weighing the important political significance that Hogg played during the period of abolitionism and emancipation from slavery in North America. Hogg was an important example of democracy for newly freed African Americans and an inspiration for self-made men in a period where the ideals of the American dream were emerging and providing hope to the Scots who emigrated there. Analysis of the marriage plot in Hogg's 'Tales of Fathers and Daughters', which he especially wrote with a multi-ethnic American audience in mind, concludes the chapter, further highlighting the weight of Hogg's democratic values in early nineteenth-century North America.

This book has therefore shown that a cultural and historical contextualisation of (im)politeness theory offers an evaluative tool for discussing theoretically the author's intentions and the readers' reception of those supposed intentions. Both the production and the perception of (im)politeness are a non-fixed continuum which changes through time, and which norms of class, gender, race, and ethnicity influence enormously: issues about prostitution and illegitimate pregnancy treated by Hogg may be acceptable to a reader of the twenty-first century; yet the British reviewers of Hogg's time perceived the same topics as unacceptable. Hogg's failed observance of politeness principles, however, did not merely threaten social taboos but it also questioned British assumptions about progress and civilisation in the mother country.

Brown and Levinson (1987) have developed politeness theories for face-to-face communication between two individuals, and only recently research in this field has focused on the dynamic within 'communities of practice', namely on the perception and evaluation of politeness by small groups of people (Mills 2003). This book utilises discursive (im)politeness theory to explore the power relations at the level of social discourse among the Edinburgh literary elite, and Scottish reviewers in particular, in the early nineteenth century, who controlled what could be published according to their sense of propriety. New research should hence be developed into how both the production and the perception of literary politeness are influenced by historically conditioned norms of gender, class, race, ethnicity, age, education and so forth, and into how an author can then challenge such norms for critical purposes. The potential of this phenomenon is enormous for literary criticism in Scottish literature and postcolonial studies, as well as for those literatures whose goal is to voice realities other than the socially accepted ones, as in Hogg's case.

Bakhtin's novelistic dialogism can be considered as a discursive (im)politeness theory in its embryonic stage because carnivalesque and *heteroglot* voices challenge the rules of literary politeness by distancing themselves from what is considered to be the centripetal language of the dominant discourse. At the same time, however, *heteroglot* voices reveal a different reality of the world outwith the text, thereby exposing that perceptions of acceptable language and behaviour—what is defined as Englishness—only represent the dominant side of the social spectrum. English contemporary critics received Hogg's use of the Scots language rather negatively, judging it beyond their comprehension. Even so, Hogg persisted in voicing characters from the margins in broad Scots, and not for mere purposes of comic effects.

The reactions to Hogg's supposed intentions by the critics of his time were prejudiced by Hogg's social origin. In the last issue of his weekly magazine *The Spy*, Hogg wrote that 'as his name became known the number of his subscribers diminished. The learned, the enlightened, and polite circles of this flourishing metropolis, disdained either to be amused or instructed by the ebullitions of humble genius' (2000: 514). In her introduction to Hogg's periodical, Gillian Hughes observes that

> [that was] a time when standards of politeness and delicacy were shifting rapidly towards later Victorian prudery' [...and] 'The Spy's Farewell to his Readers' also reveals that Hogg had utilised the work of his predecessors in the essay periodical in another way to expose the prejudices to which he was subject as a self-educated rustic.
>
> 2000a: xxxii

In the same periodical, Hogg reflects on the 'impossibility of pleasing everybody', arguing that

> [s]ince I began to publish The Spy, I am certain I have conversed with an [*sic*] hundred people about the best manner of conducting it, some who knew me, and some who did not; and I think there has never been three of them who proposed the same thing, or the same subjects: so as I find it is impossible to please every body, I will in future endeavour only to please myself; which I am convinced every writer must first do, before he can please others.
>
> 2000: 189

Though Hogg failed to meet the expectations of a number of early nineteenth-century reviewers, he did not fail to please his own wishes, in so doing fulfilling the expectations of postmodern and postcolonial critics, as well as those of twenty-first centsury readers, more concerned as they are with human rights and democratic values.

Bibliography

Works by James Hogg (in chronological order)

Hogg, James [J.H. Craig of Douglas]. 1814. 'Preface', in James Hogg (auth.), *The Hunting of Badlewe: A Dramatic Tale* (London: Colburn), pp. v–viii.

Hogg, James. 1816. 'Wat o' the Cleuch', in *The Poetic Mirror* (London: Longman, Hurst, Rees, Orme, and Brown; Edinburgh: John Ballantyne), pp. 55–129 <http://books.google.com> [accessed 6 December 2012].

Hogg, James. 1835. 'Bruce and the Spider', *Virginia Free Press* (Charlestown), 16 April, p. n/a.

Hogg, James. 1835. 'Emigration', *New-England Galaxy*, 27 June, p. 4, from *Chamber's Edinburgh Magazine* of 18 May 1833.

Hogg, James. 1839. 'Try Again', *The Emancipator* (New York), 11 April 1839, p. 202.

Hogg, James. 1976 [1818]. *The Brownie of Bodsbeck*, ed. by Douglas S. Mack (Edinburgh: Scottish Academic Press).

Hogg, James. 1985 [1831–1832]. 'On the Changes in the Habits, Amusements and Condition of the Scottish Peasantry', in *A Shepherd's Delight: A James Hogg Anthology*, ed. by Judy Steel (Edinburgh: Canongate), pp. 40–51.

Hogg, James. 1996 [1822]. *The Three Perils of Man: War, Women and Witchcraft*, ed. by Douglas Gifford (Edinburgh: Canongate Classics).

Hogg, James. 1997 [1834]. *A Series of Lay Sermons on Good Principles and Good Breeding*, ed. by Gillian Hughes (Edinburgh: Edinburgh University Press).

Hogg, James. 1998 [1825]. *Queen Hynde*, ed. by Suzanne Gilbert and Douglas S. Mack (Edinburgh: Edinburgh University Press).

Hogg, James. 2000 [1810–1811]. *The Spy: A Periodical of Literary Amusement and Instruction*, written by Hogg and others, ed. by Gillian Hughes (Edinburgh: Edinburgh University Press).

Hogg, James. 2002 [1829]. 'Tibby Hyslop's Dream, and the Sequel', in *The Shepherd Calendar*, ed. by Douglas S. Mack (Edinburgh: Edinburgh University Press), pp. 142–62.

Hogg, James. 2002 [1824]. *The Private Memoirs and Confessions of a Justified Sinner*, ed. by Peter D. Garside (Edinburgh: Edinburgh University Press).

Hogg, James. 2002 [1823]. *The Three Perils of Woman; or Love, Leasing, and Jealousy: A Series of Domestic Scottish Tales*, ed. by Antony Hasler and Douglas S. Mack (Edinburgh: Edinburgh University Press).

Hogg, James. 2004 [1834]. *Anecdotes of Scott*, ed. by Jill Rubenstein (Edinburgh: Edinburgh University Press).

Hogg, James. 2004a [1820]. 'Cousin Mattie', in *Winter Evening Tales*, ed. by Ian Duncan (Edinburgh: Edinburgh University Press), pp. 433–41.

Hogg, James. 2004b [1820]. 'Maria's Tale: Written by Herself', in *Winter Evening Tales*, ed. by Ian Duncan (Edinburgh: Edinburgh University Press), pp. 151–58.

Hogg, James. 2004–08. *The Collected Letters of James Hogg*, ed. by Gillian Hughes, associate editors Douglas S. Mack, Robin MacLachlan and Elaine Petrie, 3 vols (Edinburgh: Edinburgh University Press).

Hogg, James. 2005 [1813]. *The Queen's Wake*, ed. by Douglas S. Mack (Edinburgh: Edinburgh University Press).

Hogg, James. 2005 [1816]. *Mador of the Moor*, ed. by James E. Barcus (Edinburgh: Edinburgh University Press.

Hogg, James. 2005 [1832]. 'Memoirs of the Author's Life', in *Altrive Tales*, ed. by Gillian Hughes (Edinburgh: Edinburgh University Press), pp. 11–52.

Hogg, James. 2007. 'Donald Macdonald', in *The Mountain Bard*, ed. by Suzanne Gilbert (Edinburgh: Edinburgh University Press), pp. 108–09.

Hogg, James. 2010. 'An Essay on Sheep-Farming and Population', in *Highland Journeys*, ed. by H. B. de Groot (Edinburgh: Edinburgh University Press), pp. 195–223.

Hogg, James. 2020 [1835]. '[For the Zodiac] Tales of Fathers and Daughters. By the Ettrick Shepherd', in *Contributions to English, Irish, and American Periodicals*, ed. by Adrian Hunter with Barbara Leonardi (Edinburgh: Edinburgh University Press), pp. 144–63.

Historical Criticism on Hogg (in alphabetical order by title of work and periodical in which they appeared)

Great Britain

'[Review of] *The Brownie of Bodsbeck*'. 1818. *Clydesdale Magazine*, 1, May, pp. 24–28.

'[Review of] *The Jacobite Relics of Scotland (First Series)*'. 1820. *Edinburgh Review*, 34, August, pp. 148–60.

'[Review of] *Mador of the Moor*'. 1817. *Antijacobin Review*, 52, June, pp. 328–35.

'[Review of] *Mador of the Moor*'. 1816. *British Lady's Magazine*, 4, October, pp. 251–55.

'[Review of] *Mador of the Moor*'. 1816. *Champion*, 9 June, pp. 181–82.

'[Review of] *Mador of the Moor*'. 1816. *Critical Review*, 5th ser., 4, August, pp. 130–43.

'[Review of] *Mador of the Moor*'. 1817. *Eclectic Review*, 2nd ser., 7, February, pp. 174–79.

'[Review of] *Mador of the Moor*'. 1816. *Monthly Review*, 81, December 1816, pp. 438–40.

'[Review of] *Mador of the Moor*'. 1816. *Literary Panorama*, n.s., 4, August, pp. 731–40.

'[Review of] *Mador of the Moor*'. 1816. *Scots Magazine*, 78, June, pp. 448–51.

'[Review of] *The Mountain Bard*'. 1807. *Literary Panorama*, 2, August, pp. 957–60.

'[Review of] *Pilgrims of the Sun*'. 1815. *The Eclectic Review*, n.s., 3, March, pp. 280–91.

'[Review of] *The Poetic Mirror*'. 1816. *Eclectic Review*, 2nd ser., 6, November, pp. 507–11.

'[Review of] *The Poetic Mirror*'. 1816. *Quarterly Review*, 15, July, pp. 468–75.

'[Review of] *The Private Memoirs and Confessions of a Justified Sinner*', *British Critic*, n.s., 22, July 1824, pp. 68–80.

'[Review of] *The Private Memoirs and Confessions of a Justified Sinner*'. 1824. *The Ladies' Monthly Museum*, 20, p. 106.

'[Review of] *The Private Memoirs and Confessions of a Justified Sinner*. 1824. *London Literary Gazette*, Saturday 17 July, pp. 449–51.

'[Review of] *The Private Memoirs and Confessions of a Justified Sinner*'. 1824. *Monthly Critical Gazette*, 1, pp. 436–38.

'[Review of] *The Private Memoirs and Confessions of a Justified Sinner*'. 1824. *New Monthly Magazine*, 12, p. 506.

'[Review of] *The Private Memoirs and Confessions of a Justified Sinner*. 1824. *Westminster Review*, 2, pp. 560–62.

'[Review of] *Queen Hynde*'. 1825. *Lady's Magazine*, n.s., 6, p. 97.

'[Review of] *Queen Hynde*'. 1824. *Literary Gazette*, 414, pp. 817–19.

'[Review of] *Queen Hynde*'. 1825. *Monthly Critical Gazette*, 2, pp. 343–47.

'[Review of] *Queen Hynde*'. 1825. *Philomatic Journal*, 3, pp. 161–205.

'[Review of] *Queen Hynde*'. 1825. *Westminster Review*, 3, pp. 531–37.

'[Review of] *The Three Perils of Man*'. 1822. *Monthly Censor*, 1, pp. 467–69.

[John Wilson?] '[Review of] *The Three Perils of Woman*'. 1823. *Blackwood's Edinburgh Magazine*, 14, pp. 427–37.

'[Review of] *The Three Perils of Woman*'. 1823. *British Critic*, n.s., 20, pp. 357–61.

'[Review of] *The Three Perils of Woman*'. 1823. *The British Magazine*, 1, pp. 364–74.

'[Review of] *The Three Perils of Woman*'. 1823. *Literary Chronicle*, 228, 27 September, pp. 615–16.

'[Review of] *The Three Perils of Woman*'. 1823. *Literary Gazette*, 345, pp. 546–48.

'[Review of] *Winter Evening Tales*'. 1820. *Blackwood's Edinburgh Magazine*, 7, pp. 148–54.

'[Review of] *Winter Evening Tales*'. 1820. *British Critic*, n.s., 13, pp. 622–31.

'[Review of] *Winter Evening Tales*'. 1820. *Monthly Review*, n.s., 93, November, pp. 263–67.

'[Review of] *Winter Evening Tales*'. 1820. *The Scotsman*, 29 April, pp. 143–44.

North America

'ART. I. 1. *The Queen's Wake; a legendary Poem by James Hogg*. 2. *The Pilgrims of the Sun; a Poem by James Hogg, author of the Queen's Wake*. 3. *Mador of the Moor; a Poem by James Hogg, author of the Queen's Wake, &c.* 4. *The Brownie of Bodsbeck; and other tales by James Hogg, author of the Queen's Wake, & c.*'. 1819. *North American Review and Miscellaneous Journal*, 1st June 1819, pp. 1–23.

'Biographical Sketches. The Ettrick Shepherd'. 1836. *The Cincinnati Mirror*, 19 March, pp. 57–58.

De Witt Bloodgood, Simeon. 1834. 'Sketch of the Life of Hogg', in *Familiar Anecdotes of Sir Walter Scott*, written by James Hogg (New York: Harpers & Brothers), pp. 7–118.

G. 1818. 'ART. 2. *The Brownie of Bodsbeck; and other Tales. By JAMES HOGG, Author of "The Queen's Wake," "Pilgrims of the Sun," &c. &c. pp. 220. New York. Wiley & Co.'*, *American Monthly Magazine & Critical Review* (New York), 1st September, pp. 334–54.

'James Hogg, the Ettrick Shepherd'. 1836. *The Cincinnati Mirror*, 27 February, p. 34, from London's *Athenaeum* of 5 December.

'James Hogg, the Ettrick Shepherd: "Sweet poet of the woods! A long adieu!"'. 1836. *The Museum of Foreign Literature and Science*, 1st December, pp. 394–96.

'On the Genius of Hogg'. 1825. *Minerva* (New York), 20 August 1825, pp. 315–16.

'[Review of] *Familiar Anecdotes of Sir Walter Scott—By James Hogg, the Ettrick Shepherd, with a sketch of his life, by S. De Witt Bloodgood—New York, Harpers & Brothers*'. 1834. *New York Spectator*, 26 May, p. n/a.

'[Review of] *The Queen's Wake: a legendary poem, by James Hogg. Boston, republished by Wells and Lilly, pp. 257*'. 1815. *The North American Review and Miscellaneous Journal*, vol. 2, no. 4, 1st November, pp. 103–109.

'Review of New Books. *Altrive Tales*, collected among the peasantry of Scotland'. 1834. *The Journal of Belles Lettres*, 8 April, pp. 1–3.

'[Review of] *Sermons* by the Ettrick Shepherd'. 1834. *The Albion, A Journal of News, Politics and Literature*, 19 July, p. 227–28, from the *London Literary Gazette* of 26 April 1934.

'[Review of] *The Shepherd's Calendar*. By JAMES HOGG, Author of The Queen's Wake, &c. &c. 2 vols. 12mo. New-York republished, 1829. A. T. Goodrich, and others'. 1829. *Critic*, 16 May, p. 31.

'[Review of] *The Shepherd's Calendar*. By James Hogg, Author of The Queen's Wake, &c. In two volumes. New York: 1829'. 1829. *The Southern Literary Gazette*, vol. 1, no. 3, pp. 52–54.

'Some Particulars Relative to the Ettrick Shepherd'. 1836. *The Albion, A Journal of News, Politics and Literature*, 19 March, p. 89.

'Songs by Mr. Hogg'. 1831. *The Albion, A Journal of News, Politics and Literature*, 19 February, p. 292, from the *London Literary Gazette* of 1 January 1831, pp. 5–6.

'The Ettrick Shepherd'. 1831. *Atheneum; or Spirit of the English Magazine* (Boston), 1 March, pp. 513–16.

'The Ettrick Shepherd'. 1835. *Atkinson's Casket*. March, p. 130.

'The Ettrick Shepherd'. 1834. *The Philadelphia Album and Ladies' Literary Portfolio*, 10 May, p. 149.

'The Ettrick Shepherd and Other Scotch Poets'. 1829. *The American Monthly Magazine*, vol. 1, November, pp. 522–30.

'The Ettrick Shepherd: To the Sky Lark'. 1835. *Zion's Herald*, 15 April, p. 59.

'A visit to Hogg, the Ettrick Shepherd'. 1834. *Philadelphia Album and Ladies' Literary Portfolio*, 23 Aug, p. 270, from *The American Monthly Magazine* of 1 April 1834, p. 85.

Secondary Sources

Akbar, Na'im. 2009. 'The Conquest of African American Educational Performance', in *Educating African American Students: Foundation, Curriculum, and Experience*, ed. by Abul Pitre and others (Lanham: Rowman & Littlefield), pp. 19–32.

Alker, Sharon, and Holly Faith Nelson. 2001. 'Marginal Voices and Transgressive Borders in Hogg's Epic *Queen Hynde*', *Studies in Hogg and his World*, 12: 25–39.

Alker, Sharon, and Holly Faith Nelson. 2006. 'James Hogg as Working-Class Autobiographer: Tactical Manoeuvres in a "Memoir of the Author's Life"', *Studies in Hogg and his World*, 17: 63–80.

Alker, Sharon, and Holly Faith Nelson. *James Hogg and the Literary Marketplace: Scottish Romanticism and the Working-Class Author*, ed. by Sharon Alker and Holly Faith Nelson (Farnham: Ashgate).

Alker, Sharon, and Holly Faith Nelson. 2009. 'Introduction', in *James Hogg and the Literary Marketplace: Scottish Romanticism and the Working-Class Author*, ed. by Sharon Alker and Holly Faith Nelson (Farnham: Ashgate), pp. 1–20.

Anderson, Benedict. 2006 [1983]. *Imagined Communities* (London: Verso).

Anderson-Currie, Stephanie. 1993. *Preliminary Census of Early Hogg Editions in North American Libraries*, compiled by S. Anderson-Currie, South Carolina Working Papers in Scottish Bibliography, 3 (Department of English, University of South Carolina).

An Anti-Papist. 1757. 'Letter to the Author of the *Scots Magazine*', *Scots Magazine*, 19, 9 February, pp. 80–82.

Arnot, Hugo. 1785. *Collection and Abridgement of Celebrated Criminal Trials in Scotland, 1536–1784* (Edinburgh).

Atkinson, David. 1992. 'History, Symbol, and Meaning in "The Cruel Mother"', *Folk Music Journal*, 6·3: 359–80.

Bakhtin, Mikhail M. 1981. *The Dialogic Imagination: Four Essays*, ed. by Michael Holquist, trans. by Caryl Emerson and Michael Holquist (Austin: University of Texas Press).

Bennet, Andrew and Nicholas Royle. 1978. *Introduction to Literature, Criticism and Theory*, 2nd edn (Prentice Hall Europe).

Barcus, James E. 1995. '"When Beauty Gives Command, all Mankind must Obey!": Gender Roles in Hogg's *Mador of the Moor*', *Studies in Hogg and his World*, 6: 33–49.

Barcus, James E. 2005. 'Introduction', in *Mador of the Moor*, written by James Hogg, ed. by James E. Barcus (Edinburgh: Edinburgh University Press), pp. xi–xlii.

Berger, Dieter A. 1988. 'James Hogg as a Parodist in Verse: *The Poetic Mirror*', in *Papers Given at the Second James Hogg Society Conference, Edinburgh 1985*, ed. by Gillian Hughes (Aberdeen), pp. 79–96.

Blair, Kirstie. 2013. 'Introduction', in *Class and the Canon: Constructing Labouring-Class Poetry and Poetics, 1750–1900*, ed. by Kirstie Blair and Mina Gorji (Basingstoke: Palgrave Macmillan), pp. 1–15.

Berger, John. 1972. *Ways of Seeing* (London: Penguin Books).

Bloedé, Barbara. 1992. '*The Three Perils of Woman* and the Edinburgh Prostitution Scandal of 1823: A Reply to Dr Groves', *Studies in Hogg and his World*, 3: 88–94.

Bold, Valentina. 1992. 'Traditional Narrative Elements in *The Three Perils of Woman*', *Studies in Hogg and his World*, 3: 42–56.

Bold, Valentina. 2007. *James Hogg: A Bard of Nature's Making* (Oxford: Peter Lang).

Braun, Heather. 2005. 'The Seductive Masquerade of *The Wild Irish Girl*: Disguising Political Fears in Sydney Owenson's National Tale', *Irish Studies Review*, 3.1: 33–43.

Brown, Callum G. 2006. 'Religion', in *Gender in Scottish History since 1700*, ed. by Lynn Abrams and others (Edinburgh: Edinburgh University Press), pp. 84–110.

Brown, J. Stewart. 2012. 'Religion and Society to c. 1900', in *The Oxford Handbook of Modern Scottish History*, ed. by T. M. Devine and J. Wormald (Oxford: Oxford University Press), pp. 78–98.

Brownstein, Rachel M. 2015. 'Character and Caricature: Jane Austen and James Gillray', *Persuasions*, 37: 86–100.

Burke, Edmund. 1982. *Reflections on the Revolution in France*, ed. by Conor Cruise O'Brien (Harmondsworth: Penguin, 1982).

Camden, Jennifer. 2010. *Secondary Heroines in Nineteenth-Century British and American Novels* (Farnham: Ashgate).

Chambers, J. D. 1972. *Population, Economy and Society in Pre-Industrial England* (London: Oxford University Press).

Child, Francis James (ed.). 1957. *The English and Scottish Popular Ballads*, 5 vols (New York: The Folklore Press in Association with Pageant Book Company).

Christie, Christine. 2000. *Gender and Language: Towards a Feminist Pragmatics* (Edinburgh: Edinburgh University Press).

Cohen, Stephen. 2007. 'Introduction', in *Shakespeare and Historical Formalism*, ed. by Stephen Cohen (Aldershot: Ashgate), pp. 1–27.

A Country Elder. 1757. 'Letter to the Author of the *Scots Magazine*', *Scots Magazine*, 19, August, pp. 401–02.

Craig, Sheryl. 2015. *Jane Austen and the State of the Nation* (Basingstoke: Palgrave Macmillan).

Cramond, W. 1888. *Illegitimacy in Banffshire* (Banff).

Culpeper, Jonathan. 1996. 'Towards an Anatomy of Impoliteness', *Journal of Pragmatics*, 25: 349–67.

Culpeper, J., D. Bousfield, and A. Wichmann. 2003. 'Impoliteness Revisited: With Special Reference to Dynamic and Prosodic Aspects', *Journal of Pragmatics*, 35: 1545–79. https://doi.org/10.1016/S0378-2166(02)00118-2.

Currie, Janette. date n/a. *A Listing of Hogg Items in the American Periodical Press*, James Hogg Research Website, available from <http://www.jameshogg.stir.ac.uk> [accessed 30 September 2014].

Currie, Janette. (date n/a). 'Hogg in the Zodiac: From Altrive to Albany; James Hogg's Transatlantic Publication (i)', James Hogg Research Website, available from <http://www.jameshogg.stir.ac.uk> [accessed 30 September 2014].

Currie, Janette. 2009a. 'The "Banshee" and "The Rose of Plora"', *Studies in Hogg and His World* 17 (2009), 145–65.

Currie, Janette. 2009b. 'Hogg and the American Literary Marketplace', in *James Hogg and the Literary Marketplace: Scottish Romanticism and the Working-Class Author*, ed. by Sharon Alker and Holly Faith Nelson (Farnham: Ashgate), pp. 219–34.

Currie, Janette. 2010. '"Betwixt the Devil and the Deep Sea": Hogg's Harris Venture', in *Highland Journeys*, written by James Hogg, ed. by H. B. de Groot (Edinburgh: Edinburgh University Press), pp. 231–42.

Devine, T. M. 2004 [2003]. *Scotland's Empire 1600–1815* (London: Penguin Books).

Devine, T. M. 2006a [1999]. 'Highlandism and Scottish Identity', in *The Scottish Nation 1700–2000*, written by T. M. Devine (London: Penguin Books), pp. 231–45.

Devine, T. M. 2006b. 'The Parish State', in *The Scottish Nation: 1700–2007*, written by T. M. Devine (London: Penguin Books,), pp. 84–102.

Duncan, Ian. 1994. 'Review of The Stirling/South Carolina Edition of James Hogg, Volume 2, *The Three Perils of Woman*', *Studies in Hogg and his World*, 5: 154–57.

Duncan, Ian. 1998. 'Review of The Stirling/South Carolina Research Edition of the Collected Works of James Hogg, Volume 6, *Queen Hynde*, ed. by Suzanne Gilbert and Douglas S. Mack (Edinburgh: Edinburgh University Press, 1988)', *Studies in Hogg and his World*, 9: 137–42.

Duncan, Ian. 2004. 'Note on the Text', in *Winter Evening Tales*, written by James Hogg, ed. by Ian Duncan (Edinburgh: Edinburgh University Press), pp. 527–34.

Duncan, Ian. 2007a. 'Ireland, Scotland, and the Materials of Romanticism', in *Scotland, Ireland, and Romantic Aesthetic*, ed. by David Duff and Catherine Jones (Lewisburgh: Bucknell University Press, 2007), pp. 258–78.

Duncan, Ian. 2007b. *Scott's Shadow: The Novel in Romantic Edinburgh* (Princeton: Princeton University Press).

Duncan, Ian, and Douglas S. Mack. 2012. *Edinburgh Companion to James Hogg* (Edinburgh: Edinburgh University Press).

Eddleman, Stephanie M. 2015. 'Past the Bloom: Ageing and Beauty in the Novels of Jane Austen', *Persuasions*, 37: 129–45.

Enloe, Cynthia. 2014. *Bananas, Beaches, and Bases: Making Feminist Sense of International Politics*, 2nd revised and updated edn (Berkley: University of California Press).

Ferris, Ina. 1991. *The Achievement of Literary Authority: Gender, History, and the Waverley Novels* (Ithaca: Cornell University Press).

Ferris, Ina. 2002. *The Romantic National Tale and the Question of Ireland* (Cambridge: Cambridge University Press).

Ferris, Ina. 2009. '"On the Borders of Oblivion": Scott's Historical Novel and the Modern Time of the Remnant', *Modern Language Quarterly*, 70·4: 473–94.

Fielding, Penny. 1996. *Writing and Orality: Nationality, Culture, and Nineteenth-Century Scottish Fiction* (Oxford: Clarendon Press).

Fielding, Penny. 2011. *Scotland and the Fictions of Geography: North Britain 1760–1830* (Cambridge: Cambridge University Press).

Freedman, Jean R. 1991. 'With Child: Illegitimate Pregnancy in Scottish Traditional Ballads', *Folklore Forum*, 24·1: 3–18.

Foucault, Michel. 1990. *The History of Sexuality: An Introduction*, vol. 1, trans. by Robert Hurley (New York: Vintage Books).

Gallop, Jane. 1985. 'Keys to Dora', in *Dora's Case: Freud, Hysteria, Feminism*, ed. by C. Bernheimer and C. Kahane (New York: Columbia University Press).

Garside, Peter D. 1995. 'Introduction', in *A Queer Book*, written by James Hogg, ed. by Peter D. Garside (Edinburgh: Edinburgh University Press,), pp. xi–xxxvii.

Garside, Peter D. 2001. 'Hogg's *Confessions* and Scotland', *Studies in Hogg and his World*, 12: 118–38.

Garside, Peter D. 2006. 'The Origins and History of James Hogg's "Donald Macdonald"', *Scottish Studies Review*, 7·2: 24–39.

Gifford, Douglas. 1976. *James Hogg* (Edinburgh: The Ramsay Head Press).

Gilbert, S. M., and S. Gubar. 2000 [1979]. 'Preface to the First Edition', in *The Madwoman in the Attic: The Woman Writer and the Nineteenth-Century Literary Imagination*, written by S. M. Gilbert and S. Gubar, 2nd edn (New Haven: Yale University Press), pp. xi–xi.

Gilbert, Suzanne. 2007. 'Editorial notes to "Donald Macdonald"', in *The Mountain Bard*, written by James Hogg, ed. by Suzanne Gilbert (Edinburgh: Edinburgh University Press), pp. 454–55.

Gilbert, Suzanne. 2012. 'Hogg's Reception and Reputation', in *The Edinburgh Companion to James Hogg*, ed. by Ian Duncan and Douglas S. Mack (Edinburgh: Edinburgh University Press), pp. 37–45.

Gilbert, S., and D. S. Mack. 1998a. 'Introduction', in *Queen Hynde*, written by James Hogg, ed. by Suzanne Gilbert and Douglas S. Mack (Edinburgh: Edinburgh University Press), pp. xi–lxix.

Gilbert, S., and D. S. Mack. 1998b. 'Note on the Text', in *Queen Hynde*, written by James Hogg, ed. by Suzanne Gilbert and Douglas S. Mack (Edinburgh: Edinburgh University Press), pp. 221–34.

Goode, Mike. 2009. *Sentimental Masculinity and the Rise of History, 1790–1890* (Cambridge: Cambridge University Press).

Graham, Henry Grey. 1906. 'Religious and Ecclesiastical Life', in *The Social Life of Scotland in the Eighteenth Century*, written by Henry Grey Graham (London: Black), pp. 267–392.

Grey, J. R. Daniel. 2018. '"No Crime to Kill a Bastard–Child": Stereotypes of Infanticide in Nineteenth-Century England and Wales', in *Intersections of Gender, Class, and Race in the Long Nineteenth Century and Beyond*, ed. by Barbara Leonardi (Cham: Palgrave Macmillan), pp. 41–66.

Grice, Herbert Paul. 1989. 'Logic and Conversation', in *Studies in the Way of Words*, written by H. P. Grice (Cambridge, MA: Harvard University Press), pp. 22–40.

de Groot, H. B. 2010. 'Introduction', in *Highland Journeys*, written by James Hogg, ed. by H. B. de Groot (Edinburgh: Edinburgh University Press), pp. xi–lxvii.

Groves, David. 1982. 'Myth and Structure in James Hogg's *The Three Perils of Woman*', *The Wordsworth Circle*, 13·4: 203–10.

Groves, David. 1986. 'Stepping Back to an Early Age: James Hogg's *Three Perils of Woman* and the *Ion* of Euripides', *Studies in Scottish Literature*, 21: 176–96.

Groves, David. 1987. 'James Hogg's *Confessions* and *Three Perils of Woman* and the Edinburgh Prostitution Scandal of 1823', *The Wordsworth Circle*, 18·3: 127–31.

Groves, David. 1992. 'Urban Corruption and the Pastoral Ideal in James Hogg's *Three Perils of Woman*', *Studies in Scottish Literature*, 27: 80–88.

Harris, Jason Mark. 2003. 'National Borders, Contiguous Cultures, and Fantastic Folklore in Hogg's *The Three Perils of Man*', *Studies in Hogg and his World*, 14: 38–61.

Harris, Jason Mark. 2008. *Folklore and the Fantastic in Nineteenth-Century British Fiction* (Aldershot: Ashgate).

Hasler, Antony. 1988. 'Ingenious Lies: *The Poetic Mirror* in Context', in *Papers Given at the Second James Hogg Society Conference, Edinburgh 1985*, ed. by Gillian Hughes (Aberdeen), pp. 9–96.

Hasler, Antony. 2002. 'Introduction', in *The Three Perils of Woman*, written by James Hogg, ed. by Antony Hasler and Douglas S. Mack (Edinburgh: Edinburgh University Press), pp. xi–xliii.

Heat, James E. 1835. 'Editorial Remarks', *Southern Literary Messenger*, vol. 1, January, p. 254–55.

Hendler, Glenn. 2001. *Public Sentiments: Structures of Feeling in Nineteenth-Century American Literature* (Chapel Hill: The University of North Carolina Press).

Hook, Andrew. 1975. *Scotland and America: A Study of Cultural Relations 1750–1835* (Glasgow: Blackie).

Hook, Andrew. 1999. *From Goosecreek to Gandercleugh: Studies in Scottish-American Literary and Cultural History* (East Lothian: Tuckwell Press).

Howard, Claude. 1986. 'The Emigration of Hogg's Brothers I: Leaving Scotland', *Newsletters of the James Hogg Society*, 5: 11–13.

Hughes, Gillian. 1982. 'The Critical Reception of *The Confessions of a Justified Sinner*', *Newsletter of the James Hogg Society*, 1: 11–14.

Hughes, Gillian. 2000a. 'Introduction', in *The Spy: A Periodical of Literary Amusement and Instruction*, written by James Hogg and others, ed. by Gillian Hughes (Edinburgh: Edinburgh University Press), pp. xvii–xlix.

Hughes, Gillian. 2000b. 'James Hogg and the "Bastard Brood"', *Studies in Hogg and his World*, 11: 56–68.

Hughes, Gillian. 2006. 'Introduction', in *The Collected Letters of James Hogg, Volume 3 (1832–1835)*, written by James Hogg, ed. by Gillian Hughes (Edinburgh: Edinburgh University Press), pp. xiii–xlviii.

Hughes, Gillian. 2007. *James Hogg: A Life* (Edinburgh: Edinburgh University Press).

Hughes, Gillian. 2008. 'Essay on the Genesis of the Text', in *Midsummer Night Dreams and Related Poems*, written by James Hogg, ed. by Jill Rubenstein and others (Edinburgh: Edinburgh University Press), pp. xiii–xliii.

Hume, David. 1965 [1739]. *A Treatise on Human Nature*, ed. by L. A. Selby-Bigge (Oxford: Clarendon Press).

Hunter, Adrian. 2020. 'Introduction', in *James Hogg's Publications to English, Irish, and American Periodicals*, written by James Hogg, ed. by Adrian Hunter with Barbara Leonardi (Edinburgh: Edinburgh University Press), pp. xi–xliv.

Ide, Sachiko. 1989. 'Formal Forms and Discernment: Two Neglected Aspects of Linguistic Politeness', *Multilingua*, 8(2–3): 223–48, https://doi.org/10.1515/mult.1989.8.2-3.223.

Inglis, Katherine. 2011. 'Maternity, Madness and Mechanization: The Ghastly Automaton in James Hogg's *The Three Perils of Woman*', in *Minds, Bodies, Machines: 1770–1930*, ed. by Deirdre Coleman and Hilary Fraser (Houndmills: Palgrave Macmillan), pp. 61–82.

J. G. W. 1849. 'The Slave Poet of North Carolina', *The Western Literary Messenger*, vol. 12, p. 114.

Jacobs, Harriet. 1861. *Incidents in the Life of a Slave Girl. Written by Herself*, ed. by R. J. Ellis, Oxford World's Classics (Oxford: Oxford University Press).

Jackson, Richard D. 2003. 'Gatty Bell's Illness in James Hogg's *The Three Perils of Woman*', *Studies in Hogg and his World*, 14: 16–29.

Kribbs, Jayne K. 1977. *American Literary Periodicals, 1741–1850 an annotated bibliography* (Boston: G. K. Hall & Co.).

Killick, Tim. 2004. 'Hogg and the Collection of Short Fiction in the 1820s', *Studies in Hogg and his World*, 15: 21–31.

Landsman, Ned C. 1985. 'A Scots Community: Settlement Patterns and Family Networks in the New World Environment', in *Scotland and its First American Colony, 1683–1765*, written by Ned C. Landsman (Princeton, New Jersey: Princeton University Press), pp. 131–62.

Leneman, Leah. 1999. 'Seduction in Eighteenth and Early Nineteenth-Century Scotland', *The Scottish Historical Review*, 78·1, no. 205 (April): 39–59.

Leneman, L., and R. Mitchison. 1993. 'Acquiescence in and Defiance of Church Discipline in Early-Modern Scotland', *Records of the Scottish Church History Society*, 25: 19–39.

Leneman, L., and R. Mitchison. 1998. *Sin in the City: Sexuality & Social Control in Urban Scotland 1660–1780* (Edinburgh: Scottish Cultural Press).

Leonardi, Barbara. 2012a. 'James Hogg, "Basil Lee," and the Pragmatics of Highland Masculinity', *NAWA: Journal of Language and Communication*, 6.1: 84–101.

Leonardi, Barbara. 2012b. 'James Hogg, the *Three Perils*, and the Pragmatics of Bourgeois Marriage', *Studies in Hogg and his World*, 22: 19–38.

Leonardi, Barbara. 2016a. 'James Hogg's *The Brownie of Bodsbeck*: An Unconventional National Tale', *Studies in Scottish Literature*, 42.1: 49–67.

Leonardi, Barbara. 2016b. 'James Hogg's *The Profligate Princes*: An Unconventional Treatment of Scottish Female Sexuality in Romantic Writing for the Theatre', *Scottish Literary Review*, 6.2: 37–53.

Leonardi, Barbara. 2018a. 'Introduction: The Family Metaphor', in *Intersections of Gender, Class, and Race in the Long Nineteenth Century and Beyond*, ed. by Barbara Leonardi (Cham: Palgrave), pp. 1–13.

Leonardi, Barbara. 2018b. 'Motherhood, Mother Country, and Migrant Maternity', in *Intersections of Gender, Class, and Race in the Long Nineteenth Century and Beyond*, ed. by Barbara Leonardi (Cham: Palgrave), pp. 17–40.

Leonardi, Barbara. 2019a. 'James Hogg's "Cousin Mattie": A Maternity Gone Wrong', *Studies in Hogg and his World*, 27–28: 31–47.

Leonardi, Barbara. 2019b. 'James Hogg's and Walter Scott's Scottishness: Varying Perceptions of (Im)Politeness in Negotiating Englishness', in *Pragmatics and Literature*, Series: Linguistic Approaches to Literature, ed. by Siobhan Chapman and Billy Clark (Amsterdam: Benjamins), pp. 191–214.

Leonardi, Barbara. 2019c. 'Hunger and Cannibalism: James Hogg's Deconstruction of Scottish Military Masculinities in *The Three Perils of Man or War, Women, and Witchcraft!*', in *Martial Masculinities: Experiencing and Imagining the Military in the Long Nineteenth Century*, ed. by Michael Brown, Anna Maria Barry and Joanne Begiato (Manchester: Manchester University Press), pp. 139–60.

Leonardi, Barbara. 2020. 'Reprintings of Hogg's Works Overseas', in *James Hogg's Publications to English, Irish, and American Periodicals*, written by James Hogg, ed. by Adrian Hunter with Barbara Leonardi (Edinburgh: Edinburgh University Press), pp. 187–201.

Letley, Emma. 1990. 'Some Literary Uses of Scots in *The Three Perils of Woman*', *Studies in Hogg and his World*, 1: 45–56.

Lynch, Deidre. 1996. 'Domesticating Fiction and Nationalizing Women', in *Romanticism, Race, and Imperial Culture, 1780–1834*, ed. by Alan Richardson and Sonia Hofkosh (Bloomington: Indiana University Press), pp. 40–71.

Mack, Douglas S. 1988. 'Hogg, Blackwood and *The Shepherd's Calendar*', in *Papers Given at the Second James Hogg Society Conference (Edinburgh 1985)*, ed. by Gillian Hughes (Aberdeen), pp. 24–31.

Mack, Douglas S. 1990. 'Gatty's Illness in *The Three Perils of Woman*', *Studies in Hogg and his World*, 1: 133–35.

Mack, Douglas S. 1992. 'Hogg and the Blessed Virgin Mary', *Studies in Hogg and his World*, 3: 68–75.

Mack, Douglas S. 2006. *Scottish Fiction and the British Empire* (Edinburgh: Edinburgh University Press).

Mack, Douglas S. 2008. 'Introduction', in *The Bush aboon Traquair and The Royal Jubilee*, written by James Hogg, ed. by Douglas S. Mack (Edinburgh: Edinburgh University Press), pp. xi–lv.

Mack, Douglas S. 2009. 'Hogg's Bardic Epic: *Queen Hynde* and Macpherson's *Ossian*', in *James Hogg and the Literary Marketplace: Scottish Romanticism and the Working-Class Author*, ed. by Sharon Alker and Holly Faith Nelson (Farnham: Ashgate), pp. 139–55.

Mack, Douglas and Wilma. 2004. 'Introductory Notes' [to 'Tales of Fathers and Daughters'], *Studies in Hogg and His World*, 15: 126–27.

Malcolmson, R. W. 1977. 'Infanticide in the Eighteenth Century', in *Crime in England 1555–1800*, ed. by J. S. Cockburn (London: Methuen), pp. 187–209.

Mao, LuMing Robert. 1994. 'Beyond Politeness Theory: "Face" Revisited and Renewed', *Journal of Pragmatics*, 21: 451–86.

Martin, Maureen M. 2009. *The Mighty Scot: Nation, Gender, and the Nineteenth-Century Mystique of Scottish Masculinity* (Albany: State University of New York Press).

McClintock, Anne. 1995. *Imperial Leather: Race, Gender and Sexuality in the Colonial Conquest* (New York: Routledge).

McDonagh, Josephine. 2003. *Child Murder and British Culture, 1720–1900* (Cambridge: Cambridge University Press).

McEathron, Scott. 2012. 'Labouring-Class Poetry', in *The Encyclopedia of Romantic Literature*, ed. by Frederick Burwick, Nancy Moore Goslee, and Diane Long Hoeveler (Oxford: Blackwell), pp. 743–50.

McNeil, Kenneth. 2007. *Scotland, Britain, Empire: Writing the Highlands, 1760–1860* (Columbus: The Ohio State University Press).

Mey, L. Jacob. 2000. *When Voices Clash: A Study in Literary Pragmatics* (Berlin: Mouton de Gruyter).

Mey, L. Jacob. 2001. *Pragmatics: An Introduction*, 2nd rev. and enlarged edn (Malden, MA: Blackwell).

Mergenthal, Silvia. 2012. 'Hogg, Gender, and Sexuality', in *The Edinburgh Companion to James Hogg*, ed. by Ian Duncan and Douglas S. Mack (Edinburgh: Edinburgh University Press), pp. 82–89.

Miller, Karl. 2003. *Electric Shepherd: A Likeness of James Hogg* (London: Faber and Faber).

Mills, Sara. 2000. *Gender and Politeness* (Cambridge: Cambridge University Press).

Mills, Sara. 2009. 'Impoliteness in a Cultural Context', *Journal of Pragmatics*, 41: 1047–60.

Mills, Sara. 2011. 'Discursive Approaches to Politeness and Impoliteness', in *Discursive Approaches to Politeness*, ed. by Linguistic Politeness Research Group (Berlin: de Gruyter Mouton), pp. 19–56.

Miskin, Lauren. 2015. '"True Indian Muslin" and the Politics of Consumption in Jane Austen's *Northanger Abbey*', *Journal for Early Modern Cultural Studies*, 15·2: 5–26.

Mitchison, R., and L. Leneman. 1989. *Sexuality & Social Control: Scotland 1660–1780* (Oxford: Basil Blackwells).

Mitchison, R., and L. Leneman. 1998. *Girls in Trouble: Sexuality and Social Control in Rural Scotland 1660–1780*, rev. edn of *Sexuality & Social Control: Scotland 1660–1780*, first published by Blackwells in 1989 (Edinburgh: Scottish Cultural Press).

Morini, Massimiliano. 2009. *Jane Austen's Narrative Techniques: A Stylistic and Pragmatic Analysis* (Farnham: Ashgate).

Mott, Frank Luther. 1957. *A History of American Magazines 1741–1850* (Cambridge, Massachusetts: The Belknap Press of Harvard University Press).

'The New Copyright Law'. 1838. *The American Monthly Magazine*, February, pp. 105–112.

O'Halloran, Meiko. 2012. 'Hogg and the Theatre', in *The Edinburgh Companion to James Hogg*, ed. by Ian Duncan and Douglas S. Mack (Edinburgh: Edinburgh University Press), pp. 105–12.

O'Halloran, Meiko. 2016. *James Hogg and British Romanticism: A Kaleidoscopic Art* (Basingstoke: Palgrave Macmillan).

Oxford Dictionary Online, <WWW.OED.com> [accessed 27 April 2013].

Petrie, Elaine E. 1988. '*Queen Hynde* and the Black Bull of Norroway', in *Papers Given at the Second James Hogg Society Conference (Edinburgh 1985)*, ed. by Gillian Hughes (Aberdeen), pp. 128–39.

Parrinder, Patrick. 2006. *Nation & Novel: The English Novel from its Origin to the Present Day* (Oxford: Oxford University Press).

Pittock, Murray G. H. 1991. *The Invention of Scotland: The Stuart Myth and Scottish Identity, 1638 to the Present* (London: Routledge).

Pittock, Murray G. H. 2002. 'Introduction', in *The Jacobite Relics of Scotland, First Series*, written by James Hogg, ed. by Murray G. H. Pittock (Edinburgh: Edinburgh University Press), pp. xi–xxxviii.

Pittock, Murray G. H. 2003a. 'Introduction', in *The Jacobite Relics of Scotland, Second Series*, written by James Hogg, ed. by Murray G. H. Pittock (Edinburgh: Edinburgh University Press,) pp. xi–xix.

Pittock, Murray G. H. 2003b. 'Narrative Strategies in 'The Brownie of the Black Haggs'', *Studies in Hogg and his World*, 14: 30–37.

Pittock, Murray G. H. 2011. 'Introduction: What is Scottish Romanticism?', in *The Edinburgh Companion to Scottish Romanticism*, ed. by Murray Pittock (Edinburgh: Edinburgh University Press), pp. 1–9.

Pocock, J. G. A. 1985. *Virtue, Commerce, and History* (Cambridge: Cambridge University Press).

'Present State and Prospects of the English Emigrants in South Africa'. 1974 [1824]. In *The South African Journal*, ed. by John Fairbairn and Thomas Pringle, reprint edn (Cape Town: South African Library), pp. 151–60.

'Politeness'. 1826–1827. *The Album, and Ladies' Weekly Gazette*, vol. 1, no. 22, p. 5.

'Politeness'. 1836. *New-York State Journal*, 3 February, p. 161.

Radcliffe, David Hill. 2003. 'Crossing Borders: The Untutored Genius as Spenserian Poet', *John Clare Society Journal*, 22: 51–67.

Redekop, Magdalene. 1988. 'Trials, Dreams, and Endings in the Tales of James Hogg', in *Papers Given at the Second James Hogg Society Conference, Edinburgh 1985*, ed. by Gillian Hughes (Aberdeen), pp. 32–41.

Richardson, Thomas C. 2009. 'James Hogg and *Blackwood's Edinburgh Magazine*: Buying and Selling the Ettrick Shepherd', in *James Hogg and the Literary Marketplace: Scottish Romanticism and the Working-Class Author*, ed. by Sharon Alker and Holly Faith Nelson (Farnham: Ashgate), pp. 185–99.

Rowland, Ann Wierda. 2004. '"The fause nourice sang": Childhood, Child Murder, and the Formalism of the Scottish Ballad Revival', in *Scotland and the Borders of Romanticism*, ed. by Leith Davis, Ian Duncan, and Janet Sorensen (Cambridge: Cambridge University Press), pp. 225–44.

Rudanko, Juhani. 2006. 'Aggravated Impoliteness and Two Types of Speaker Intention in an Episode in Shakespeare's *Timon of Athens*', *Journal of Pragmatics* 38: 829–41, https://doi.org/10.1016/j.pragma.2005.11.006.

Rudanko, Juhani. 2017. 'Towards Characterizing a Type of Aggravated Impoliteness, with Examples from *Timon of Athens*', *Language and Literature*, 26.1: 3–17, https://doi.org/10.1177/0963947016663588.

Scott, Walter. 1815 [1808]. *Marmion: A Tale of Flodden Field*, 9th edn (Edinburgh: Archibald Constable).

'Slavery'. 1835. *The American Magazine of Useful and Entertaining Knowledge*, vol. 2, September, pp. 22–23.

Sell, Roger D. 2000. *Literature as Communication: The Foundation of Mediating Criticism* (Amsterdam/Philadelphia: John Benjamins Publishing Company).

Sell, Roger D. 2011. *Communicational Criticism: Studies in Literature as Dialogue* (Amsterdam: John Benjamins Publishing Company).

Sell, Roger D. 2015 [1991]. 'The Politeness of Literary Texts', in *Literary Pragmatics*, ed. by Roger D. Sell, 2nd edn (London: Routledge), pp. 208–24.

Shields, Juliet. 2010. *Sentimental Literature and Anglo-Scottish Identity, 1745–1820* (Cambridge: Cambridge University Press).

Shumway, Suzanne Rosenthal. 1994. 'The Chronotope of the Asylum: *Jane Eyre*, Feminism, and Bakhtinian Theory', in *A Dialogue of Voices: Feminist Literary Theory and Bakhtin*, ed. by Karen Ann Hohne and Helen Wussow (Minneapolis: University of Minnesota Press), pp. 152–70.

Sigler, David. 2015. '"It is Unaccountable": Anxiety and the Cause of Desire in *Pride and Prejudice*', in *Sexual Enjoyment in British Romanticism: Gender and Psychoanalysis, 1753–1835*, written by David Sigler (Montreal: McGill-Queen University Press), pp. 57–91.

Smith, Adam. 1976 [1759]. *The Theory of Moral Sentiments*, ed. by D. D. Raphael and A. L. Macfie, Glasgow Edition of the Works and Correspondence of Adam Smith (Oxford: Clarendon Press).

Smout, Christopher. 1980. 'Aspects of Sexual Behaviour in Nineteenth-Century Scotland', in *Bastardy and its Comparative History: Studies in the History of Illegitimacy and Marital Non-Conformism in Britain, France, Germany, Sweden, North-America, Jamaica, and Japan*, ed. by P. Laslett and others (Harvard: Harvard University Press), pp. 192–216.

Sorensen, Janet. 2000. *The Grammar of Empire in Eighteenth-Century British Writing* (Cambridge: Cambridge University Press).

Sudan, Rajani. 1996. 'Mothering and National Identity in the Works of Mary Wollstonecraft', in *Romanticism, Race, and Imperial Culture*, ed. by Alan Richardson and Sonia Hofkosh (Bloomington: Indiana University Press), pp. 72–89.

Symonds, Deborah A. 1997. *Weep not for Me: Women, Ballads, and Infanticide in Early Modern Scotland* (University Park, Pennsylvania: The Pennsylvania State University Press).

Tait, William. 1840. *Magdalenism: An Enquiry into the Extent, Causes, and Consequences of Prostitution in Edinburgh*, 1st edn, (Edinburgh: P. Rickard, South Bridge) <http://books.google.com> [accessed 18 Feb 2022].

Tait, William. 1842. *Magdalenism: An Enquiry into the Extent, Causes, and Consequences of Prostitution in Edinburgh*, 2nd edn (Edinburgh, Glasgow, and London: 1842) <http://books.google.com> [accessed 18 Feb 2022].

Tracy, Thomas. 2004. 'The Mild Irish Girl: Domesticating the National Tale', Éire-Ireland, 39.1&2: 81–109.

Trumpener, Katie. 1997. *Bardic Nationalism: The Romantic Novel and the British Empire* (Princeton: Princeton University Press).

Tulloch, Graham. 2004. 'Writing "by advice": *Ivanhoe* and *The Three Perils of Man*', *Studies in Hogg and his World*, 15: 32–52.

Tulloch, Graham. 2012. 'Hogg and Scott in Early Australian Newspapers', *Studies in Hogg and his World*, 22: 39–59.

Webb, Samantha. 2002. 'In-Appropriating the Literary: James Hogg's *Poetic Mirror* Parodies of Scott and Wordsworth', *Studies in Hogg and his World*, 13: 16–35.

Wills, Clair. 2001. 'Upsetting the Public: Carnival, Hysteria, and Women's Texts', in *Bakhtin and Cultural Theory*, ed. by David Shepherd and Ken Hirschkop (Manchester: Manchester University Press, 2001), pp. 85–108.

Wohlgemut, Esther. 2002. '"What do you do with that at home?": The Cosmopolitan Heroine and the National Tale', *European Romantic Review*, 13.1: 191–97.

Womack, Peter. 1989. *Improvement and Romance: Constructing the Myth of the Highlands* (Basingstoke: Macmillan).

Wrightson, Keith. 1975. 'Infanticide in Earlier Seventeenth-Century England', *Local Population Studies*, 15: 10–22.

Wrigley, E. A. 1966. 'Family Limitation in Pre-Industrial England', *Economic History Review*, 2nd ser., 19: 82–109.

'The Zodiac'. 1836. In 'Reviews', *The New-York State Journal*, 9 March, p. 204.

Digital Platforms

19th Century US Newspapers (Gale).
American Antiquarian Society (AAS) Historical Periodical Collections (Ebsco).
America's Historical Newspapers (Readex).
Gale News Vault.
Newspapers.com.
Nineteenth Century British Library Newspapers (Gale).
ProQuest American Periodicals.
ProQuest Historical Newspapers.

Index